Absolute Justice, Kindness and Kinship

The Three Creative Principles

Consists of Four Addresses
by
Ḥaḍrat Mirza Tahir Ahmad
Khalīfatul Masīḥ IV

ISLAM INTERNATIONAL PUBLICATIONS LTD.

إسلام كا نظام عدل، إحسان اور ايتاء ذی القربی

Absolute Justice, Kindness and Kinship—
The Three Creative Principles

by: Ḥaḍrat Mirza Tahir Ahmad[rh]
The Fourth Successor of the Promised Messiah[as]

First Edition of the first part published in UK (ISBN: 1 85372 567 6)
Present Edition comprising all four parts published in UK in 2008

Published by:
Islam International Publications Ltd.
'Islamabad' Sheephatch Lane,
Tilford, Surrey GU102AQ
United Kingdom.

Printed in the UK by
CPI William Clowes
Beccles NR34 7TL

ISBN: 1 85372 741 5

إِنَّ اللهَ يَأْمُرُ بِالْعَدْلِ وَالْإِحْسَانِ وَإِيتَآئِ ذِى الْقُرْبِى وَيَنْهِى عَنِ الْفَحْشَآءِ وَالْمُنْكَرِ وَالْبَغْيِ ۚ يَعِظُكُمْ لَعَلَّكُمْ تَذَكَّرُونَ ٥

Verily, Allah requires you to abide by justice, and to treat with grace, and give like the giving of kin to kin; and forbids indecency, and manifest evil, and transgression. He admonished you that you may take heed.

(Sūrah al-Naḥl; 16:91)

Contents

Part I

Part IV

Ḥaḍrat Mirza Tahir Aḥmad (1928–2003)
Khalifatul Masih IV
The Fourth Successor of the Promised Messiah

About the Author

Hadrat Mirza Tahir Ahmad[rh] (1928-2003) was a man of God, the voice articulate of the age and a great orator. He was a deeply learned scholar of phenomenal intelligence, a keen student of comparative religions and a prolific and versatile writer. He was loved and devoutly followed by his more than 10 million Ahmadi Muslim followers all over the world as their Imam, the spiritual head, being the fourth successor of Hadrat Mirza Ghulam Ahmad (the Promised Messiah and Mahdi[as]), to which august office he was elected as Khalīfatul Masīḥ in 1982.

After the promulgation of General Zia-ul-Haq's anti-Ahmadiyya Ordinance of 26th April 1984, he had to leave his beloved country, Pakistan, and migrated to England from where, among many other achievements, he launched Muslim Television Ahmadiyya International (MTA) which would (and still does) telecast its programmes 24 hours a day to the four corners of the world.

Besides being a religious leader, he was a homeopathic physician of world fame, a highly gifted poet and a sportsman.

He received his schooling in Qadian, India, and later joined the Govt. College, Lahore, Pakistan. After graduating from Jāmi'ah Ahmadiyya, Rabwah,

Pakistan with distinction, he obtained his honours degree in Arabic from the Punjab University, Lahore. From 1955 to 1957 he studied at the School of Oriental and African Studies, University of London.

He had a divinely inspired and very deep knowledge of the Holy Quran which he translated into Urdu. He also partially revised and added explanatory notes to the English translation of the Holy Quran by Ḥaḍrat Maulawī Sher Ali[ra]. 'Revelation, Rationality, Knowledge and Truth' is his magnum opus.

Though he had no formal education in philosophy and science, he had a philosophical mind and tackled most difficult and abstruse theological-philosophical questions with great acumen and ease and his intellectual approach was always rational and scientific. For a layman he had an amazingly in-depth knowledge of science, especially life sciences which attracted him most. He also had deep knowledge of human psychology. His was an analytical mind of high intelligence—an intellect scintillating with brilliance, capable of solving the knottiest of problems with ease, leaving his listeners and readers spellbound.

Introduction

Ḥaḍrat Ṣāḥibzāda Mirza Tahir Ahmad (1928-2003), the Head of the Worldwide Ahmadiyya Muslim Community (Jamā'at) from 1982-2003, began a series of lectures in Urdu at Jalsah Sālānah (the Annual Convention of the Community) in Rabwah, Pakistan, in 1982, the year in which he was elected Khalīfatul Masīh, on the subject:

(Absolute Justice, Kindness and Kinship—The Three Creative Principles)[*]

The second lecture was delivered the following year, in December 1983, also in Rabwah, Pakistan. In 1984, Ḥuḍūr migrated to England where he delivered two more lectures on the same subject at Jalsah Salana, UK. The first of these (i.e., the third lecture of the series) was delivered on 2nd August 1987, and the second (i.e., the fourth and last lecture of the series) on 24th July 1988. The first lecture was translated into English and published in 1996, by Islam International Publications Ltd., England, under the title: Absolute Justice, Kindness and Kinship—The Three Creative Principles.

---

[*] Ḥuḍur[rh] himself gave this title to the English version of these lectures. (Publishers)

Later on Ḥuḍūr himself revised the text of all the four lectures, and made many additions and changes. Realizing that there was a big time lapse between the different lectures with the result that many repetitions had inadvertently found their way into them, he extensively revised the whole manuscript, shortened many passages and deleted many, to spare the reader the botheration of going through unnecessary repetitions, without any loss to the continuity of the subject.

The following were some of those who had the honour to work with Ḥuḍūr on this project: Munir Ahmed Javed (Private Secretary), the late Pir Muhammad Alam, Mrs. Saliha Safi and Mrs. Fauzia Bajwa.

For the English Edition, the first two lectures were dictated anew in English by Ḥuḍūr himself to Mrs. Farina Qureshi and Mrs. Farida Ahmed. The third and fourth lectures were revised with them and simultaneous revisions to the Urdu lectures were also done in these sittings.

I was, by the blessings of Allah, very fortunate to have the privilege and honour of sitting at the feet of Ḥuḍūr daily for hours on end for many months. In these blessed sessions, Ḥuḍūr went through the Urdu script of all four lectures—I would read out the script to Ḥuḍūr, and he, in spite of his illness, would make corrections, revisions, amendments, etc; he would also give me instructions regarding other related matters. Mrs. Farina Qureshi and Mrs. Farida Ahmed, also, had the blessed opportunity for several months to spend many hours with Ḥuḍūr for his guidance and worked on the manuscript in accordance with the instructions of Ḥuḍūr. With the blessings of Allah, Ḥuḍūr dictated the final amendments just a few weeks before he passed away.

References were checked carefully by a team in Pakistan headed by Wakīl-ul-Ishā'at Mirza Anas Ahmad, M.A. M.Litt (Oxen). Sheikh Naseer Ahmad, typeset the manuscript and Mahmood Ahmad Malik (Incharge Central Computer Department London) made the final corrections and designed the book for publishing. Please remember all those in your prayers who contributed in any way in priniting this edition.

I feel very sad that, for some unavoidable reasons, the manuscript, when it was at last finalized, could not see the light of publication during the life of Ḥuḍūr. Now at last, with a mixed feeling of sadness and delight, we look forward to its publication under the auspices of Ḥaḍrat Khalifatul Masih V, Ḥaḍrat Ṣāḥibzāda Mirza Masroor Ahmad.

These lectures are now for the first time being published in one volume with four parts, each part comprising one lecture as per the wishes of Ḥuḍūr. The contents and glossary of all the parts are given in the beginning of the book; the subject-headings of each part are also given on the title of each part.

Munīr-ud-Dīn Shams
Additional Wakīl-ut-Taṣnīf
London
April 2008

Publisher's Note

In this book the name of name of Muhammad[sa], the Holy Prophet of Islam, has been followed by the symbol [sa], which is an abbreviation for the salutation (ﷺ) *Ṣallallāhu 'Alaihi Wasallam* (may peace and blessings of Allah be upon him). The names of other Prophets[as] and messengers are followed by the symbol [as], an abbreviation for (عليه السلام) *'Alaihissalām/ 'Alaihimussalām* (on whom be peace). The actual salutations have not generally been set out in full, but they should nevertheless be understood as being repeated in full in each case. The symbol [ra] is used with the name of the Companions of the Holy Prophet[sa] and those of the Promised Messiah[as]. It stands for (رضي الله عنه) *Raḍī Allāhu 'anhu/'anhā/ 'anhum* (May Allah be pleased with him/with her/with them). [rh] stands for (رحمه الله) *Raḥimahullāhu Ta'ālā* (may Allah's blessing be on him). [at] stands for (أيده الله) *Ayyadahullāhu Ta'ālā* (May Allah, the All-Mighty help him).

In transliterating Arabic words we have followed the following system adopted by the Royal Asiatic Society.

ا	at the beginning of a word, pronounced as *a*, *i*, *u* preceded by a very slight aspiration, like *h* in the English word 'honour'.
ث	*th*, pronounced like th in the English word 'thing'.

ح   *ḥ*, a guttural aspirate, stronger than h.

خ   *kh*, pronounced like the Scotch ch in 'loch'.

ذ   *dh*, pronounced like the English th in 'that'.

ص   *ṣ*, strongly articulated s.

ض   *ḍ*, similar to the English th in 'this'.

ط   *ṭ*, strongly articulated palatal t.

ظ   *ẓ*, strongly articulated z.

ع   ', a strong guttural, the pronunciation of which must be learnt by the ear.

غ   *gh*, a sound approached very nearly in the r '*grasseye*' in French, and in the German r. It requires the muscles of the throat to be in the 'gargling' position whilst pronouncing it.

ق   *q*, a deep guttural k sound.

ء   ', a sort of catch in the voice.

Short vowels are represented by:

a   for ——— (like *u* in 'bud');

i   for ——— (like *i* in 'bid');

u   for ——— (like *oo* in 'wood');

Long vowels by:

ā   for ——— or آ (like *a* in 'father');

ī   for ى ——— or ——— (like *ee* in 'deep');

ū   for و ——— (like *oo* in 'root');

Other:

ai   for ى ——— (like *i* in 'site')*;

---

* In Arabic words like شيخ (Shaikh) there is an element of diphthong which

xiv

au   for و ─╰── (resembling *ou* in 'sound').

Please note that in transliterated words the letter 'e' is to be pronounced as in 'prey' which rhymes with 'day'; however the pronunciation is flat without the element of English diphthong. If in Urdu and Persian words 'e' is lengthened a bit more it is transliterated as 'ei' to be pronounced as 'ei' in 'feign' without the element of diphthong thus 'کے' is transliterated as 'Kei'. For the nasal sound of 'n' we have used the symbol 'ṅ'. Thus Urdu word ' میں' is transliterated as 'meiṅ'.[*]

The consonants not included in the above list have the same phonetic value as in the principal languages of Europe.

We have not transliterated Arabic words which have become part of English language, e.g., Islam, Mahdi, Quran[**], Hijra, Ramadan, Hadith, ulema, umma, sunna, kafir, pukka etc.

For quotes straight commas (straight quotes) are used to differentiate them from the curved commas used in the system of transliteration, ' for ع, ' for ء. Commas as punctuation marks are used according to the normal usage. Similarly for apostrophe normal usage is followed.

---

is missing when the word is pronounced in Urdu.

[*] These transliterations are not included in the system of transliteration by Royal Asiatic Society. [Publisher]

[**] Concise Oxford Dictionary records Quran in three forms—Quran, Qur'an and Koran. [Publisher]

Glossary of Terms

Part I

'Abd: slave, servant.

'Adl: absolute justice.

Aḥsani Taqwīm: The best creative process which results in the creation of well-balanced, straight, accurate, exact and rightly proportioned creatures.

'Adalaka: Proportioned thee correctly and perfectly balanced.

Ajrun Ghairu Mamnūn: an unending reward.

Ambatnā: 'We caused to grow'.

Asfala Sāfilīn: The lowest of the low.

'Azīz: Mighty with honour, Commanding respect.

Darūd: The Holy Quran (33:57) enjoins upon Muslims to invoke blessings on the Holy Prophet[sa] and to salute him with the salutation of peace. *'Darūd'* is the name for this act of prayer.

Dhikrā: reminder, exhortation.

Dīni Qayyim: the right religion.

Fujūr: sinfulness, unrighteousness, viciousness, wickedness.

Fa Sawwāka Fa 'Adalaka: Perfected you and proportioned you to the point of perfect balance, consummated you (in respect of your innate faculties) and made you well balanced in your nature.

Ghafūr: most forgiving.

Guru: God, avatar, saint, religious teacher. Here it is used in the sense of saint.

Ḥadīth: sayings and traditions of the Holy Prophet[sa].

Ḥaḍrat: title of respected for eminent religious personages

Ḥūr: companions promised in the hereafter to the righteous believers.

Iḥsān: to grant someone more than his due; a reward in excess of the labour involved.

Ītā'i Dhil-Qurbā: To treat with such grace and benevolence as one would treat one's kindred, where the labour-reward relationship is no longer in play and favours are done with natural urge.

Istaqāma: remained steadfast.

Kūnū Qiradatan Khāsi'īn: 'Be ye apes despised'.

Mauzūn: perfectly proportioned, well-balanced.

Mīzān: balance, measure, weight.

Millah: religion, creed, a people belonging to a creed or faith.

Nabātāt: vegetation, green foliage. *Ambatnā* is a verb from the same root and means 'caused to grow'.

Nafkh-i-Rūḥ: Allah's act of giving breath of life, breathing of the spirit, revelation from God, the Word of God.

Nafs: life.

Qāma: stood up.

Qawwām: guardian, someone who does something resolutely and keeps others upright, one having authority over others.

Qisṭ: justice, equity.

Ravāsiya: deeply and firmly rooted

Rūḥ: soul, spirit, the Word of God.

Sat-Sri-Akāl: salutations or greetings of the Sikhs. Its literal meanings are 'Truth is eternal'.

Ṣirāṭi Mustaqīm: straight or shortest path (which has no bend or turns).

Sūrah: A chapter of the Quran. The Quran has one hundred and fourteen chapters in all.

Taʻdīl: to bring into play the principles of absolute justice.

Tamīda Bikum: feeds you, provides you with the requirements and support of life.

Taqwīm: to apply the principles of absolute justice both in inanimates and animals.

Taqwā: the fear of Allah. The expression *Taqwa* in fact denotes that the true believers keep a vigilant watch over themselves and always try their best to refrain from doing anything which is not approved by Allah.

Taswiyah: the act of making something perfect.

Umma: people, nation.

Ummatan Wasaṭan: exalted nation, the best of nations, a nation which always treads the middle path.

Wasṭ: the best, exalted, the middle.

Wazn: weight.

Part II

Adhān: the Islamic call to prayer.

Ajr: reward.

Dīn: faith, religion, custom, godliness.

Fajr: The first of the five daily prayer services, offered any time during the period starting from dawn and ending a few minutes before sunrise.

Ikrāh: coercion.

Jāhada: to struggle against anyone (including oneself).

Jihad: struggle, war in self defence. See page 180 for the difference between jihad and *Qitāl*.

Kalima: the credo of Islam, 'There is none worthy of worship except Allah; Muhammad is the Messenger of Allah'.

Kalima-e-Tauḥīd: profession of the Unity of God.

Qātala (verb): He waged war.

Qitāl: waging of war. For explanation see page 180.

Tahajjud: Optional prayer of great merit offered in the latter part of the night.

Tayammum: To put or strike lightly the hands over clean earth and then pass the palm of each on the back of the other, blow off the dust and then pass them on the face. This is performed instead of ablution and *Ghusl* (bath).

Ẓuhr: The midday prayer of the five mandatory daily prayers, offered any time during the period starting from decline of sun and ending before doubling of the shadows.

Part III

Bi'ilmihī: based on His knowledge.

Dhimmatun: protection.

Dhimmī: Christians and Jews and other non-Muslims living under Muslim rule and Muslim protection. A *Dhimmī* does not pay Zakat. He is levied a special tax to meet the monetary requirements for his protection and welfare in a Muslim state.

Ḥikmah: wisdom.

Khalīfatullāh: vicegerent of Allah.

Khātamun Nabiyyīn: seal of the Prophets.

Khatm-e-Nabuwwat: the seal of Prophethood.

Malā'ikah (plural of *Malak*): angels.

Qāimam bil Qisṭ: in accordance with justice; maintaining justice.

Sawwā: to make perfect.

Sawwaituhū: Fashioned him in perfection.

Sū'uddār: grievous abode.

Tazkiyah: purification.

Part IV

Ar-Raḥmān: one of the attributes of Allah meaning the Gracious.

Aulād: children.

Qauli Sadīd: a true and straightforward statement, (a speech which has no tilt in any direction but in the direction of the truth).

Raḥmān: Gracious (Allah's attribute).

Riḥm: uterus.

Sadīd: right, just, well directed.

Sharīka: spirit of fraternity, solidarity with your kin and clan or tribe etc.

Walad: a child, son, daughter; offspring. The word is used both in singular and plural and masculine and feminine. (Lane)

Waqf-e-Nau: A scheme launched by Ḥaḍrat Khalīfatul Masīḥ IVth that parents should dedicate the lives of their newborn and expected children to the service of Ahmadiyyat, the true Islam. *Waqf-e-Nau* literally means new (*Nau*) dedication (*Waqf*).

Absolute Justice, Kindness and Kinship

The Three Creative Principles

Ḥaḍrat Mirza Tahir Ahmad

Part I

Speech delivered at the Annual Convention
of the Ahmadiyyah Muslim Jamā'at
in Rabwah, Pakistan in December 1982

LIST OF CHAPTERS IN PART I

Foreword to the First Edition

of the First Part

Ever since its formation more than one hundred years ago, it has been customary for the Ahmadiyya Muslim Community to host an Annual Convention, which is attended by delegates from all over the world. In December 1982, the Annual Convention was held in Rabwah, Pakistan. On that occasion, Ḥaḍrat Mirza Tahir Ahmad, the then Supreme Head of the Ahmadiyya Muslim Community, delivered an Urdu address entitled *'Adl, Ihsan aur Ita'i Dhil-Qurba'*.

This book developed out of that speech. In addition to translating the Urdu speech into English, various themes have been expanded upon, which time had not permitted in the original address. The Holy Quran is quoted extensively and many Arabic words have been retained in this book. A Glossary of Terms is included which gives an English rendering of Arabic words used.

Publishers

Prologue

When I woke up this morning and proceeded towards
the mosque for prayers, I noticed that the sky was
overcast, threatening rain. I thereupon examined my
inner thoughts; there was no trace of ingratitude in
relation to God for bringing this rain upon us at such
an inopportune moment. It was the day of the Annual
Gathering (*Jalsah*) and it seemed that if it were to rain
heavily, the *Jalsah* proceedings would be completely
disturbed.

'All praise belongs to Allah' was the spontaneous
response of my heart because I found not a flimsiest
trace of ingratitude anywhere in the recesses of my
heart. At this very moment I was moved to send
Darūd (salutations) to Prophet Muhammad^{sa}, who is
the greatest benefactor of mankind. The Quran
cultivates among us the attitude of total submission to
the will of God. In response, God listens to the
supplications of such dedicated servants more than

5

those of others and further reciprocates this act of
goodness by bestowing His numerous favours upon
them. This is expressed beautifully in the verse of an
Urdu poem by Ḥaḍrat Mirza Bashīr-ud-Dīn Mahmood
Ahmad^ra, Khalīfatul Masīḥ II:

هو فضل تيرا يارب يا كوئى ابتلا هو

راضى هيں هم اسى ميں جس ميں تيرى رضا هو

O Lord, bestow Your blessings, or test us with trials,
Contented and at peace are we, in that wherein lies
Your will.

Also we find in the Holy Quran a verse discussing the
same subject in a different way:

اَلَاۤ اِنَّ اَوۡلِیَآءَ اللّٰہِ لَا خَوۡفٌ عَلَیۡهِمۡ وَ لَا هُمۡ یَحۡزَنُوۡنَ ۝

Behold! the friends of Allah shall certainly have no
fear, nor shall they grieve—
(Sūrah Yūnus; Ch.10: V.63)

It is a boundless bounty of Allah that we, belonging to
the Ahmadiyya Community, are a people who remain
always content with the will of Allah; because this is
the very essence of the philosophy of Allah's
protection extending to His humble servants—if
people are completely content with all the
manifestations of Allah's will they become the living

symbols of His design. So much so that He sees to it that they are neither overpowered nor destroyed.

There were other thoughts too which filled my heart with Allah's praise—among them was the zeal of our community. I fully appreciate that the Promised Messiah's[as] community has such willingness in making sacrifices that if their *Khalīfah* orders them to go and sit in the rain, they will not hesitate for a minute to obey him. They will come running in obedience. This is the trait of the Promised Messiah's[as] community. Yet I would hesitate to require this of them, knowing that among them there are some who are poor, some who are indisposed and also some who are weak. But as far as the spirit of the sacrifice is concerned, it is best expressed in someone's comment which was brought to my attention today: 'The spirit of zeal and sacrifice of this community makes one shudder.'

We are definitely not among those whose example can be illustrated in the following joke. It is said that a cart belonging to a group of non-Muslims got stuck in mud and they invoked their *'sat-sirī-akāl'* prayer to pull the cart out. They also used other gurus' names to make their pull more effective, but nothing would work. It so happened that a group of Muslims walked by; they offered to help and gave a mightier pull in the name of Ali, a saintly figure who is popularly held to possess special powers. By this time obviously more men had joined, therefore they were able to get the cart out of the ditch. But the non-Muslims became worried that the Muslims' guru would now be labelled as 'the more powerful one'. They were naturally reluctant to pay such a tribute to Muslims, which would go against their own faith. Therefore, instead of admitting plainly that the Muslims' guru was mightier than theirs, they said that the Muslims' guru was mightier in only muddy situations, implying that they had not accepted the superiority of the Muslims' guru. As we would say in Punjabi:

مُسلے دا گرو کھوبے دا تگڑا اے

'*Muslei dā gūrū, Khobei dā tagrhā aiy*'. (The Muslim's gūrū is mightier indeed in muddy situations).

We are not the followers of such a guru who possesses powers confined only to certain areas; we are the disciples of One Guru who is the Master in all situations and is Superior and excels in His dignity over everything. He guides us from darkness into light. His followers are never subdued or apprehended by darkness; they walk in any condition. They are not like the ones mentioned in the Holy Quran thus:

… اِذَآ اَظْلَمَ عَلَیْهِمْ قَامُوْا …

…When the darkness falls on them, they stand still … (Sūrah al-Baqarah; Ch.2: V.21)

8

On the contrary they walk in light and in darkness, come rain or shine. Pondering over this subject my heart was filled with even greater praise for Allah.

1 The Three Creative Principles Defined

Three Stages of Human Relations

1. *'Adl* (absolute justice).
2. *Iḥsān* (to grant someone more than his or her due).
3. *Ītā'i Dhil-Qurbā* (to treat others with such grace and overwhelming benevolence as one would treat one's kindred).

The Quranic verse which I have chosen for today's address is extremely vast and comprehensive:

اِنَّ اللهَ يَأْمُرُ بِالْعَدْلِ وَالْاِحْسَانِ وَ اِيْتَآئ ذِى الْقُرْبٰى ...

Indeed Allah requires you to abide by justice, to treat with grace and to give like the giving of kin to kin. ... (Sūrah al-Naḥl; Ch. 16: V.91)

Allah does not command us to exercise justice *('Adl)* alone, but also desires us to voluntarily add benevolence *(Iḥsān)* to the act of justice and then to move further to the third stage of human relationships, which is *Ītā'i Dhil-Qurbā*—a spontaneous expression of love and care as experienced by a mother for her child. When a mother loves her child, she does so without any element of design and without any trace

11

of affectation. It is but a natural flow which she does not generate, but one with which she is carried away. Spontaneity is always central to her expression of love for her dear ones. The above example illustrates fully the spirit of *Ītā'i Dhil-Qurbā*.

To recapitulate, the first part of this verse sets out three stages of human relations. The least demand, yet at the same time the most important one that Allah makes on the believers, is absolute justice. However, they are not expected to stop short at only justice; they are required to move on to the domain of benevolence. They will then not only be just towards mankind, but will also learn the art of returning more than the others' dues; their generosity will benefit people without obligation. This, in Quranic terminology, is called *Iḥsān* or benevolence.

It should be remembered, however, that the term *Iḥsān* is not limited to one subject matter alone as there are several underlying meanings. When this term is used in relation to God and His servants, a change in its application takes place accordingly. I will mention this aspect later at the appropriate juncture.

The third term used in this verse is *Ītā'i Dhil-Qurbā*, i.e. kindness to one's kindred. According to this, we are expected to extend our favours to others in such a way that no feeling of pride finds any place in this relationship. Our benevolence is extended in such a manner that we consider it to be our duty or obligation and not a favour to others.

The next part of this verse deals with some traits which a believer should eschew; these traits run counter to the virtues which God requires to be cultivated among the believers. Allah says:

$$\ldots \text{وَ يَنْهَى عَنِ الْفَحْشَآءِ وَالْمُنْكَرِ وَ الْبَغْيِ ۚ يَعِظُكُمْ لَعَلَّكُمْ تَذَكَّرُونَ}$$

...And He forbids indecency, and manifest evil, and wrongful transgression. He admonishes you, so that you may take heed.
(Sūrah al-Naḥl; Ch.16: V.91)

Indecency, blatant evil and wrongful transgression are the negative terms used in the Holy Quran, in contrast to justice, beneficence and kindness to one's kindred. Initially, I intended to speak on the first half of this verse, hoping that the time in today's address would be enough. But when I started working on it, I was amazed at the depth and the vastness of the subjects covered by this verse. New gates were being opened to me in different vistas, each of which appeared to be a wonderful universe of knowledge and wisdom. Thus I gave up the idea of covering the subject of the verse even partially during this session. Then I focused my attention on the aspect of justice alone but found it in turn to be so vast that the whole of God's creation was found to be governed by the principle of universal justice. This is not a boastful claim. In truth, each word of what I say is based on solid facts. Justice is not only vast in its application, but it is also profound in its meanings. It is extremely intricate and refined, and leads us to the secrets of nature lying hidden, tier under tier. In today's session, with Allah's grace, we shall attempt to understand the principle of absolute justice.

Humanity is in dire need of the application of this universal principle. All of its ills which are responsible for polluting and contaminating human relationships, are directly born out of lack of its application. Mankind stands in need of justice so desperately that if we do not teach it to people in the light of the Quranic teachings they will continue to wander astray, losing their way in a labyrinth of utter ignorance. Man will continue to suffer heavily at the hands of man. Therefore, it is our utmost duty to enlighten the world with the Quranic principle of absolute justice.

The Most Elaborate Verse of the Holy Quran

When Ḥaḍrat 'Abdullāh bin Mas'ūd[ra] contemplated on the above mentioned verse, he spontaneously exclaimed that it was the most comprehensive verse of the Holy Quran. This observation by Ḥaḍrat 'Abdullāh bin Mas'ūd[ra], who was one of the greatest commentators of the Holy Quran, is indeed of great import. It seems to be the fruit of an entire lifetime dedicated to the study of the Holy Quran. He seems to draw our attention to the fact that the subject of the verse relates to all the teachings of the Holy Quran.

In addition to 'Abdullāh bin Mas'ūd[ra], Ḥaḍrat 'Umar bin 'Abdul 'Azīz[rh] also had a special regard for this verse. It was he who introduced its recitation into the second sermon in Friday prayers. In this respect he emerged as a benefactor of all Muslims. As far as its impact on Muslims is concerned, the two examples which I have related demonstrate the point clearly. However, the impact did not remain confined to the Muslims alone. It is reported that even among the severe enemies of Islam, at the time of Prophet Muhammad[sa], there were some who were overwhelmed with the profound wisdom of this verse. It is narrated that when one of the chiefs of the Quraish of Mecca, Walīd, heard this verse he exclaimed, 'What a verse indeed! How fresh and pleasant, as if spring had blossomed forth!'

We notice that the principle of justice at work in the creation of the universe is so wide in its application that it seems as if a whole new universe of meaning is born of it. Then we find the channel to the second and higher stage of beauty in the word *Iḥsān,* and from this avenue of beauty springs forth many a path leading to the last and final stage of perfection which is *Ītā'i Dhil-Qurbā.*

The Application of this Verse to the Domain of the Plant and Animal Kingdoms

The plant and animal kingdoms are both equally governed by this fundamental principle of *'Adl, Ihsān* and *Ītā'i Dhil-Qurbā*. When the same evolutionary process of all beings, from a lower order to a higher order of perfection, reaches the stage of man, it acquires an even wider dimension.

In respect to the application of this principle, creation can be classified into three categories. The first category is that of an inanimate form of creation. The second category begins from the emergence of life and extends to the time when man emerged as the ultimate product of evolution, thus creating a category of its own. The third and final stage is occupied by man alone. All of these groups are governed by the same principle, but among the first two categories, i.e. the inanimates and the lower animates, this principle works in them as a law with consciousness apparently playing no role. It flows in all of their creative processes effortlessly, like the flow of rivers. They follow the laws of nature without any option. But when it comes to the category of the comparatively higher stage of animals, below human beings, they do not take their decisions unconsciously like the inanimate but do it as governed by their intuition. Intuition seems to be placed halfway between unconsciousness and the full consciousness reached at the stage of man. We observe for the first time that only one form of life i.e. human life, has been granted options and it no longer compulsively follows the path of intuition. Of all the life forms, it is man alone who has been granted the choice of making conscious decisions as to whether he should follow the path of absolute justice or the path of transgression and iniquity.

The Principle which Governs the Law Responsible for the Creation of Equilibrium and Balance

The principle of absolute justice when applied to the realm of human beings includes the new aspect of free will. If man misuses the free will granted to him by God and chooses the wrong path, he no longer continues to rise in his journey to higher achievements but turns volte-face and begins a descent back to the lowliest of the lowly state of his origin. This natural evolutionary process has been established in these verses of the Holy Quran:

$$لَقَدْ خَلَقْنَا الْإِنْسَانَ فِيْ أَحْسَنِ تَقْوِيْمٍ ۞ ثُمَّ رَدَدْ نٰهُ أَسْفَلَ سَافِلِيْنَ ۞ إِلَّا الَّذِيْنَ اٰمَنُوْا وَعَمِلُوا الصّٰلِحٰتِ فَلَهُمْ أَجْرٌ غَيْرُ مَمْنُوْنٍ ۞$$

Surely, We have created man in the best make; Then, *if he works iniquity*, We reject him as the lowest of the low, except those who believe and do good works; so for them is an unending reward.
(Sūrah al-Tīn; Ch.95: Vs. 5-7)

17

An 'unending reward' means a form of continuous unbroken moral and spiritual evolution. Literally, 'Taqwīm' (تَقْوِيم) means straightening something into a continuously improving form and, according to *al-Munjad* (an Arabic Lexicon) it also means *Ta'dīl* which can be translated as application of justice.

These verses of the Holy Quran refer to the evolutionary process of animals leading up to its culmination in man. They also cover man's intellectual and moral evolution. Animals with lower intelligence turn into more intelligent life forms as they evolve. It is essentially through the instrument of justice that God initiated the creation of life, and it is through the application of the same principle of absolute justice that life began to evolve, stage after stage, until it reached its final destination.

The Quranic expression *Aḥsani Taqwīm* points to the fact that the evolution of life was carried out in the best of manners. At every stage it took a step forward in a way which could not be bettered. Evidently, blind evolution is ruled out by this term.

This phenomenon when observed among humans, with their consciousness and voluntary decisions to take a just and equitable course, is referred to in the Quran as *Ta'dīl* meaning application of justice. Hence, the entire evolutionary process which guides God's creation from lower to higher stages, is dependent on *Taqwīm* and *Ta'dīl*.

Having been trained and cultivated over billions of years of evolution, the question now arises as to what should be the next destination, if any, for man in this journey of evolution? Has it come to an end? Or is it an ongoing process set in an eternal motion?

Common sense requires that if human beings attained such marvellous progress through the blessings of justice over this period, then the converse should also be true, i.e. negation of justice should be instrumental in reversing man's direction and making him retrace his steps to the earliest rudimentary stages of life. Of course, the physical development of man will not be reversed. But in his intellectual and moral state, and in the perfection of his five faculties, it is possible that he should revert to a subhuman level of attitudes and become so perverted that he reaches a stage of beastlike behaviour.

The second scenario deals with options open to man once he is carried to the summit of evolutionary progress. If he displays wisdom enough to draw his lessons from his own evolution and if he realises that in essence he is the fruit of absolute justice in operation through the billions of years of evolution, then he will chart a course for himself which will never disregard the dictates of justice. In this case his evolution would not come to a halt. It would continue to move forward slowly but constantly, raising man from lower human orders to higher human orders. The only difference between this and the previous evolution is that while the previous evolution was mainly physical and mental, the latter one will be mental, moral and spiritual. The mental aspect of evolution comprises the evolution of all five senses.

The subsequent verse of the same Surah throws light on this subject and gives solutions to these issues. The first question which the Holy Quran raises in this Surah is the same as has just been discussed. It pointedly speaks of the danger of man reverting to his earlier lowly states if he abandons the principle of justice.

ثُمَّ رَدَدْنٰهُ أَسْفَلَ سَافِلِيْنَ ☐

Then We degraded him to the lowest of the low.
(Sūrah al-Tīn; Ch.95: V.6)

In the above verse, the Arabic expression *Asfala Sāfilīn* is translated as 'the lowest of the low'. But it cannot be inferred from this that man will begin his physical devolution and would ultimately sink to the lowest form of life, maybe becoming an amoeba or sinking even lower.

Yet at the same time a door of hope is opened, leading to a path of never ending eternal progress for those who would believe in Allah and do righteous deeds. It is promised that their journey into spiritual evolution will never come to an end. It should be remembered that it is the course of justice which provides the basis for righteousness. No act which is devoid of this attribute can be termed as righteous. This is the least that is expected of those who hope to qualify for the journey of eternal progress. Yet there is more to it and many factors, when added to the attribute of justice, contribute to the improvement of the quality of righteousness raising it to higher levels of excellence. In the light of what precedes, *Ajrun Ghairu Mamnūn* (Sūrah al-Tīn; Ch.95: V.7) will mean that so long as man observes righteous deeds, he will not be denied his reward—the reward being that he will continue progressing towards higher goals of attainment.

This aspect of the matter under discussion has now been clarified to some extent. But when we agree with this viewpoint, a question that arises naturally is: what is meant by man's reversion to the lowest stages of his origin? According to some medieval Muslim scholars, man can indeed physically revert to some lower orders of life and taking some verses of the Holy Quran too literally, they conclude that he can definitely be reverted to the stage of monkeys and pigs and perhaps even asses!

Several bizarre stories based on this view are in circulation. For example, the medieval Muslim scholars misconstrue some verses of the Holy Quran and some traditions, and tell the tale of an imaginary township where some of the rebellious Jews were turned into apes, while some others were turned into pigs. Of course, they cannot name that township because historically it does not exist. Again they do not enlighten as to how the natural phenomenon of reproduction played its role in that subverted community. All they tell the world is that one fine morning they all died suddenly and disappeared, along with the remains of that unfortunate township. It happened so completely that no trace of them remained for the poor archaeologists to dig for.

But among the old scholars, Mujāhid seems to have found the right answer when he explains that God did not command them to become actual apes, but just as foolish or shameless people are derided as being donkeys or dogs, similarly these people have been given the epithet of monkeys[1]. Again, *Asfala Sāfilīn* could in no way have referred to their physical retrograde because obviously apes and swine do not belong to the lowest forms of life. There exist millions of life forms below them.

When we say that man has been given the freedom of adopting or rejecting absolute justice, we certainly do not mean to say that he has limitless freedom in this regard. In fact there are many spheres in which this principle of absolute justice works by itself, without the least conscious control of man, and he does not have the power to change the course of those natural phenomena. This can be illustrated well with reference to the bricks of life of which all life forms are created. Within each brick there lies a vast and complex system of a character-bearing mechanism.

There is little that man can do to interfere in this micro-universe within him. Thus another meaning of his transgression into lower forms of animal life could refer to the possible degeneration of his mental facilities. Such people as have lost control of their mind can sometimes behave in a manner of lower animals. These similarities are more mental than physical and the possibilities are almost limitless. Mad men can behave and act like dogs or pigs or imitate much lower forms of animal life.

Man's life, even today, is governed by the vast and grand system of *Taqwīm* and it is fortunate that he cannot interfere with the grand scheme of things, except superficially. He transgresses in the area of his moral life and sinks even lower than the behaviour of lowly placed animal species emerging as a man of bestial attitude. In fact, in that area alone we can say with certainty that this Quranic principle of *Asfala Sāfilīn* can, and does, apply fully. He can cross all limits in his transgressions against his own fellow human beings, surpassing the beastliest of beasts.

It is important for us to identify the areas of life over which man has power to interfere, as the process of *Asfala Sāfilīn* will only operate within the boundaries of those spheres. The behaviour of life at subhuman level shows that the behaviour of animals is governed largely by instinctive forces. The process of their minds and decision-making have little to do with their day-to-day activities. They are not provided with any code of life to influence their behaviour, almost all they have is intuition. Hence all spheres of their lives are controlled by the laws of nature which they must follow. If for instance, beasts require a particular food for their sustenance, they will do whatever they can to obtain it. No code of conduct will impose any restriction on their mode of hunt. No one can tell them to get food in this way or that. Their act of killing an animal for their own survival is not considered as contrary to the principle of justice, neither will their action of sparing a life be counted as a display of justice.

Among animal life, there is no responsibility or code of life as such. Hence the terms *Qawwām* and *Taqwīm* are widely applicable even in such areas where according to human understanding, the issue of *'Adl* is irrelevant. This variation in the usage of the above mentioned terminology is to avoid confusion and to differentiate their spheres.

It should be remembered that *Taqwīm* is an act of creating balance in all such situations where the animal involved is incapable of consciously realising the importance of balance and poise. Yet this is what he needs. Hence *Taqwīm* should be understood as an act of God expressed through various laws in nature largely responsible for confining the progress of life to the middle path.

All through its journey towards man, life has been subjected to a course of *Taqwīm* by the decree of

Allah, so that its ultimate direction towards its destination is clearly defined and set.

Unworded lessons drawn from the long journey of evolution are all that guide the steps of life as it enters the phase of man. From then on, other factors such as environment, family and racial influences attempt to deviate the course of man from its middle path. Then a conscious effort on his part to resist these influences is termed as *Ta'dīl* in the Holy Quran.

Although man has reached a stage where he can consciously make free choices to adhere to, or to deviate from the middle path, yet within a system, *Taqwīm* continues to work unruffled and without his conscious knowledge of what is happening to him. Fortunately for him, he cannot interfere with the course of *Taqwīm* working internally. He can only superficially interfere with it when, accidentally or consciously, he fails to do justice to his health. This neglect or accident damages a minute portion of one of his internal organs thereby upsetting the whole ecosystem of kinds of balance and counterbalance. Thus, just a tiny disease can influence the entire body and make it unhealthy in its totality. All the natural laws operating within him which are taking care of his health and physical behaviour, are a result of an extremely long course of *Taqwīm* during his evolution.

A study of the ecosystem will also help a researcher to understand the wisdom which lies behind absolute justice in the animal kingdom but this will be dealt with at a later stage.

The dividing line between man and pre-human forms of life is simply this: man is often in a position to choose freely from the many options available to him whereas animals do not have such options. Whatever options they have are imposed and free will has little role to play. This separates man from lower orders of life. This area of options provides him with distinctive advantages as well as disadvantages in comparison to animals. If man follows and adopts the principle of justice in these areas, he is promised boundless progress. But if he chooses to reject these principles, he is warned that he will revert to the early stages of *Asfala Sāfilīn.*

2 The Creation of the Universe

We will now see how all constituent parts of the universe work according to the principles mentioned in the following verse of the Holy Quran:

وَالسَّمَآءَ رَفَعَهَا وَوَضَعَ الْمِيزَانَ ۩ أَلَّا تَطْغَوْا فِي الْمِيزَانِ ۩ وَأَقِيمُوا
الْوَزْنَ بِالْقِسْطِ وَ لَا تُخْسِرُوا الْمِيزَانَ ۩

And the heaven He has raised high and set up the measure, that you may not exceed the measure. So weigh all things with justice and fall not short of the measure.
(Sūrah al-Raḥmān; Ch.55: Vs.8-10)

In these verses, God says that He has created the heavens high, pointing out its loftiness as well as its grandeur. Both of these characteristics depend totally upon balance; this celestial universe is not only made on the principle of justice but also works as a touchstone for it.

The word *Mīzān* (مِيْزَانَ) includes the principles as well as the instruments by which justice can be measured. The message for man implied in this word is that if one were to cast a glance at the heavens and whatever they contain as created by God, one would find therein absolute balance and nothing but perfect symmetry. With the help of this grand plan of God's creation one can truly understand the meaning of absolute justice.

The whole universe is subject to one uniform law and its constituent parts unite to form a glorious harmony of structure and motion. If this harmony or equilibrium between different things is in the least disturbed, a universal chaos would result. But God has kept all the laws that regulate the world under His exclusive control beyond the reach of man. This supreme principle operates everywhere in the creation of the universe and intrinsically possesses poise and balance. Had there been an absence of absolute justice in the operation anywhere in the universe, utter disorder would have ensued.

Balance and symmetry in the inanimate world are expressed in terms of absolute justice and equity, clearly indicating that not only is the universe the handiwork of one Creator, but it is the same single Supreme Being who constantly maintains the running of this enormous edifice. The point can be further explained by examining the work of an artist, whose masterpieces are easily recognised by the supremacy of his talent and skill.

An in-depth study of the universe reveals the amazing fact that despite its almost limitless vastness, there is not the slightest evidence of any contradiction between the laws of nature and the creative process which they govern. This state of perfect unison and harmony inevitably leads one's mind to God—the Supreme and Perfect Creator, the One and Only God.

However, there seem to be some chaotic states and apparent conflict as one casts a superficial glance over God's creation. Things appear to be in conflict with varying interests and opposing motives. Yet, in that unending state of conflict, there lies a hidden hand of justice which is constantly at work. A most beautiful and amazing balance of symmetry is created which, when applied to the struggle of existence between animal and animal, and species and species, is termed as the 'ecosystem'.

In the grand plan of creation, animal life also occupies a sphere of activity or function. The laws that we observe in the entire cosmos as being in perfect agreement with each other, are simulated in the comparatively smaller sphere of the laws which govern life. Each section of the universe moves within its sphere under the specific laws designed for that particular domain. The laws of chemistry, physics, nuclear behaviour and their mutual interplay give birth to the animal kingdom. A new code of life suddenly appears as they emerge into existence and in the area of each species, certain laws specific to these species appear to gain control and command of their lives.

The study, if correct, leads to the inevitable conclusion that at every later stage of creation, as it spirally moved forward and upward, had there been any other interfering force outside the agency of the Primary Creator, there would certainly have erupted a chaos and disorder which could quake the entire creation. Once such a balance as this is disturbed it can never be restored again. This exactly is the Quranic statement regarding perfect harmony and order as one may observe in Allah's creation.

The following verse speaks eloquently on this subject:

لَوۡ كَانَ فِيۡهِمَاۤ اٰلِهَةٌ إِلَّا اللّٰهُ لَفَسَدَتَا ۚ فَسُبۡحٰنَ اللّٰهِ رَبِّ الۡعَرۡشِ عَمَّا يَصِفُوۡنَ ☐

If there had been in them (the heavens and the earth) other gods beside Allah, then surely both would have gone to ruin.
(Sūrah al-Anbiyā'; Ch.21: V.23)

Nowhere in the vast expanse of the universe does there appear to be the slightest sign of duality. Everything continues to run in smooth and perfect harmony in relation to each other, and in relation to all other spheres in creation. The eternal march forward for evolution would be inconceivable without this perfect universal harmony. If there had been more than one maker, then more than one law would have governed the universe. For each god, it would have been necessary to create the universe with his own special laws and hence disorder and confusion would have been the inevitable result and the whole universe would have gone to pieces.

We should also bear in mind that everything in the universe is constantly changing; if the change is for the better, then we call it progress or evolution. Most often, what makes a thing better than the earlier state is the reorganisation of components that adds to its quality and beauty. In short, disorder is ugliness and order is beauty. This exactly is the nature of evolution that we observe on earth. The quality of life is gradually becoming more complex. The higher the step in the tree of evolution, the more organised its constituents. Looking at it from this perspective, we can briefly describe evolution as a journey from disorderliness to orderliness, from a loosely organised state to an ever-increasing complexity. This indeed is the dividing line between life and death.

Although this is a complex scientific subject, a poet of the Urdu language, B. Narayan Chakbast, has brought it within our grasp by expressing it simply and beautifully in the following words:

زندگی کیا ہے عناصر کا ظہور ترتیب

موت کیا ہے انہیں اجزاء کا پریشاں ہونا

which translates as: 'What is life but the end product of organised elements and what is death other than the disorganisation of the same again?'

When matter goes through a chain of chemical reactions, newer and more complex molecular combinations are evolved. A stage is reached at last where, with the help of enormously advanced and complex organic chemicals, it is possible to build the first brick of life, which is DNA. All the constituents of life begin to acquire different new shapes, meanings, looks, depths and heights with the reorganisation of the bricks of life into new patterns. The elements are set in well-designed formations like jewels embedded in an ornament, and the elements begin to emanate the brilliance of life and life begins to sparkle. Break this organisation and smash the jewels into their initial chemical states and you are left with nothing but dead carbonates.

So the Holy Quran is most certainly right when it draws the conclusion that, had there been more than one Master of the universe, the gods would have vied with each other for the rights of possession and the universe would have ended in disorder and chaos. In other words we can describe life as the outcome of balance and poise, and what ensues from their absence is death. If mankind had understood this in-depth message of the Holy Quran, and had acknowledged and adhered to the Unity of God, it would have been a different world indeed.

The Universal Law of Gravitation

There is enough scientific evidence and ample material at hand to substantiate the claim that justice played a crucial role in the creation of the universe, but it would suffice here to illustrate the point under discussion with reference to the universal law of gravity. According to this law, any two particles of matter in the universe are attracted to each other with a force whose magnitude is directly proportional to the product of their masses and inversely proportional to the square of the distance between them. This mutual attraction is called gravitation. Without the perfect equation and balance in opposing forces, the universe could not have achieved its ultimate balance. This applies to the macro as well as the micro universe of molecules and atoms.

Everything in orbit is made to stay in orbit as a result of perfectly balanced centripetal and centrifugal forces. A highly complex net of such forces binds the heavenly bodies and results in the maintenance of the universal stability.

The Holy Quran refers to the same creative genius of God when it speaks of every heavenly body as being set in an elliptical orbital motion. This applies to all solar systems as well as to the galaxies and the groups of galaxies. Not a particle of nature is exempt from this all-embracing law. One observes the same orbital motions when one peeps into the exceedingly diminutive world of molecules and atoms.

The orbital motion of a planet has to be perfectly balanced in relation to the counter forces of gravity, which constantly pull it inwards. This depends on the exactness of the speed by which it is moving around the centre. Add a few miles to, or subtract a few miles from the speed, and the bodies in orbit will either break loose from their orbits and run amok or collapse within them. Such perfectly matched and balanced forces and counter forces are not a matter of a few examples alone. The universe abounds in billions upon billions of such star systems which present the same mathematical precision in their orbital design. To simplify numbers to a layman's understanding, we can say that the existing universes and galaxies are virtually innumerable.

The wonderful harmony in the universe is termed as *Mīzān* in the Holy Quran. Numerous scholars have spoken and written on this subject from different angles, for the exploration of the universe is an inexhaustible subject. The explorers have not even penetrated the peripheral secrets of the universe. Thousands upon thousands of studies have been made and books written, each bringing to light more aspects of the grand balance of things in the universe. Each testifies again and again to the truth of a single word used by the Holy Quran to indicate the central principle which governs the entire universe, i.e. *Mīzān,* meaning perfect balance or absolute justice.

Einstein pondered upon this subject during his study and exploration of the astronomical laws which govern the motion of the heavenly bodies. He was amazed beyond expression to find perfect symmetry and poise within the universe. Wonder-struck, he said, this perfect symmetry compels us to believe that there has to be a Supreme Creator and Designer of the universe. He perhaps did not believe in a personal God who could commune with man and reveal religion, but at least he had to admit the existence of a Supreme Creator who could think and plan perfectly and implement His design to the ultimate perfection.[2]

The following verses from the Holy Quran illustrate the wonder of Allah's universe:

تَبٰرَكَ الَّذِيْ بِيَدِهِ الْمُلْكُ ۫ وَهُوَ عَلٰى كُلِّ شَيْءٍ قَدِيْرُ ۙ الَّذِيْ خَلَقَ الْمَوْتَ وَالْحَيٰوةَ لِيَبْلُوَكُمْ اَيُّكُمْ اَحْسَنُ عَمَلًا ۭ وَهُوَ الْعَزِيْزُ الْغَفُوْرُ ۙ الَّذِيْ خَلَقَ سَبْعَ سَمٰوٰتٍ طِبَاقًا ۭ مَا تَرٰى فِيْ خَلْقِ الرَّحْمٰنِ مِنْ تَفٰوُتٍ ۭ فَارْجِعِ الْبَصَرَ ۙ هَلْ تَرٰى مِنْ فُطُوْرٍ ۙ ثُمَّ ارْجِعِ الْبَصَرَ كَرَّتَيْنِ يَنْقَلِبْ اِلَيْكَ الْبَصَرُ خَاسِئًا وَّ هُوَ حَسِيْرٌ ۙ

Blessed is He in Whose hand is the Kingdom, and He has power over all things;

It is He Who has created death and life that He might try you—which of you is best in deeds; and He is the Mighty, the Most Forgiving, *The Same* Who has created seven heavens in stages. No incongruity can you see in the creation of the Gracious *God*. Then look again: Do you see any flaw?

Aye, look again, and yet again, your sight will *only* return to you frustrated and fatigued.

(Sūrah al-Mulk; Ch.67: Vs.2-5)

Allah is the One who has created death and life and between the two He has caused a constant struggle. These verses of the Holy Quran actually enumerate the principle of the survival of the fittest. As a result of this struggle, God determines which of His living creation acts in the most befitting manner. What these verses deal with is that in the struggle between right and wrong, right must emerge victorious and wrong must be annihilated.

In comparative terms applicable to the evolutionary processes, it is the direction which would determine the fate of a living object. If a thing is moving towards death, it constantly loses some of its quality of life and the converse is also true. Between these two opposite ends lie innumerable stages of comparative life and death. These are the only two directions in which every living being in the universe is moving. Things are improving or deteriorating while they are moving upwards or falling downwards. Whichever life form moves along the course to a comparative state of higher consciousness seems to be moving in the direction of man. Every species of a lower order, when seen from the vantage point of a higher species, appears to be relatively closer to death. Each step that it takes in the direction of life is a step in the direction of comparative perfection and beauty. Although there is an end to everything which moves towards death, no end lies in the direction of life because this path leads to Allah, and Allah is infinite.

The above quoted verse numbers 2–3, mention two attributes of God at their end, '*Azīz-ul-Ghafūr*. '*Azīz* means He is powerful and worthy of respect because of the powerful knowledge He possesses, and *Ghafūr* means He is very forgiving. These attributes signify that the more knowledgeable the living become, the more worthy of respect they would be and also more powerful. The second attribute means that although the living would make many mistakes during their progress, God would forgive most of these mistakes and they will not suffer a setback because of them.

It is He who created the seven heavens in the rightful proportion. Not the slightest flaw or contradiction can be found in His creation. We are challenged to look around the universe and detect any flaw in God's creation. One is amazed that this challenge was given to mankind through Prophet Muhammad[sa] at a time when the understanding of people regarding the earth and heavens was childishly naive and was based on ancient philosophy. Nothing then of the vision of the universe could prompt anyone to throw a challenge in the defence of its beauty and perfection. This challenge is repeated once again, coaxing man to explore the vast expanse of the universe in search of a flaw. But answering the challenge itself, the Quran points out that we will find no flaw and our searching sights would return to ourselves, vain, tired and totally defeated.

3   The Ecosystem

Balance between Earth and the Heavenly Bodies

The function of the atmospheric phenomena operative between the earth and the heavenly bodies is amazing. One is astonished to notice the complex scientific observations found in the Holy Quran, revealed to Prophet Muhammad[sa] over fourteen hundred years ago. Today's scientists have spared no effort to discover the mysteries of the universe, yet the Holy Quran is far ahead of them in the grasp and profound understanding of the laws of nature and its workings. The fruits that their efforts have borne are praiseworthy indeed, but they have their limitations.

The Earth's Atmosphere

The Holy Quran dictates:

فَقَضٰهُنَّ سَبْعَ سَمٰوٰتٍ فِيْ يَوْمَيْنِ وَاَوْحٰى فِيْ كُلِّ سَمَآءٍ اَمْرَهَا ۚ وَزَيَّنَّا السَّمَآءَ الدُّنْيَا بِمَصَابِيْحَ ۚ وَحِفْظًا ۚ ذٰلِكَ تَقْدِيْرُ الْعَزِيْزِ الْعَلِيْمِ □

So He completed them into seven heavens in two days, and He revealed to each heaven its function. And We adorned the lowest heaven with lamps *for light* and for protection. That is the decree of the Mighty, the All-Knowing.
(Sūrah Ḥā Mīm al-Sajdah; Ch.41: V.13)

39

God has perfected the heavens, and each one of them is functioning in accordance with the purpose of its creation. Then the Holy Quran refers to the lowest atmospheric layer as the nearest heaven to the earth, and points out that it has been created for the protection of the earth. The most that man of that age could understand was that heaven was somehow protecting them. No one had the faintest idea as to what he was being protected from and why he was being protected.

One definition of justice is to fully comprehend what we are drawing attention to. It is essential to observe that absolute justice does not permit any part to interfere with the role of other parts. As far as the harmful effects are concerned, every part of the system is fully protected and insulated against their negative influence. For the beneficial aspects of the mechanism, their flow is not barred from reaching other parts but instead is promoted to the maximum (this is not against the concept of justice). Having understood this, we shall realize that the function the nearest heaven is performing for the implementation of justice, in application to the material world, should be described as perfect balance and harmony.

Let us now examine the role that various layers of atmosphere around the globe are playing. It should be remembered that although the nearest heaven seems to indicate one single entity of a heaven, in reality this heaven is further divided into many spheres. It is with reference to some of these spheres that we will further elaborate our study.

The Troposphere

To define troposphere, the following excerpt by William Van Der Bijl is quoted:

'The first sphere is termed as the 'troposphere'. The troposphere is a layer of atmospheric air extending about seven miles upward from the earth's surface, in which the temperature falls with height. As it is directly above the earth's surface, it is of most immediate concern to mankind. This seven mile layer of gases skirts the earth's surface and is held there by the force of gravity. It has many functions to perform, the entire life system is supported by this part of the nearest heaven. Moreover, this layer works as a protective cushion. Suspended in the gases are a countless number of particles of solid matter, specks of inanimate dust, and tiny living organisms which are swept aloft from the earth's surface by the incessant movement of the air. It is this cushion which protects the earth and life on earth from the constant bombardment of stray heavenly bodies. Without this cushion, it would have been impossible for life of any sort to be sustained on earth. Another point worthy of note is that the density of this layer is exactly what is needed and that the size of the layer is made to measure.

If the balance were somehow disturbed, this layer would be of no benefit to life on earth. It would rather work to the contrary; the light of the sun and other beneficial rays which must reach the earth, would be fogged out.'[3]

The Stratosphere

The stratosphere as defined by William Van Der Bijl is:

> 'The stratosphere is the second lowest of the four atmospheric layers. Its lower boundary is called the tropopause and its upper boundary, the stratopause. The underlying troposphere is characterised by vertical temperature gradient and vertical instability (weather changes). In contrast, temperatures in the stratosphere remain the same, or even increase with increasing height, which indicates vertical stability. The stratospheric air flow is mainly horizontal. Ultraviolet absorption by the ozone cause the high temperatures of the stratosphere which is usually between 48 & 53 km or 30 & 33 miles above the earth's surface.'[4]

This brief study of the functioning of the two spheres as part of the nearest heaven, mentions but only a few of the complex functions they perform. But even this preliminary knowledge is quite sufficient to astound man and drown him in an ocean of bewilderment. How precisely and thoughtfully the nearest heaven is organised and split into spheres to perform specific functions. Disturb the balance by the slightest degree and life as such will be rendered insupportable on earth. Any reduction in the ozone layer would be enough to destroy all forms of life as intense cosmic radiation would reach the earth undeterred. This study is not only useful to demonstrate the deeper meaning of *'Adl* and balance, as reflected in the universe, but it also creates a bridge between man and his Creator. The deeper one delves into the mysteries of nature, the higher is raised the level of gratitude and sense of awareness of what God has done for man. No game of chance could create and support life on earth and help it reach the dizzy heights occupied by man. Billions of measures are taken to maintain balance among various forces to make this world a befitting abode for the sustenance of life.

The Magnetosphere

The magnetosphere is a region in the atmosphere where magnetic phenomena and the high atmospheric conductivity caused by ionisation are essential in determining the behaviour of charged particles. Its function is to absorb infinite cosmic energy and to stop most of it from reaching the earth.

There are two basic types of cosmic rays, primary and secondary. Primary cosmic rays consist chiefly of protons (hydrogen nuclei) and alpha particles (helium nuclei). The majority of primaries have energies of nearly one billion electron volts. Although some primaries originate from the sun, the majority come from sources far from the earth (possibly violently exploding stars called super-novas) and at the highest energies from outside the Milky Way. Some primary cosmic rays enter the earth's atmosphere where they collide with oxygen and nitrogen nuclei, giving rise to secondary cosmic rays. These secondary cosmic rays include subatomic particles such as electrons, positrons, mesons, neutrinos, as well as photons. Highly energetic secondary cosmic rays interact with other nuclei in the atmosphere and generate still more secondary cosmic rays. Such successive collisions and the resultant proliferation of cosmic rays is termed as the cascade shower.

Cosmic radiation originally received the attention of the scientists simply because the phenomena posed a challenge to their understanding. The cosmic rays acquired great importance because of their influence on many areas of the life-support system on the earth. In fact human life on earth largely depends on secondary cosmic rays. They play a primary role in the making of chlorophyll in plants which is the pigment that gives them their green colour. Chlorophyll plays an essential role in photosynthesis, the process through which elements like carbon, oxygen and hydrogen are converted into such complex organic materials as constitute all forms of vegetative products. Starting from the root, leaves, stem, flowers and fruit, all owe their existence to the role of chlorophyll which works as an efficient factory run with combined energies of the sun's rays and secondary cosmic rays.

These secondary cosmic rays are highly penetrating and will pass through a great thickness of lead. They have been detected, still travelling downwards, at the bottom of the deepest mines, and also on the ocean floor. It has been estimated that a human is bombarded by some 25,000-30,000 cosmic ray particles every minute. Cosmic rays must be prevented from reaching the earth's surface in their primary form. This is achieved by the protective layers mentioned above. It is only the secondaries, resulting from their repeated collisions with oxygen and nitrogen atoms, which ultimately reach the earth.

As mentioned before in relation to the heavens, the Holy Quran uses the term *Mīzān,* which means balance or something which can be instrumental in determining balance. In relation to earth and earthly things, the Holy Quran uses another derivative from the same infinitive. The infinitive of *Mīzān* is *Wazn* (i.e. weight). *Mīzān* is derived from the connotation of both meanings just mentioned. Another derivative of the same root is *Mauzūn,* which literally means something made perfectly balanced or proportioned.

Is there any other book apart from the Holy Quran in the entire world which discusses such complex subjects with such ease and simplicity and such masterly command? A book with profound academic and scientific subjects, with a fluency and familiarity that is absolutely astounding. Although it discusses the problems and interests of today, the Holy Quran does not belong to this age but was revealed fourteen hundred years ago in a completely different era of knowledge and understanding. For it to discuss and reveal complex secrets of nature and the underlying phenomena in every creative process is mind boggling.

Some critics of Islam, and those who do not believe in the existence of God, allege that the Holy Quran was not authored by God but is merely the word of Prophet Muhammad[sa]. If so, the Holy Quran itself would then seem to present a mystery and dilemma of a much greater proportion than the mysteries of nature it discusses. It is amazing how they can afford to ignore the fact that Prophet Muhammad[sa], the person to whom they attribute the authorship of the Holy Quran, was unlettered. He was born in a country which was derogatorily referred to as the 'Land of the Illiterate'. On one side of Arabia was the highly advanced civilisation of Persia. On the other lay the great and vast Roman Empire, which was the cradle of knowledge where philosophies and sciences flourished like nowhere else in the world at that time. Both these contemporary superpowers looked down on Arabia with derision and contempt as a breeding ground of ignorance. The authorship of this great fountain of knowledge in such a land can in no way be attributed to the Holy Prophet[sa]—it can only be the Word of God.

The Earth

Among the principles of balance relating to the creation of the earth, the Holy Quran mentions a few for the purpose of illustration. For example,

وَٱلْأَرْضَ مَدَدْنَٰهَا وَٱلْقَيْنَا فِيهَا رَوَاسِيَ وَأَنۢبَتْنَا فِيهَا مِن كُلِّ شَىْءٍ مَّوْزُونٍ ☐

And the earth have We spread out, and set therein firm mountains and caused everything to grow therein in proper proportion.
(Sūrah al-Ḥijr; Ch.15: V.20)

This verse of the Holy Quran indicates that God has created the heavens and the earth on similar principles of perfect balance. Consequently whatever is created within the earth and the heavens follows the principles of justice. Hence, God most appropriately declares the heavens to be *Mīzān* and the earth to be *Mauzūn,* indicating that the earth did not become balanced by itself but was balanced by an outside superior balancing.

The word *Mīzān,* relating to heavenly principles of justice, also has a clear connotation of being instrumental in creating balance in other things. Therefore, the principle of justice as observed on earth is not born out of its own intrinsic quality but out of something which is bestowed upon it in the heavens. Here we are led to the recognition of another reality;

the excellence of all material forms of existence on earth depend upon their being in harmony with heavenly principles. Likewise, it is quite sensible to draw the lesson that genuine heavenly people are better fitted to lead the rest of the world in everything good.

$$\cdots \Box\text{وَأَنۢبَتۡنَا فِيهَا مِن كُلِّ شَيۡءٍ مَّوۡزُونٍ}\Box$$

...And We caused everything to grow therein in proper proportion.
(Sūrah al-Ḥijr; Ch.15: V.20)

Everything in the earth grows under the influence of the supreme law of nature of absolute justice. There is no option but to follow it. The Divine laws of nature seem to control all areas of growth on earth.

In this context the use of the Arabic word *Ambatnā* or 'we caused to grow' requires special attention. Commonly it is believed that this word is used only in reference to the phenomena of vegetative growth. This is not true. The Holy Quran uses the same word in application to human birth and development as well.

In Sūrah al-Nūḥ verse 18, the same word *Nabāt* is used in direct application to the creation of man on earth and his subsequent development. The verse runs as follows:

$$\Box\text{وَٱللَّهُ أَنۢبَتَكُم مِّنَ ٱلۡأَرۡضِ نَبَاتًا}\Box$$

And Allah has caused you to grow as a *good* growth

from the earth.
(Sūrah Nūḥ; Ch.71: V.18)

Here, addressing man, God categorically declares the birth and growth of man to have taken place through the same processes as are covered by the word *Nabatāt,* meaning vegetative growth.

Mountains

We will now look at Sūrah al-Ḥijr verse 20 again, along with verses 11 and 12 of Sūrah Luqmān, and see how the latter talks about the same phenomena in more detail regarding the subject under discussion.

وَالۡاَرۡضَ مَدَدۡنٰهَا وَاَلۡقَيۡنَا فِيۡهَا رَوَاسِيَ وَاَنۡۢبَتۡنَا فِيۡهَا مِنۡ كُلِّ شَيۡءٍ مَّوۡزُوۡنٍ ☐

And the earth have We spread out, and set therein firmly rooted mountains and caused everything to grow therein in proper proportion.
(Sūrah al-Ḥijr; Ch. 15: V.20)

...وَ اَلۡقٰى فِى الۡاَرۡضِ رَوَاسِيَ اَنۡ تَمِيۡدَ بِكُمۡ وَبَثَّ فِيۡهَا مِنۡ كُلِّ دَآبَّةٍ وَاَنۡزَلۡنَا مِنَ السَّمَآءِ مَآءً فَاَنۡۢبَتۡنَا فِيۡهَا مِنۡ كُلِّ زَوۡجٍ كَرِيۡمٍ ☐ هٰذَا خَلۡقُ اللّٰهِ فَاَرُوۡنِىۡ مَاذَا خَلَقَ الَّذِيۡنَ مِنۡ دُوۡنِهٖ بَلِ الظّٰلِمُوۡنَ فِىۡ ضَلٰلٍ مُّبِيۡنٍ ☐

...and He has placed in the earth firm mountains so that they may provide you with food and He has scattered therein all kinds of creatures and We have

49

sent down water from the clouds, and caused to grow therein noble pairs from every species. This is the creation of Allah. Now show me what others beside Him have created. Nay, but the wrongdoers are in manifest error.
(Sūrah Luqmān; Ch.31: Vs.11-12)

The word employed here to refer to mountains is *Ravāsiya,* meaning something which is deeply and firmly rooted. The Arabs, because of this connotation, refer to mountains by the same word. Most translations of the Holy Quran translate the expression *Tamīda bikum* in relation to mountains, to mean that mountains are created to save mankind from earthquakes. This translation cannot be accepted in view of the fact that the role of mountains is not to save the earth from earthquakes. On the contrary, most centres of the earthquakes are situated in mountains above the surface of the earth, or in volcanic mountains hidden deep in the oceans. It is not appropriate to translate the word of God in contradiction to His act of creation.

Maddā Yamuddu, from which the word *Tamīda bikum* is derived, reveals another meaning indicating the setting of the table in preparation for a meal. Thus the translation should be, 'We created firmly rooted mountains so that they would work as a source for providing you with food.'

In short, God has created the mountains not because they protect mankind from earthquakes but because sustenance of life depends on the existence of mountains. The system supporting the food chain necessary for life is maintained and supported by them which creates a perfect image for the word *Mauzūn.*

Only 30% of the global surface is made up of dry land which is divided into five continents. The remaining 70% of the earth's surface is covered with oceans and lakes. But this water that we see is not all the water that there is. It is most amazing that actually 75% of the total water is locked up in the form of ice in mountain tops in the Northern Hemisphere. If mountains did not work as a reservoir for frozen water, and if the ice melted and returned to the oceans, then the 30% of available dry land would be completely submerged. There would be nothing but oceans covering the entire surface of the earth.

Mountains play a significant role in maintaining the balance of water on earth. Purification of water for human consumption and vegetative life is also another important function performed by mountains. The process by which water circulates from the oceans to the mountains and returns again to the oceans is a long story. However, in this cycle, clean water is consumed by the vegetative and zoological life on earth and polluted water flows back to the sea again.

The mountains also play an important role in the precipitation of moisture. In polar and high mountain regions, most moisture precipitation is in the form of snow rather than rain; there the snow is compacted into ice sheets and glaciers.

There is a constant gravitational force working on these huge mountains of ice. This gravitational force plays an important role in releasing the entrapped potential energy of the ice. It is a natural law that when ice is pressed hard, the surface where the pressure is the greatest gains a much higher temperature and begins to melt the ice. Even in areas where the temperature falls below -60°C, the underside of the glacier is always melting. Consequently, a glacier touching a mountain surface rises in temperature and melts. Thus the entire glacier loses its grip upon the mountain and begins to slide downwards. As it slides, it carries along huge boulders and rocks embedded within, and also destroys other obstructions on the way during its downward journey. This results in the grating of boulders and rocks etc. into many smaller stones and pebbles. Grains of salt are also created as an end product.

But for this law, all the water of the oceans could have been transformed and transported back to the mountains and poles. Eventually all human life would cease to exist as all water would be converted into oceans of ice.

Again, there is another role mountains play in the support of life as they provide fertility to the soil of the earth by different means. It should be remembered that artificial manure used for fertilising soil consists mostly of various ammonium salts. When highly electrically charged rain clouds are carried by strong air currents towards mountains, they break into electrical storms, lightning and thunderbolts, which in turn disintegrate water particles and nitrogen gases in the air into many ammonium salts, enriching the rain or snow. According to some estimates, the entire production of fertilisers in the man-made industry in the world in one year equals the fertilisers manufactured by this process in one hour.

A detailed study of all these operations will truly illustrate the wealth of knowledge found in the Holy Quran regarding the blessings of mountains for human life on earth. A verse from Surah Ḥā Mīm al-Sajdah is quoted below:

وَجَعَلَ فِيهَا رَوَاسِيَ مِن فَوْقِهَا وَبَٰرَكَ فِيهَا وَقَدَّرَ فِيهَآ
أَقْوَاتَهَا فِىٓ أَرْبَعَةِ أَيَّامٖ سَوَآءٗ لِّلسَّآئِلِينَ ☐

He set therein firm mountains rising above *its surface*, and placed blessings therein and finely balanced its means of sustenance in four periods—alike for *all* who seek.
(Sūrah Ḥā Mīm al-Sajdah; Ch.41: V.11)

In short, when we observe the manifestations of the laws of nature in the way the affairs of earth and the surrounding heavens are governed, we find perfect unison, coordination and balance. The changes of day into night and night into day, the alternation of different seasons from winter to summer, autumn to spring, from hot to cold and their specific effects on life upon earth, are factors which have a profound effect on our life supporting system.

Balance in the Atmospheric Gases

Each season has its own significance, whether welcome or not. Each of them is essential, jointly or separately, for maintaining the ecosystem on earth – not only in relation to the various forms of life but also by keeping balance in the elements.

Why should there be a certain proportion of nitrogen, oxygen and carbon dioxide in the air and why should there be the presence of rare gases? These are the questions drawing the ever-growing attention of the scientists to resolve and tackle. One thing for certain is that these proportions are not accidental, and a disturbance in the balance will disrupt the entire ecosystem of life. Even if the proportion of carbon dioxide were to rise by as much as 1% in the atmosphere, the effect could be devastating. What one reads in the newspapers about the greenhouse effect is little understood by the common reader. But readers become deeply concerned when the scientists inform them as to the real significance of this effect. If, for example, carbon dioxide were to rise by as much as 4-5%, the planet earth would no longer be fit for hosting life. It is not just a question of the proportion of carbon dioxide alone. Each element found in the atmosphere serves a purpose and is needed in exactly the proper proportion at which it is found. The same applies to the upper layers of the earth's atmosphere.

In the stratosphere, the layer of the ozone is said to extend from eighteen to thirty miles in thickness. If by some accident this balance of the ozone layer were upset, there would be every danger for the earth to be bombarded by cosmic radiation at short wavelengths which are extremely destructive to life. Ozone specifically destroys ultraviolet at short wavelengths.

Balance in the Vegetative and Animal Kingdoms

The balance within species in relation to each other and the balance between the animal and the vegetative domains, are increasingly attracting the scientists' attention. These kinds of balance comprise many categories. We enumerate some of them as below:

- the balance of living organisms in relation to the habitat where they belong
- the balance between the predator and it's prey
- the balance in migration of fish from their breeding grounds in mountain tops to oceans, and their counter migration back to their breeding grounds
- The maintenance of balance between rivers and lakes and the interchange of the various life-forms they contain to and from the oceans.

Scientists are involved in these and many other similar studies, and each discovery leads them on to another underlying mystery of such balances, layer after layer.

In order to describe the principle of justice operative in the entire ecosystem, covering both the inanimate and the animate, and their mutual co-ordination, one cannot conceive of a better expression or description than the word *Mauzūn*.

In short, the principle of justice found in the Holy Quran is so vast that one finds it operative in every particle of the universe. Much has been said and written on this topic, but the subject is inexhaustible. It would not be appropriate therefore to make an attempt here to discuss this subject in intricate scientific terms. The discussion, however interesting it may be, will remain out of reach of the layman.

4   The Animal Kingdom

As far as the approach of philosophers is concerned, some among them believe that the creation of the universe does not require a Creator. They argue that it is an ongoing automatic, blind, evolutionary process. On this basis they obviously try to understand and tackle human nature with the same blind principle.

Such Philosophers propose that there should be no special moral and ethical restrictions on man and that he should be as free to shape his life as animals are. In this scenario we do not find any role for an outside agency like God to legislate for man as a Supreme Lawgiver. In their opinion, the concept of justice is born merely out of the exercise of the human intellect which, in relation to its long chain of human experiences from time immemorial, gradually began to deduce rules and regulations for human society as it developed. So they began to legislate, among other things, in matters relating to justice too.

The religious doctrine is in direct clash with this secular social theory. Religion teaches us that the faculty of discretion is granted to man by God with a specific purpose—to decide whether he should allow himself to follow his instinctive desires like animals, or whether he should refrain from following a course of action in certain situations.

Conclusively if we believe that this attribute has been granted to mankind by God, it logically follows that the guidance on what he should do or should not do must also come from God, through His revealed guidance.

However, this argument needs to be elucidated with the help of some illustrations. For instance, a lion's natural instinct will tell him to go and kill an animal for the satisfaction of his hunger, but his ability to determine that his animal should be killed in the least painful manner is beyond his creative limitations. It is God who has intuitively taught him ways to kill his prey in a mode that would be least painful, in the sense that the affliction of unnecessary pain is avoided.

Over a long period of gradual implementation, the process of *Taqwīm* resulted in a slow but definite and well oriented transformation, whereby animals gradually gained awareness of the pain and suffering of others. Among humans, it began as a first step with the closest kith and kin and gradually it extended to the wider family circles and ultimately into the much larger sphere of all fellow human beings. Then came the turn of feeling for the suffering of lower forms of life as well. This attribute was born out of the same sense of belonging to one another as observed in the entire animal kingdom. At the time of crisis, animals of the same species flock together. This intuitive tendency is perhaps responsible for the group awareness among dogs and wolves as well, who move in packs in the wilderness as hunting parties. These are but some examples in the evolutionary trend born out of same widening awareness of others' feelings. Also at times of danger, elephants and wild beasts, zebras and deer etc. react as a group or class against the common enemy. It is here that we see a diffused awareness of belonging to one species or group widening its borders. As man evolved, the same animal tendencies grew stronger and more distinct in him. His sense of feeling and care for others no longer remained confined to his own family or to the human species, but spilled over into the animal kingdom of lower order as well. At this stage, one realises the need for a code of behaviour for mankind whose sensitivity has extended even beyond human borders.

Ultimately, this plan of natural education and instructions resulting in material changes in the character-bearing genes of living animals, continued unbroken from one species to another higher species until it reached the stage of man. As nature broadened awareness in the evolving species of their surroundings, it also seems to have etched upon their character-bearing genes some of their behavioural patterns so that we can see specific behavioural patterns in each species as distinct from others. When one reaches the stage of man, one is astounded to discover that there is not just a drift of one or two notches between man and earlier life, but that there is a vast difference. Man has not only become alive to what he sees around him, but has also become aware of some forms of existence which he cannot see, hear or feel directly. He is provided with the faculty of imagining various forms of possible existence and it is this higher stage of evolutionary development which broadens his vision limitlessly, far beyond the confines of the planet earth. This awareness prepares him to fulfil the next higher role that he is destined to play and provides him with the capability of boundless progress. This new faculty builds a bridge between him and the Creator and provides him with a means of communion with God.

As far as food for the sustenance of man is concerned, potentially he can be both carnivorous and herbivorous. Animal flesh has been a part of his diet from time immemorial. At the same time, he can also live entirely on vegetative products alone. This in itself illustrates the evolutionary direction of expansion. Apart from that, a very important social and moral question can be raised. One must also take into account a very important distinctive feature of man, viz., that he has been given the option to follow his instinctive desires or to refuse to act according to their dictates.

Here, when we re-examine the whole issue of man's options and the exercise of his options, the need for legislation and code of conduct becomes self evident. Now returning to the same issue, which relates to the food consumption of man for his survival, we take up the question of the eating of animal flesh once again. If man had free choice, he could hunt any animal to satiate his basic urge for survival and also satisfy his personal tastes and likings. It is not possible to expect each man to achieve the same tenderness and taste as others, and so the spectrum of choices grows very wide. Also, this offers a good opportunity to compare man's instinctive features to the lower stages of animal life.

The food habits in the animal kingdom are specifically programmed and individual variation of taste and value play little role in their overall behaviour. In man, however, the widening of options and choices has greatly enlarged the field of his eating habits. Man has now evolved to a stage where, in spite of his urge for meat eating, he can control and suppress his desire in favour of other options—a completely different trend from other animal behaviour. Here his developed mental faculties and a much wider spectrum of awareness, make it possible for him to reject his inner impulses for the sake of a higher ideal. This ideal becomes so important for him that he is able to sacrifice his natural urges and find satisfaction in an alternative, and despite his strong urge for eating flesh, he can command himself not to submit to that urge.

Animals are only controlled by their intuition while humans can make choices. They can behave like carnivorous animals as well as herbivorous ones. Amazingly, human teeth are also adapted to both dietary systems.

There is another large difference between animal and human behaviour. In certain situations, humans can act in a more beastly manner than the beasts themselves. Beasts can never become cannibals, they never eat their own species; humans can. Even in this age in certain dark patches in Africa, one can find cannibals. There are certain tribes who capture some members of other tribes living across their political borders, to abduct and kill them for their flesh. They do so with the beating of drums celebrating this great festival. It is hard to imagine lions, wolves and dogs behaving in the same manner towards their fellow lions, wolves and dogs. Beasts are never cannibalists even when stricken with starvation.

This apparent reflection on man's character should be studied in further depth, lest we draw the wrong conclusions. When man abstains from eating the flesh of his fellow human beings it is not merely intuitive; in fact he has both options available to him. There is no law of nature that stands between this malpractice and him. It is merely a higher stage of refinement in matters of values which prevents most men from such acts.

To illustrate this point in greater depth it must be stated that on the basis of non-cannibalistic tendencies, the lion may appear to be more civilised than man, but this is not necessarily conclusive. A lion only acts as he has been taught by nature, he does not deviate from a prescribed pattern. Man, on the other hand, must choose his own path. An award is merited only when there is an option of choice. When there is no option, the question of award does not come up. But where there are options there is also a need for legislating a code of conduct in the areas of rights, obligations, proprieties, improprieties etc. Therefore to make the right choice man stands in need of guidance from God. It is needed because of varying customs, habits, traditions, values and social backgrounds which prevail differently in different parts of the world. This is the philosophy of the Divine teachings which all the major religions of the world share.

Hence through a long, meandering course of gradual and steady instruction, man has ultimately reached the stage of humane conduct which distinguishes him from the animal kingdom of the lower order. This instruction comprises the inculcation of values not only belonging to the domain of *'Adl,* but also to the areas of *Iḥsān* and *Ītā'i Dhil-Qurbā.*

Moreover, light is also thrown on the meaning of *Ajrun Ghairu Mamnūn* which speaks of an endless journey of achievements and rewards, further refining man's conduct as he progresses. But it all hinges on the right choices on the part of man. If man continues with the right options, he will perpetually tread the path of constant refinement. However, if at any time he begins to abuse his freedom of choice he is bound to slide down the path of retrogression, the lowest stage of which is *Asfala Sāfilīn*; and it becomes quite unlikely for him to evince concern for his fellow human beings. He could become so callous and selfish in his behaviour as to degrade himself to an order lower than the order of beasts.

All the same, man has the exceptional ability to rise to the level of such refinement as is unseen in the rest of the animal kingdom. Man can achieve the highest form of nobility by performing righteous deeds while firmly adhering to the course of justice and fair play and can reach even the highest level of *Ītā'i Dhil-Qurbā* when he sacrifices his personal gain or comfort for the sake of others who are not actually his kith and kin.

We have demonstrated many exceptions to this. A slightly different exception is found in the case of some depraved humans who kill innocent children just for the sake of consumption of their flesh without any compulsion. Again, child abuse also belongs to the same category. Here the warning of the Holy Quran regarding the potential danger that man may return to the lowest rung is demonstrated.

Even as a group, man is known to indulge in heinous crimes of torture of his fellow human beings merely because of religious and political differences.

When bigoted, small minded religious clergy or despotic, immoral politicians gain ascendancy they lose all sense of balance and justice. The Spanish Inquisition is such a case in point.

Similarly the Muslim history of the Middle Ages is also blemished with such atrocious incidents, where governments took no measures to stop religious zealots from putting people to death merely because of differences of opinion in religious matters. Even a cursory glance at such beastly acts of human deprivation makes one shudder. Alas these chapters are not fully closed and still no one can say that man has now become so refined that now there is no danger of him reverting to his subhuman stage of conduct. The Ahmadiyya Muslim Community has itself been long subjected to religious persecution of a worse nature, making it no longer necessary for scholars to search through the pages of history for such evidence.

As against this, we also come across examples of such cultured and decent behaviour on the part of man which brings to mind the Quranic teachings of *'Adl, Iḥsān* and *Ītā'i Dhil-Qurbā*. Even when on the whole man seems to be sliding down the course of moral degradation, there are such singular examples of excellence that one's confidence in man's future is restored.

There is an interesting story which can be related here. A story it may be, but whoever wrote it provided us with an excellent opportunity to understand the relationship between *'Adl, Iḥsān* and *Ītā'i Dhil-Qurbā* and their respective merit in relation to each other.

It is said that once a holy man was sitting in an open field when suddenly an exhausted dove who was being chased by a falcon fell into his lap. He gave protection to the wretched dove but the falcon protested bitterly saying it was against the principle of justice and that it did not behove a holy man to deprive him from the hard earned fruit of his labour. He said, 'This is how nature has provided me the means of my sustenance.' The holy man accepted this argument but his benevolence would not permit him to hand over the helpless dove to the falcon.

As the story goes, he decided to cut a portion of his own flesh and offer it to the falcon, saying that he justly deserved a portion of fine meat, but his insistence that he must eat the flesh of that dove had no logic. He said, 'Nowhere has nature specified the dove for you. The meat you need is the meat I offer and that should suffice.'

This story is amazingly appropriate in illustrating the subject under discussion. It explains the true meaning of justice and the principles of its implementation in relative terms and in situations where one's life depends on the death of another.

In this scenario, an explanation of the principle of *Taqwīm* and justice would be that each animal has been granted provisions for his livelihood and the means to achieve them. At the same time, every animal faces perils related to the grand scheme of the 'struggle for existence'. Hence a well-balanced ecosystem is created which runs on the fundamental principles of justice.

The second aspect highlighted in this illustration is that justice is fundamental and absolute, and will be given priority over kindness whenever kindness comes into clash with the requirements of justice. Kindness can only be achieved if justice is maintained and not at its cost.

Central to this illustration is the question, that when justice seems to clash with benevolence what would be the third option that could resolve this dilemma? The option which the holy man chose was to sacrifice his own flesh to satisfy the simultaneous requirements of justice and benevolence. His conduct can also be called an act of *Ītā'i Dhil-Qurbā* because such an extreme sacrifice cannot be offered but for one's kith and kin.

This is the real meaning of *Ītā'i Dhil-Qurbā* in relation to *Iḥsān* and *'Adl*, that emerges from the study of the Holy Quran, and which governs the universe. However, it should be remembered that these three principles did not begin to operate simultaneously from the beginning of creation. In fact, the world of matter (inanimates) seems to be governed entirely by the principle of absolute justice.

With life was born the element of consciousness. As it grew stronger and as life evolved to a higher stage of awareness, both *Iḥsān* and *Ītā'i Dhil-Qurbā* began to evolve and they started to play an ever-growing role in guiding the steps of life. Until life reached the stage of man, it moved with a slow and steady pace as if in a continued procession. But as it reached the stage where there is a large gap between animal life and the life of human beings, it seems to have taken a gigantic leap forward which completely transformed the conduct of life, as if a new creation was begotten.

The adoption or rejection of the above principles by man brought about epoch-making changes, and trends developed in the history of man with far reaching effects.

The Role of Sensitivity and Consciousness in Relation to *'Adl*, *Iḥsān* and *Ītā'i Dhil-Qurbā*

Now the question arises as to why man's sensitivity, in comparison to that of an animal, became so significantly refined and developed. This is because sensitivity evolved gradually with the evolution of life and, having reached the stage of man, it suddenly started moving forward in leaps and bounds. This was so as the emphasis of evolution, after reaching the human stage, was not as much on his physical evolution as it was on his sensual and spiritual evolution.

After a long period of passing through several stages of progress, it widened its circle. Individuals became conscious of their surroundings and acquired awareness and sensitivity for their own species. At a higher stage than this their sensitivity and awareness extended to other species.

The presence of sensibility as observed among humans has become amazingly vast and intense. Here consciousness and sensibility are at play together. The difference does not relate only to comparative areas of operation but also applies to the quality of awareness and sensibility. There is no longer a vague sense of something, like a worm being in pain or the pleasure of an insect finding food, but it is far more clearly defined and intense. It is more intricately related to various functions of the human body and its memory; as such it becomes an intricate phenomenon.

It is is evident from this that these two faculties have played an important and complex role in refining and cultivating human behaviour in all its spheres, leaving indelible marks on all aspects of human conduct.

Among humans, sensitivity and consciousness work hand in hand with *'Adl, Ihsān* and *Ītā'i Dhil-Qurbā*. They give birth to new ideas, theories, concepts and beliefs and enlarge the spectrum of all that goes towards the making of human life. In short *'Adl, Ihsān* and. *Ītā'i Dhil-Qurbā* play a pivotal role in the making or breaking of man in relation to his ultimate destination.

5   Further Evolution of Man

A Study of the Micro-Universe of Man

Man presents the greatest miracle of creation. In him are concentrated and compacted a billion years of biotic evolution. This is no exaggeration whatsoever. In every human being there exists a complete and utter record of the entire history of animal evolution. Man is a micro-universe, indeed a living symbol of a perfect blending together of space and time. But before discussing this further, it is impossible not to mention the most amazing fact that the Holy Quran covers all the important stages and fundamental features of human creation, omitting no step and no stage worthy of mention.

Of all the forms of creation, it is man whose creation is mentioned in the Holy Quran to be the most symbolic and representative in demonstrating the role of justice in its perfection:

يَـٰٓأَيُّهَا ٱلْإِنسَـٰنُ مَا غَرَّكَ بِرَبِّكَ ٱلْكَرِيمِ ٱلَّذِى خَلَقَكَ فَسَوَّىٰكَ فَعَدَلَكَ فِىٓ أَىِّ صُورَةٍ مَّا شَآءَ رَكَّبَكَ

O Man! What has made you arrogant in relation to thy Noble Lord? The One who created you and perfectly proportioned you and fashioned you with justice. This

He did at every stage and in every form in which He
compounded and fashioned you.
(Sūrah al-Infiṭār; Ch.82: Vs.7-9)

Let us now re-examine the above verse at greater
length. God seems to address man as such: 'O Man!
on what grounds are you behaving so arrogantly
towards your Lord who created you? If it is beyond
you to comprehend the grandeur and limitless wonder
of the universe, you can at least delve into your own
being and wonder at the perfect balance with which
God has created you i.e. the universe within yourself.
Yet you have the audacity to question the existence of
God. Again, we reiterate the above, that it is He who
created you, then fashioned you, then proportioned
you.'

One of the verses just referred to, though revealed
fourteen hundred years ago, seems to have been
revealed in the contemporary air of advanced
knowledge to which we belong. At the time of the
revelation of the Holy Quran, there was no concept of
man having passed through embryonic stages; so
many different stages, so many shapes and organic
proportions reminiscent of the history of evolution.
Verse 9 of Sūrah al-Infiṭār quoted above simply could
not have been a product of the human mind of that
age. It reminds man that he has been passing through
so many different shapes and forms before his birth,
going through innumerable changes requiring
different organic proportions. One wonders what

message earlier people could have received from this verse that belonged to an age yet to dawn.

The theme is further developed in Surah al-Qiyāmah:

بَلِ الْاِنْسَانُ عَلٰى نَفْسِهٖ بَصِيْرَةٌ ۙ وَّ لَوْ اَلْقٰى مَعَاذِيْرَهٗ ۚ

Nay, man is fully aware of his ownself; Even though he puts forward his excuses.
(Sūrah al-Qiyāmah; Ch.75: Vs.15-16)

That is to say that man may hide behind his excuses, yet he has the ability to discover the ulterior motives behind his intentions. Again the Holy Quran speaking of the same innate capacity of man to understand himself, declares in Sūrah al-Shams:

فَاَلْهَمَهَا فُجُوْرَهَا وَتَقْوٰىهَا ۙ

And He revealed to it what is wrong for it (Fujūr) and what is right for it (Taqwā).
(Sūrah al-Shams; Ch.91: V.9)

This means that God has imbued in every soul the ability of knowing what is good for it and what is bad for it; what he should do and what he should abstain from doing. Hence, in referring to the innate messages computed into his nature, man is capable of judging right from wrong.

In other words, God has instilled in man's nature the faculty of intuition which warns him of the ever impending danger attendant upon his decisions. Likewise, he is provided with the faculty of caution which constantly discriminates between right and wrong and makes it practically impossible for him to do wrong without knowing it.

When these verses are studied in conjunction with each other, they seem to open up new avenues of knowledge. Scientists have attempted to explore these avenues to the full, but the more they explore the more they seem to grow in size and dimension. In fact they appear to be boundless. A comprehensive study of the secrets encoded in the character-bearing genes of life of all species would require hundreds of generations of scientists without their ever being able to exhaust the subject.

The Bricks of Life

When we examine human physique and its constituents, we are amazed to see the most complex system at work within our bodies. Man's body is made up of billions of cells. Each type of cell is different and each has special features which vary according to its function. The cells are of various shapes and sizes and are composed of many different parts. Each part is responsible for a specific function in the body. Although each part of the cell performs its relative function, central to it is the role of the nucleus whose functions are enormously complex and intricate.

The nucleus is positioned inside the cell in a membrane of its own. Inside the nuclear membrane there is the nucleoplasm, which has a concentration of RNA and DNA—the substance which plays a key role in the replication of the cell. The existence of a healthy cell depends upon its nucleus. It is an essential agent in the growth, metabolism, reproduction and transmission of characters.

By way of illustration we can say that the information stored in one body cell (of the billions we have in our body) is much more than the information stored in the most advanced and complex man-made computer memories. This means that billions of cells are built with exactly similar information, each having its own role to play in the body-complex. At the right moment, in the right direction, a reaction begins to take place within the cell organism which activates functions for which the cell is built and created. Similarly, the information is transmitted to all other relevant areas in the body with the help of RNA messenger cells. All this is carried out in perfect unison without any clash or discrepancy.

We should appreciate the fact that God revealed this information a long time ago to Prophet Muhammad[sa] through the Holy Quran—long before the scientists could examine the cellular wonders of man with the aid of microscopes—and thus one wonders at the perfect and most suitable expression used in the Holy Quran, viz., He created you, perfected you and fashioned you with justice and shaped you into so many different forms of perfect balance (see Sūrah al-Infiṭār; Ch.82: Vs.7-9). Man of that age probably wondered as to why the Holy Quran had used the word *'Adalaka* (عَدَلَكَ) to describe balance for the creation and structure of mankind. No previous book of philosophy or religion had described the creation of man in such clear terms.

Balance and Consciousness

It is interesting to note how Quranic expressions used in different places are intricately correlated. For instance, the phenomenon of balance is prevalent in all earthly objects. While *'Adl* is used to describe the principle of justice operative among human beings, this does not mean that man is not *Mauzūn*. *'Adl* encompasses *Mauzūn* as well as *Mīzān*, and also has the connotation of conscious realisation of balance and justice. Hence the question of *'Adl* indicates a far more advanced stage of balance with the added factor of consciousness. Man is described in the Holy Quran as the one who is created on the principle of *'Adl*, which puts him at the highest order in the grand Heavenly plan of justice and makes him most outstanding among all of God's creatures.

From the beginning, the principle of justice played a completely unconscious role in the form of the laws of nature. At a later stage, when evolution of the universe reached the threshold of life, the unconscious application of justice changed into an intuitive form of balanced behaviour. Also, the creative principles which run through all the evolutionary stages are all strictly governed by either complete unconsciousness or the intuitive operation of various kinds of balance. As has been emphasised before, only man reaches the third higher stage of consciousness.

Through billions of years of progress, life is constantly ushered into a gradually raised level of awareness. All that was meant and aimed at was the attainment of the final stage of conscious justice. This was essential for the further progress of human mind and soul, and for the journey to the unknown forms of a higher and more ethereal forms of existence. Each rung of this progressive ladder is made of *'Adl*. No higher forms of existence can be reached without moving from one stage of *'Adl* to another stage of *'Adl*. Justice was to give birth to *Iḥsān* and *Iḥsān* was to be transformed ultimately into that sublime relationship referred to as *Ītā'i Dhil-Qurbā* (treatment of others like one's kindred).

In short, the expression of *'Adl* has a special bond with consciousness of actions and behaviour. It is used to describe the behaviour of human beings, as their actions are determined by full consciousness and they do not have the tendency to sway in the direction of the left or the right. Here begins a new stage of life.

6 Different Kinds of Balance within Man's Body

The Inbuilt Criterion for Good and Bad

Previously we discussed verse 9 of Sūrah al-Shams elaborating on one of its meanings. Now we turn to another aspect of the same.

God has endowed the human physiology with the intrinsic potential to distinguish disease from health and creative phenomena from destructive phenomena. This system of discrimination works without the knowledge of human consciousness and as an ongoing self-flowing phenomenon. In fact, this applies not only to human beings but to all forms of life. Each species, whether elementary or advanced, is well equipped with an inbuilt ability which informs each individual of what is good for it and what is bad for it, within its own tiny world of the barest form of existence. Even the amoeba has its limitations of health and disease, what it should endeavour to possess, and what it should avoid and evade. But in man this is so highly developed and complex that even a cursory glance at its function is absolutely astounding.

The process of selection and rejection is observed in perfect operation at every level of human existence.

The following simple illustration will help elaborate the case in point: the appetite in man creates in him the awareness of the requirements of energy. The sense of sight, smell, touch and taste, and even in some cases the sense of hearing, all immediately begin to take an active part in determining what is good and what is bad for the man in need of some form of energy. When man begins to chew a morsel of food, the taste buds, heat buds, sensory organs relating to touch etc., teeth and salivary glands, jaw bones, and muscles of the jaws, all begin to play a perfectly balanced role. At last when something is swallowed, the selection process begins to play a more profound role in disintegrating the food into its constituent materials and purifying it from alien matters not needed by the body. Again, every step is taken to protect man from the harmful effects of bacterial or viral impurities. After these stages the partially digested food is broken into such chemical elements as can be readily assimilated and recycled into other more complex organic materials.

These are but a few oversimplified examples of how the human body is well equipped for the safe consumption of its food. If the balance is disturbed, the quality of life and health would be adversely affected. The balance has to be so perfectly measured and precisely proportioned that even a slight disturbance within it can pose a threat of death to life.

Here it would be logical to interpret the word *Fujūr*, used in verse 9 of Sūrah al-Shams, as changes threatening the healthy progress of life, while *Taqwā* in the same verse refers to the potential ability to avoid the dangers which may lead to illness and death. So in terms of human physique, this verse of Sūrah al-Shams indicates that the human physiology, anatomy, nervous system, portal system, intravenous system, glandular system and the immune system are all well equipped with the knowledge of what is good and bad for them. A minute study of just one of the systems alluded to would virtually require volumes to be written, yet by no means would the subject be exhausted. To say that this is magical and wonderful would be naive. To compare the intricacies and the tiers upon tiers of mysteries with which human life is endowed, is like placing Alice in Wonderland. In comparison to the wonders of human creation, all fiction relating to mystery and wonder is paled into insignificance.

We are amazed to notice how perfectly the human bodily functions verify the relevant Quranic statements. Man's propensity to catch diseases and fall ill and at the same time, his potential ability to cure himself of almost all diseases that he suffers from, is phenomenal. Even cancers can be cured without intervention of physicians or oncologists. In fact there are some terminal cases of cancer which are duly recorded in medical history where the patient made a complete recovery, defying the oncologists' understanding of how it could have happened. The specialists' know-how is disregarded when terminally ill patients begin to recover and return to life without any understandable cause of cure. The scientists are in unanimous agreement, however, that the intricacies of the human immune system are only superficially understood. Yet this much we can say with certainty that our defence system is provided with limitless possibilities.

Despite its perfection, no defence apparatus in man can bring him eternity. In each system that man is endowed with, there is an inherent counter-system which works in measured tones for its ultimate destruction. Everything is precisely measured and proportioned. The estimated duration of the life of each cell of the human body is predetermined by the most intricate dominant and recessive characteristics etched on the genes. It is clearly predetermined as to how long the growth rate for certain organs would move at a faster pace than the death rate of the same organ. Also it is clearly predetermined as to the age at which the pace of growth and destruction would remain perfectly matched, and when it is to be tilted in favour of death, so that the process of disrepair outpaces the process of repair. None of this is accidental.

Physical Growth

Let us study by way of illustration the simple example of the growth of teeth. Milk teeth as we know them, are governed and are being constantly monitored in the rate of growth and decay, so that for some years the rate of growth outpaces the rate of decay. Then a balanced stage is reached where the rates remain constant. After this the balance is tilted again in favour of death and decay, and the days of the milk teeth are numbered. Now begins the age of the growth of adult teeth. The rate of growth in the beginning is much faster in this case than the rate of wear and tear. Up to a certain stage, when they reach their predetermined size of length, breadth and thickness, the balance in favour of growth remains intact. After a pre-calculated size is reached, suddenly a perfect balance between the rate of growth and the rate of wear and tear is delicately maintained. So, leaving aside injury through disease and accident, they remain in a perfectly healthy state with no apparent changes occurring in their length and size.

Ordinarily, people think they (the teeth) have grown and stopped growing, and that is all that there is to it. This naive concept is farthest from the truth. If they had stopped growing they would have been ground into nothingness within a matter of weeks or months. If on the other hand, the rate of growth continued to remain the same as was operative in the initial stages, they would have continued to grow longer and longer till the lower teeth would have jutted out of the top of the human skull and the upper teeth would be seen hanging below the jaw!

Thus it is not an unmeasured, uncontrollable phenomenon that we are observing. All the factors responsible for maintaining the rate of growth to a certain period and the consequent change in that rate are intrinsically balanced. It is specifically and clearly written into the blueprint of human creation. It is mind boggling to realise how the blueprint of human design and engineering timely unfolds itself and works in such an intricate manner.

The safe removal of waste products through the human excretory system is also a perfect system in itself. Here of course the principle of *'Adl* is applicable with no awareness on the part of the person who is provided with this excellent mechanism of excreting the toxic remains after he has digested the healthy part of food. If a man treats the teeth with injustice only then does he begin to realise the outcome of his folly through the damage that he inflicts on his own health. Over and imprudent eating not only damages the teeth, but also both the digestive and excretory system. Some types of diabetes are caused because of this. At the same time man is equipped with many countermeasures to meet the challenges of dietary excesses.

To illustrate this we further consider the example of diabetes. Diabetes is a common disease but in fact it is not just one disease. Hundreds of types of diabetes have so far been diagnosed. Against almost all of them, the body is provided with internal remedial measures. Some types of diabetes are caused by glandular disorders such as that of the pancreas.

The pancreas produces two types of secretions. One is called insulin and is largely responsible for the assimilation of sugar into all cells of the human body which constantly require energy for their survival. Even if man does not eat sugar directly, the carbohydrates he consumes in different forms are broken down into sugar. If insulin is produced in excessive quantities it results in hypoglycaemia—a disease in which the sugar level suddenly falls to a dangerously low level. If not immediately rectified this can result in sudden death or a deep coma damaging the brain cells and other vital organs.

To keep a countercheck on the production of insulin, there is a complex signalling system at work in the body, sounding an alarm as if announcing the fact that all the insulin that was needed has been produced and no more is required. This counter insulin secretion is also produced in the same area of the glandular system responsible for the production of insulin. When this secretion is released, the production of insulin is suddenly halted and man seems to enter a state of perfect satiation. Tilt the balance to either side and the health will be adversely influenced to that degree.

But this is not all there is to the story of insulin and the measures created by God to keep it in check and balance. Other rare elements, apart from insulin, are also needed to support this complex system. Every cell in the bloodstream constantly needs energy and after the energy has been consumed, the waste product needs to be thrown out. For this, adequate measures are taken whereby the waste product and toxins etc. are secreted out of the system.

All the above functions are performed through the agency of the bloodstream. This in itself offers limitless wonders but it can also become self-destructive. The medium of liquid in which blood cells of different types are suspended can destroy the nucleus of the cell immediately, if it is permitted to flow into the cell freely. To counter this danger there is a bi-layered envelope around each cell preventing any direct penetration of electrolytes into it. Thus this bi-layered envelope provides a perfect preventive against mishaps.

Both covers have certain pores through which a molecule of sugar, with an attached molecule of insulin, is transported into the heart of the cell where it is immediately consumed. The waste products are carried back through the pores of the same covers to the bloodstream where they are washed out to the porous skin in the form of perspiration, or highly complex mucous membranes in the kidney etc. This transportation of sugar into the cell and the expulsion of waste product occurs at unbelievably high speeds.

This is the energy transportation system, but this again is not all. There is far more to it. Each human organ, including the cells in the bloodstream, constantly require a certain amount of sugar for survival. But of course there are priorities. The priority of the brain is supreme over all the organs of the body. If the sugar level in the bloodstream sinks, the brain must somehow be guaranteed a constant supply till the entire reserve of sugar is depleted. If every organ and cellular tissues of the body had equal access to the consumption of sugar, there would always be a danger of the brain being deprived of its vital supply of sugar because of over-consumption elsewhere. Thus to keep the balance between various priorities, glands also create secretions to stop consumption of sugar in every part of the body except the brain.

The kinds of balance are not only in one place. Tier after tier of extremely delicate balances are created and maintained. This is absolute justice which works unconsciously in man at different levels of his existence. Hence, though it may not be referred to as absolute justice, one cannot escape the fact that justice and perfect balance are two names for the same phenomenon. In other words, we can say, without fear of contradiction, that perfect health is another name for perfect justice.

To understand the issue of balance in relation to sugar in the human body, let us discuss the specific example of how much sugar is needed and what are the minimum and maximum levels. For each 100ml of blood there must always be at least 60mg of sugar available for consumption. But on the other side of the equation the sugar level must not exceed 180mg per 100ml of blood.[5] If it exceeds that level then the state of imbalance is referred to as blood sugar.

If, to keep the balance correct, the insulin fails to maintain the balance, the excess sugar in the blood is washed out by the kidneys so that the excessive presence of sugar in the blood may not corrode the cellular tissues of the body. When the excess is passed out into the urine, what we have is a case of diabetes with the unwarranted presence of sugar in the urine. Sometimes the threshold of the kidneys is high and the excess sugar in the blood is not washed out, resulting in dangerously high levels of sugar in the blood. This has a corrosive effect on some organs; the heart valves can also be eaten up by the excessive flow of sugar through them (like acid corroding the channels it flows in). The extra sugar is somehow deposited where the flow of the blood is slow, in places like the capillaries, causing many types of irritation and damage. When this happens in the blood capillaries of the eyes, the person may suffer from cataract, glaucoma and other types of eye diseases. It can slow down the impulses carried through the nerves creating other dangers directly resulting from this lethargic state of transport through the nerves.

Through everyday experience, we find that some diabetic patients remain unaware of pain they should feel as a result of spasms around the heart. By missing these signals they may be taken by a surprise heart attack. So talking of the balance of justice is not just an academic luxury. The persistent lack of justice or disproportion in balance is unlikely to go unpunished in nature. Alas, this lesson is ignored by man and he lives under the illusion that he can escape the consequences of injustice. But to that we will turn later.

Protection against Disease

Let us now turn our attention to certain other examples of balance created by Allah for the healthy maintenance of human life. Not only human life, but the entire universe of innumerable species of life are firmly controlled and run under the absolute and unwavering principle of balance. Where violated, inadvertently or intentionally, one will never fail to discover the emergence of disease.

In His extreme beneficence, God has taken measures to provide an additional system of cushioning and resilience to the working of the human body, which strictly speaking does not belong to the realm of *'Adl* or justice alone. It is something extra, as if unearned, granted to the body entirely by way of special kindness. Looking at it from another angle one can say that in view of human faults, excessive negligence and even accidents, a system of compensation is provided by God. When viewed from the vantage point of conscious human actions, it appears much like the term *Ihsān* in action, as we have previously discussed at some length.

The benefaction of *Ihsān* and *Ītā'i Dhil-Qurbā* is over and above justice. For instance, if man was provided with digestive juices sufficient only to meet the daily requirements of food, that would imply that each animal eats exactly what he requires with there being no room for excess. This is only the dictate of justice. But God has treated animals with amazing benevolence. The excessive foods that he eats is preserved for him in the form of fats to maintain his life during lean days. Of course excessive fat is a burden but a moderate quantity of fat is needed by every living animal for the sake of his survival. Normally everyone can digest twice the amount of food required for healthy living. When he exceeds even this limit, then the domain of punishment begins. He cannot be a habitual violator of justice without suffering the consequences.

We still do not know enough of this delicate system of maintaining balance. How unfortunate is the case of man, otherwise such a proud animal, conscious of being at the head of all evolutionary achievements of life and equipped with the most complex faculties of thinking and computation, yet he remains unthankful for what God has provided him with. How unjust he is to his Creator Who treated him with such perfect justice. In fact there is a vast internal universe of innumerable correlating factors, suspended in perfect balance and harmony constantly taking care of life in every aspect of its requirements. This micro-universe of symphony in man is the most sublime music in him. He is the masterpiece of God's creation, but is so naively unaware of the universe of wonders created within him.

The Role of Benevolence in Production of Insulin

In order to elaborate this point further we again look at the example of the daily requirement of sugar for every animal and see how the factors of benevolence perform rescue operations and shield the patient's health from the bad effects of indulgent eating. For instance, if the insulin produced by the pancreas was in exact proportion to the daily requirement of sugar then this would only be sufficient for day to day living and no more. Benevolence would have no part to play. But God has granted the pancreas the capability to produce more insulin than is his ordinary requirement. If a healthy man consumed sugar many times his requirement, God's Benevolence would see to it that mostly he escapes the consequences.

It is also interesting to note here that if the pancreas is damaged and produces one-seventh of the insulin required, this small amount of insulin is still sufficient to meet the daily needs. It would be befitting here to elaborate this discussion a little further for the benefit of the layman, who may not understand the intricacies of this scientific phenomenon.

The production of insulin is not in any way accidental. Animals have no knowledge of what they require; they have only a vague craving for eating which compels them to eat whatever relieves their hunger and is palatable to their taste. Yet they are internally warned at a certain stage to stop eating. Had it not been so a proportion of the world would die of hunger because there would be no food left for them by the over-indulgent eaters.

Even in normal healthy animals the production of insulin has a controlled variation. An animal at rest requires a very little amount of insulin, but when he is suddenly agitated and bursts into activity the release of insulin is proportionally raised to a corresponding higher level. But for this, to achieve a higher excellence in all sports and games would be otherwise impossible. Particularly, most participants in the Olympics would die a sudden death rather than live to receive their medals.

If the human body is healthy and enjoys a balanced diet, the metabolic waste would require a certain size and weight for the kidney to perform its function of excretion. But the potential of the kidney to excrete waste product is much greater than the daily requirement. One-eighth of the size of the kidney would be sufficient to do the routine work and it would require no extra cushioning in case of accidental disease or due to the excesses of gourmet eaters. It is a fascinating display of *Iḥsān* and *Ītā'i Dhil-Qurbā* together.

If there is a constant disregard towards the dictates of justice and towards the beneficence of God and if man were to lose seven parts out of eight parts of his kidney, still he could survive as a healthy person, provided he learns his lesson and returns to a normal balanced diet.

Thus we see that in most situations absolute justice and benevolence can flourish together without one interfering with the other. However, if there is a danger of a clash occurring between the two, then benevolence is not permitted to play a role and absolute justice must prevail especially if the coming into play of benevolence requires the sacrifice of justice i.e. if favours can only be shown at the cost of justice. As long as benevolence can coexist with justice it will be permitted to survive and function. Although benevolence is a thing of a higher order, justice is more fundamental and fundamentals are never sacrificed on the altar of the extra and optional.

In relation to the same subject, once the Holy Prophet[sa] observed:

الْمُؤْمِنُ يَأْكُلُ فِى مِعَى وَّاحِدٍ وَّالْكَافِرُ يَأْكُلُ فِى سَبْعَةِ اَمْعَاءٍ

A non-believer may eat seven times more, in comparison to a believer.[6]

This tradition accurately demonstrates the minimum-maximum capacity of the digestive system.

Hundreds of other factors other than the absence of insulin are also responsible for causing diabetes. Hence it is possible for a patient to suffer from diabetes despite the pancreas working normally. So far, scientists have discovered many such factors which play a role in the maintenance of the complex sugar absorption system in the blood. Yet in the final analysis, the emphasis is always on the perfect balance of diet, or in other words on justice.

Calcium

Calcium also plays an important role in keeping the health of animals in good order. Their health is at great risk if the balance of calcium is somehow disturbed even ever so slightly. In this respect, the margin between health and disease is much narrower than in the case of the glucose level in the blood. Any rise or fall in the proportion of calcium may cause severe damage to health, even resulting in sudden death. A study of a disease not uncommon among cattle would be helpful in demonstrating how important it is for calcium to be present in the body in exactly the right proportions.

Sometimes due to viruses or environmental factors, cattle begin to show signs of sudden loss of energy which is very perplexing for a farmer, as there is no outward reason for this to happen. For example a cow, perfectly healthy the night before, suddenly buckles at the knees, drops like a dead weight and simply cannot rise again. There is no fever and no sign of any disease, just a slump into death. A capable veterinary surgeon could of course save the cattle by the injection of readily soluble calcium, miraculously injecting life into the dying animal. This is how important it is for calcium not to drop below the minimum required level. A healthy human needs a minimum amount of 9.2% calcium and a maximum of 10.4% calcium.[7]

Sometimes persistent progressive debility among humans is traced to a gradual decrease in calcium. So far, the principle to understand is that the delicate levels of calcium should not be disturbed, as this would be dangerous for human health. Generations of scientists working on this may not have quite understood all the factors responsible for the maintenance of this delicate balance.

The role of calcium in the composition of the human body is a complex one. Calcium phosphate gives rigidity to the human skeleton and the calcium salts provide the hard structure of the bones and teeth and give hardness to the membranous tissues covering the cell. A poor condition of the cells and teeth and excessive irritability are among the possible symptoms for indicating a shortage of calcium, whereas too much calcium may result in mental confusion and the lethargic condition of the body.

Inside the cell is the living protoplasm which is surrounded by a tough membrane. Any deficiency of calcium in the membrane removes its toughness, consequently making the cell weaker. This may result in the protrusion of protoplasm. Among humans, the intake of calcium varies according to what they consume and where they live. Thus any deficiency of calcium or its excessive intake can make their lives vulnerable to disease. An imbalance of calcium in the bone tissue and bloodstream can be responsible for the following disorders:

- Vasodilation resulting in a drop in blood pressure.
- Reduced contractility of the heart muscles.
- A change in bone tissue which results in rickets.
- Serious osteoarthritis, where the ratio of calcium is disturbed and which also involves angina attacks. The drop in the calcium level is because of the drop in the blood pressure and causes serious and permanent damage to the brain cells and other tissues.

Hence God has provided man's body with another protective system which keeps the balance of calcium in order. The factors responsible for maintaining the delicate balance in calcium are numerous and intricately interrelated. This monitoring and corrective system can be likened to the phrase in Sūrah al-Shams, verse 9. *Taqwā*, in this context would mean, 'We have computed into the building material of life the instructions concerning the areas of dangers to be avoided, as well as the detailed instructions of how they could be avoided.' Accordingly, the calcium balance also has many inherent monitoring systems constantly guarding over it and, whenever necessary, calling for remedial measures. The call is immediately responded to by the complex glandular system, which is well equipped with the necessary mechanism to create the supply of much needed remedies.

A small amount of calcium is needed by the blood and soft tissues, the rest is stored in the teeth and bones. If calcium in the blood is in short supply, it is replenished from the store in the bones. The body adjusts its absorption rate according to the supply of calcium in the diet. A low dietary intake means the absorption is high, and a high intake means that the excess will be stored in the bones until an optimum is reached, then the absorption from the gut is slowed down. The presence of vitamin D increases the absorption of calcium. Hence, in tropical countries, even though the diet may be deficient in calcium, the high level of vitamin D in the body from exposure to the sun will make the absorption of calcium more efficient.

Regulation of the calcium balance is under the control of a hormone called parathormone, produced by the parathyroid glands. This works in conjunction with vitamin D adjusting the absorption of calcium to meet the bodily needs. Calciton is another hormone which also plays a role in regulating the balance of calcium. If there is too much calcium in the blood, calciton takes the excess back to the bone and moreover it slows down absorption from the gut.

Sodium and Potassium

Let us illustrate the system of *Fujūr* and *Taqwā* from another angle. Sodium and potassium are two elements essential for the maintenance of life. A balance has to be kept between them. However, the necessary sodium-potassium ratio varies in different parts of the body. For example, the bones and the flesh require more potassium than sodium whereas blood cells need more sodium than potassium. An imbalance between these salts can lead to dangerous consequences. The balancing of these two chemicals in all parts of the body is not accidental but is part of a well organised scheme.

Likewise, the health of the nervous system is largely dependent on both sodium and potassium but the requirement of nerves for each chemical varies according to the situation. A message is passed from one nerve cell to another in a chain, so that the messages eventually reach the part of the body where they are intended to be delivered. In the transfer of messages from nerve cell to nerve cell, sodium flows into the cell while potassium flows out. If this process is then not reversed immediately and if the potassium is not rehabilitated to its normal level, spontaneous death would result.

It is from this that we can deduce the meaning of the Quranic expression *Fa Sawwāka Fa 'Adalaka* (Sūrah al-Infiṭār; Ch.82: V.8). This short phrase summarises the entire complex system of kinds of balance and counterbalance that exist in our bodies.

Cell Division

The process of cell division is also very interesting. Every seven years, each cell in the body is replaced under the highly complicated system of catabolism. Catabolism is the process whereby cells are constantly consumed and destroyed. However, we are not aware that this phenomenon is taking place as none of our physical features change radically.

It is possible that with the passage of time one may improve in health and gain weight, or deteriorate and lose flesh, but the personality of one's physical being remains exactly the same. Each newborn cell which replaces the dying one is born almost in the image of its predecessor which is destroyed in the process of catabolism.

To illustrate this further perhaps the most commonly known example is that of fingerprints. The thumb impression of the new-born babe, in its intricate pattern, remains exactly the same as he grows to a ripe old age.

This system is related to *'Adl* working within the human body. The body organs need constant repair because every organ would diminish in size unless the cells lost in the process of its function are replaced. If the rate of supply of cells rises higher than the requirement, the organ will continue to grow beyond its designed size and shape. If it is less than the needed rate then the organ in question will shrink in size.

In case the consumed cells are not replaced by almost exactly the same number as those lost, an imbalance will occur. By applying this principle to any organ of the body one can easily visualise the abominable consequences. For instance, let us consider the eyeball. During the daily function of the eye, we are constantly using life cells in every part of the eye. If replacements are made at a rate faster than consumption, the eyeball will begin to grow out of its socket. If the balance is tilted on the other side the eyeball would reduce in size until it becomes a mere dot before passing into nothingness.

To sum up, if the balance in any organ of a living body is disturbed, it will either grow out of proportion or fade out of existence.

An Insight into the Insect Kingdom

Although we have so far discussed some cases of advanced animals and humans, it should be borne in mind that this system of absolute justice encompasses all forms of life. Justice, in application to the governing of life processes, means that everything is kept within its designed limits and is not permitted to transgress.

In application to the insect kingdom this control system is also highly essential. Each insect has a predetermined dimension, which could be disturbed to an unmanageable degree if strict controls were not constantly applied. Insects consume certain types of food suitable for the maintenance of their life. If unchecked by the laws of nature, they would grow to such gigantic sizes as could fill the earth from end to end. Why should their growth come to a halt at a certain stage? What are the forces that impose such limits? What is the system which keeps them within a limited level of growth? These are questions that have yet to be better understood. To let them grow limitlessly would appear to be an act of kindness but at what cost—at the cost of all other forms of life.

So balance, or absolute justice in human terminology, is not kept automatically but is imposed and controlled by certain forces. Previously we mentioned the example of growth within each organ of the body. The mechanism which controls the growth of teeth and eyeballs etc. within the aforesaid animals, is universally applicable to all animal species.

Alas, man is ungrateful. In spite of intelligence he remains heedless of that Omnipotent Being while every particle of the universe bears witness to His existence!

Imbalance and Disease

If man were to reflect on his true worth, he would realise that he is no more than a mere handful of dust. All that he is arrogant about is vain pride, while he possesses nothing of his own. All belongs to Allah. Man has been granted such a perfect body, but when in health, he fails to comprehend that he is dependent on a grand and intricate system of balances. When he falls ill, his discomfort, pain and suffering bring out the realisation of his own frailty. It is then that his dependence on God begins to dawn upon him. It is God who prevents him from falling victim to the countless diseases surrounding him on all sides. He is protected from each by an inbuilt defensive mechanism which is constantly on the watch.

The point to be highlighted here is that even if a small and insignificant part of the body is permitted to fall ill, while the remaining parts stay perfectly healthy, the diseased person suffers in totality. A small sore on the tip of a finger, a corrosion of a tooth, an infection in a part of the eyelid, can make one suffer so intensely that people are known to have taken their own lives in order to escape the agony caused by such limited ailments. The growth of a gland in the brain could make a person epileptic, a suffering not only to himself but to his entire circle of family and friends. Only in such cases can the immense beneficence of God be fully realised; a beneficence constantly showered on every living creature. This realisation can only dawn on those who have the faculty to think and be grateful.

In the final analysis, disease is nothing but the disturbance of balance i.e. justice. When afflicted with disease, many great men, who commanded respect and earned renown at various times in history, lost all dignity and stooped to the abject level of begging for help from those of their attendants who had no power to help them. Such is the case of mighty emperors who, when afflicted with some disabling disease, appeared so small and insignificant that even the lowest of their slaves would not exchange their slavery with the sovereignty of their masters.

Julius Caesar is just such an example who once, during a majestic and awe-inspiring moment of oratory, suddenly fell victim to an attack of epilepsy writhing in agony and pain. Describing this event, Shakespeare writes:

'And when the fit was on him, I did mark
How he did shake; 'tis true, this god did shake;
His coward lips did from their colour fly,
And that same eye whose bend doth awe the world
Did lose his lustre'
(Julius Caesar, Act I, Scene II)

But little do these observations make an impression on the ego of man. The moment he returns to health, he completely forgets these belittling moments of his life and loses no time in returning to his vanity.

Epilepsy, which can make a person feel as if he had been robbed of his dignity, is in fact caused by a minor imbalance in the nervous system. Very often it is not possible to determine the part of the nervous system at fault.

Guardian Angels

The path to progress is fraught with pitfalls and dangers. Each step towards advancement can, if carelessly taken, lead to annihilation. Even the minutest details of the workings of life and death seem to go hand in hand. Protection of life is a profoundly well organised mechanism as yet not fully comprehended, but whatever of it has been understood is astounding indeed.

Behind this apparently self-flowing mechanism, according to religious understanding, there are some invisible conscious forces who have different dimensions than ours and are known as angels. The entire universe is run by the laws of nature which are governed, maintained and implemented to the minutest detail by these agents. The same applies here. One can visualise for instance, any unit of life advancing in time. At every minute step it takes, there is always the attendant danger of taking the wrong turn to death. The angels of life guide each step of the components of life in the right direction, but when the moment of death is decreed every step of the living is turned towards death.

The Excesses of Man

If given leave, man would transgress all boundaries but it is a great bounty of God that he has little control over the enormous workshop which operates within his body. He is unaware of what goes on inside him and is incapable of manipulating his own internal mechanisms. An overwhelmingly large number of functions of life run without the conscious control of the possessor of life.

There are of course some limited areas where man is able to exert his influence. For example excessive eating and drinking, indulgence in carnal pleasures, over indulgent habits and lifestyles are a few areas where he is free to exercise his will. We know full well the havoc man plays in these areas.

In spite of the license he takes, and the excesses he commits against himself, there runs an innate system of well cushioned protection within his physical mechanism. This protective system is designed to cope with many faults to a certain extent. But if man continues to commit mistakes or takes suicidal steps beyond all limits, then the punitive system takes over. Even then, a struggle begins between health and disease, life and death, each step provided with all of the requisite devices for prolonging this struggle against the destructive forces.

What we understand in religious terminology as indecency or transgression is in fact applicable to the physical world as well. Of course we do not mean to apply the same terms to the physical counterparts of spiritual behaviour, but the similarities are so strong that one is tempted to use the same terminology. Yet it should not be forgotten that even at such extreme stages, the benevolence of God and His limitless mercy can still come to man's rescue.

7   Violations of Justice

If someone investigates with an open mind the root cause of all evils, whether social, political, economic or moral, he will always find it to be injustice. The world cannot become an abode of peace until man adheres to justice. When injustice, tyranny and oppression take hold, evil is born and destruction is let loose.

If man is not just in his obligations to God, then it is quite unlikely that he will be just to his fellow human beings. It must be remembered that no one can trifle with the dictates of justice without exposing himself to the danger of falling victim to the punishing consequences. Such punishment is not related to the wrath of God as if descended from heaven, but is a natural outcome of the violation of the laws of nature. None is above the dominion of natural laws.

Here too God's mercy, forgiveness and benevolence become operative, with the result that man is not punished for each and every sin. But when his transgression exceeds certain prescribed limits, the protective shield of benevolence is withdrawn and nothing can stand between him and punishment. The Quran describes this as follows:

وَمَآ اَصَابَكُمْ مِّنْ مُّصِيْبَةٍ فَبِمَا كَسَبَتْ اَيْدِيْكُمْ وَ يَعْفُوْا عَنْ كَثِيْرٍ ۝

وَمَآ اَنْتُمْ بِمُعْجِزِيْنَ فِى الْاَرْضِ ۚ وَمَا لَكُمْ مِّنْ دُوْنِ اللّٰهِ مِنْ وَّلِيٍّ وَّلَا نَصِيْرٍ ۝

And whatever misfortune befalls you, is due to what
your own hands have wrought. And He forgives many
of your sins. And you cannot frustrate *God's plan* in
the earth; nor have you any friend or helper beside
Allah.
(Sūrah al-Shūrā; Ch.42: Vs. 31-32)

In other words, man brings misfortunes upon himself,
but it is God who often forgives his sins and saves
him from his self-inflicted ruin. A scan of the history
of wars would establish that the underlying cause of
every disruption of peace is, without fail, the violation
of the principles of justice.

The Doctrine of Trinity

The Christian doctrine of Trinity is a befitting
example of the gross injustice of man in relation to
God. According to the Holy Quran:

تَكَادُ السَّمٰوٰتُ يَتَفَطَّرْنَ مِنْهُ وَ تَنْشَقُّ الْاَرْضُ وَتَخِرُّ الْجِبَالُ هَدًّا ۝
اَنْ دَعَوْا لِلرَّحْمٰنِ وَلَدًا ۝

The heavens might well-nigh burst thereat, and the
earth cleave asunder, and the mountains fall down in
pieces, because they ascribe a son to the Gracious
God.
(Sūrah Maryam; Ch.19: Vs.91-92)

108

A deep contemplation of the causative factors of war and disorders in human affairs would ultimately lead to the conclusion that the above Quranic statement is certainly applicable here, as we shall establish presently.

Yet in the history of Christianity, we cannot find any direct evidence of the Christian nations being the target of Allah's wrath and displeasure due to their beliefs. On the contrary, it is they who appear, in worldly terms, to be the favoured nations. They have jointly ruled the entire world and still hold the balance of power over the non-Christian nations, so that they can be classed as being the supreme masters of the globe. Although in the last few decades, we have observed the gradual rise of the nations of the third world with a measure of independence, there is very little that has changed and the supremacy of the Christian West still prevails. In view of this, one wonders at the true import of the aforementioned Quranic statement.

A study of Christianity shows that originally the belief in the Unity of God was the only belief that Christians held. The concept of Trinity and the belief that God has a son was introduced later, mainly by St. Paul. Ever since, it has been evolving into many specific understandings of this dilemma. Different sects of Christianity have been following different paths of development. The larger denominations, from the beginning of the fourth century onwards, were mainly engaged in a grim battle of gaining ascendancy on this very issue. Each sect claimed to be on the right path regarding their concept of Trinity and its constituents. Despite this, they all claimed to be believers in one God. In other words, the one God that they believed in had a sort of split personality. It is largely because of this attitude that the Holy Quran has not labelled them as idolaters, but extends to them the right to continue to profess their belief in Unity.

Yet despite their lip service to the Unity, in reality they act as idolators. The question arises as to the manner in which this prophecy of the Quran has come to be fulfilled. A deeper study of the verse will reveal that the displeasure of God mentioned in this regard will manifest itself in the form of great global turmoil.

This indicates that inherent in the Christian beliefs is the danger of their mutual split. Hence the punishment mentioned corresponds to the crime committed. Trinity attempts to create splits within the single Person of God. As a consequence the believers in Trinity are split within themselves. The colonial policy of Christian nations of divide and rule also falls into step with this attitude.

Consider now the point in time when the Renaissance, i.e. the birth of reason, logic and the quest for truth, began to blow a new breath of life into the Christian West. During this period the Christian doctrines were doubted and questioned as they clashed with man's intellect. The Church reacted

110

strongly to these intellectual rebellions by condemning and punishing those who questioned the validity of their doctrines. When the scientists and philosophers could not find the answers to the questions they posed to the Church, they began to move away from religion altogether. They were entirely disillusioned with the Church and distanced themselves from God. The segregation between scientific rationale and religious dogma became total.

As long as the Christian world remained blanketed in ignorance, there was no problem. But as the sun of rationality, research and quest for knowledge began to dawn upon the West, they began to see things from a completely different perspective. They had come to realise that the earth was certainly not stationary. The sun did not circuit around it, paying homage to the birth place of Jesus. The scientific revolution completely transformed the vision of the universe. It was the earth, after all, which revolved around the sun showing no respect to the planet of Jesus' birth.

When the Christian intellects began to discover the realities of nature, afraid of an open rebellion to a powerful Church, they maintained their doubts privately. Agnosticism was born and in turn, gave birth to godless philosophies, Communism being a direct result of the same.

The split between the doctrine of Trinity further divided the Christian world into two opposing camps, distancing themselves and hardening their attitude towards each other. Perhaps one could raise an eyebrow at declaring the entire world as being divided into two, while in fact only the Christian West was thus polarised. But the centre of gravity as far as human power is concerned, lay firmly rooted within the combined might of the Christian powers and the Communist Block, an erstwhile stronghold of Christianity.

In this context, we can say that the two world wars have amply demonstrated the impact of human ideologies, doctrines and philosophies on man's political, economic and social behaviour.

A Warning System to Indicate Violations of Justice

Let us now examine an efficient warning system which is related to the violations of justice within the human body.

At the slightest sign of disease the entire human body becomes restless. Superficially this may seem to be an unnecessary encumbrance, while in reality it is highly essential for the survival and preservation of life. For it is the signals of pain that awaken the normally dormant defence system in every living form. The pain and discomfort serve not only as a general alarm, they are also specific in guiding the steps of the defence system to the precise location in the body where the impending danger lies. They also define the danger and its location so precisely that the defence mechanism takes countermeasures exactly to the proportion and locality of the threat. The entire immune system of life is awakened not only to the presence of pain but also to the types of danger confronting the life of the individual concerned.

There then follows a highly complicated and intricate response from the immune system of every living form. This simultaneously ensures the production of defensive agents and their transportation to the exact location where they are needed.

The alarm system specifically provided to humans, setting them apart from other animals, signals not only the body and its susceptibility to disease, but also alerts the moral awareness of man to himself as well as to God, and plays a vital role in the relationship that exists between God and him.

A similar system of alert and defence works in relation to the religious and moral functioning of man. The Holy Quran presents the history of religion in relation to the treatment of Prophets[as] at the hands of their opponents. It goes into a detailed analysis of the moral and social degradation of man in the various ages. When messengers were sent to a nation to save them from the impending ruin, very often they were bitterly opposed but their opponents had to suffer the consequences of this blind opposition. They were either rapidly wiped out of existence or subjected to a long course of gradual decline until they were no longer worthy of being mentioned as players on the stage of life.

The Holy Quran mentions many cases of such people who ignored the demands of justice. This provides a warning for the generations to come.

This system of warning extends to the entire spectrum of human faith and belief. At the highest point, faith can be summed up as a total dedication to the Oneness of God. At the lowest level, there is the day to day pattern of one's conduct, which in the case of the true believer distinguishes him from the non-believers.

At this level of the day to day conduct of a believer, the Holy Prophet[sa] admonishes him to develop the habit of removing all potential dangers to man. Elaborating this point further he[sa] mentions many such articles on pathways and roads that could in any way be injurious to passers-by. According to the Prophet's[sa] warning, if a believer does not remove for instance, a nail, a thorn or any other similar article which could hurt an unwary passer-by, he would be deficient by that much in his faith. The path to God is also fraught with similar dangers, smaller in the beginning but gradually assuming more dangerous proportions.

It is an interesting area of Islamic instruction, a study of which helps to widen and deepen one's understanding of Islam as a whole. Speaking of the same on another occasion, Prophet Muhammad[sa] warned the believers that just as man has rights on other things, so all other things have rights on man. Market places, roads and highways have their rights on those who use them. Regarding the rights of markets, the Prophet[sa] reminds us that to stand in public places or roads without purpose and interfering with the free flow of traffic is objectionable. Similarly to make encroachments for the purpose of extending shops etc. is against the spirit of his[sa] admonition. The Holy Prophet[sa] said that faith is divided into seventy tiers, the lowest of them being the habit of cleaning pathways of all obstructions.

How on earth could this be a constituent of faith, one may wonder? A second glance at the same, however, can easily make one understand the wisdom underlying this statement. True faith in God requires that security and protection which one receives from God, should also be extended to His other creatures. Hence, if someone is remiss in discharging his responsibility of extending security and protection to others, he would have faltered in his faith.

It is evident from this that Islam's sphere of instruction comprises everything that he may require even at the lowest levels. How ironic and tragic indeed it is, that in most Muslim countries today these basic instructions are so commonly violated. The roads and pathways are often in a miserable state of non-repair. Even the government agencies which dig channels on the main highways for the purpose of laying pipelines or cables etc. leave them in a perilous state for traffic without erecting warning posts or illuminated signs for the night travellers.

Unfortunately many accidents happen on the roads and mishaps occur as a result of ignoring this warning system. For example, once, while driving with dipped headlights in Islamabad, I suspected something unusual in the middle of the road and applied the brakes with a sudden sense of alarm. I discovered that a few yards ahead a huge pit had been dug across the road, yet there was no warning sign posted and no adequate lighting either. This was despite the fact that the earth from around the pit had been removed which itself could have worked as a substitute signal. Thus it was only Allah's Grace that saved us. I was travelling with my family and had I not abruptly applied the brakes, we would certainly have had a fatal accident. The next day I heard the news that a German tourist while driving his Mercedes had fallen into the same pit, hopefully with no fatal consequences.

Another incident happened when I was travelling on the Shaikhupura-Gujranwala road in Pakistan. In this instance the road had been dug up but the soil and concrete had not been removed from the site. I was travelling in the dark when I glimpsed the heap on the road and managed to apply my brakes on time, thus stopping my car some feet away from the hazardous spot. Here again there was no sign to warn the drivers of the dangers ahead. When we disembarked from the car to take a closer look, we saw to our horror that the excavation was so huge that it had accommodated an entire bus now reduced to wreakage. These are just two instances I am quoting from a catalogue of such mishaps which occur daily.

This serves to establish that where justice is withheld from people even at its rudimentary level, the consequences may be enormous. We can imagine the state of other fundamental rights in such a society. Thus the essence of the message is that a Muslim society should not ignore the dictates of justice even at its lowest level.

8   The Role of the Three Creative Principles in the Shaping of Religion

The principles of justice are also applicable to human conduct in the area of religion.

We start our discussion with reference to religion prior to the revelation of the Holy Quran. In other words we begin at the beginning and turn to the first religion ever revealed for the guidance of mankind by God through Adam[as]. With reference to that elementary teaching, we immediately notice that the features of religion as preserved by the Holy Quran pertain mainly to the mention of social and economic justice.

The religion of Adam[as] seems to have laid down firm foundations for the step by step building of the Divine teachings. With the passage of time they widened in their coverage and moved from the bare discussion of justice to the more sophisticated teachings of *Iḥsān* and *Ītā'i Dhil-Qurbā*. In short, a definite evolutionary trend is witnessed with different stages of development from the time of Adam[as] to the time of Prophet Muhammad[sa], where religion seems to have reached the ultimate stage of perfection. All other forms of so-called religions are either mythical and legendary or decadent versions of Divine religions manipulated by human interference.

The Era of Adam[as]

The institution of Prophethood seems to bring a message of enlightenment from on high which the people of the time must either obey or else face the natural consequences of their blunders and sins. The question is, what kind of justice can be ascribed to this authoritative role of the Prophets[as]? Prior to the introduction of Divine religion, society was completely free to choose its leaders and to obey or not to obey them, so why should man suddenly be made to obey another man, that is the question. The Holy Quran resolves this dilemma by pointing out that Adam[as] in himself had no personal superiority over others and was equal with his fellow human beings. Adam[as] as such had no right to command obedience from others, but when Allah breathed into him His Word and Authority, only then did he do so.

The breath of God, according to Quranic terminology, is the origin of revelation to man. The Holy Quran says in regard to this:

وَاِذۡ قَالَ رَبُّكَ لِلۡمَلٰٓئِكَةِ اِنِّیۡ خَالِقٌۢ بَشَرًا مِّنۡ صَلۡصَالٍ مِّنۡ حَمَاٍ مَّسۡنُوۡنٍ ☐ فَاِذَا سَوَّیۡتُهٗ وَ نَفَخۡتُ فِیۡهِ مِنۡ رُّوۡحِیۡ فَقَعُوۡا لَهٗ سٰجِدِیۡنَ ☐

And *remember* when your Lord said to the angels, 'I am about to create man from dry ringing clay, from

black mud wrought into shape; So when I have fashioned him *in perfection* and have breathed into him of My Spirit, fall you down in submission to him.'
(Sūrah al-Ḥijr; Ch.15: Vs.29, 30)

A similar mention is found in reference to the Holy Prophet[sa] in Surah al-Kahf. The verse runs as follows:

قُلْ إِنَّمَا أَنَا بَشَرٌ مِّثْلُكُمْ يُوحَى إِلَيَّ أَنَّمَا إِلَهُكُمْ إِلَهٌ وَّاحِدٌ ۖ ...

Say, 'I am only a man like yourselves. It is revealed to me: Verily your God is only One God.' ...
(Sūrah al-Kahf; Ch.18: V.111)

The prerequisite for the breath of God is *Taqwā*, that is the fear of Allah. The one who fears Allah in the true sense of the word is the one who is worthy of becoming the recipient of His revelation. Hence, it is *Taqwā* and *Taqwā* alone which is the mark of honour.

The expression *Nafkh-i-Rūḥ*, (Sūrah al-Ḥijr, V.30) 'a breath of life from God' is invariably used in application to human beings alone, never in relation to other animals. To do *Nafkh* means to breathe into something. The primary meaning of this term would simply be the breath of life, but in this context it is a specific term for human life alone. All living things have an ego and a centre of consciousness, but this consciousness in itself is not capable of outliving the physical 'life'. The term *Rūḥ* should be translated as 'soul' as against 'life' which all animals possess, whereas the soul is granted only to humans.

There is another term extensively used in the Holy Quran which is *Nafs*. *Nafs* simply means 'life' and as such it is not a specific term like *Rūḥ*. All living things have *Nafs*—life, but all living things do not have *Rūḥ*—soul. This is the basic difference between the terms *Nafs* and *Rūḥ*. *Rūḥ* is the secondary and more advanced state of consciousness capable of living by itself after it is separated from the body at the time of death. This unit of energy is inexplicable because the knowledge of man has not yet reached the stage where he can understand the nature of *Rūḥ*. The Holy Quran simplifies it for man's understanding by declaring *Rūḥ* to be the Word of God. That is all that man can understand.

The central meaning of the term *Nafkh* is 'revelation from God'. Hence the process of revelation is covered by the same term. The creation of soul is a gradual evolutionary step of life. It is not introduced from outside, but is the first higher order granted to humans by Allah. Revelation from God is the second higher order by which some chosen servants are raised above the level of ordinary people. Among those who are recipients of revelation, there are some who are deemed worthy of rising to the next higher rank and this is what is termed as Prophethood. Thus a vicegerent of God is created on earth through *Nafkh-i-Rūḥ* in a higher and more refined connotation of this term. From this angle the requirement of obedience to a Prophet of God is not unjust or unreasonable because a Prophet[as] commands obedience only in his capacity as vicegerent of God.

Again, the person deemed fit by God to represent Him is always worthy of this trust because of his absolute adherence to truth. As such, it is impossible for him to commit injustice either in relation to God and His message or in relation to mankind. But this only happens when the faculties of such a person have been cultivated by God to reach a stage of perfect proportion and poise; only then is he considered fit by God to act as His messenger. God thereby places His trust in him and this trust is never betrayed. Some of these vicegerents are Law-bearing Prophets[as] who usher in a new era of Divine law. For as long as that era lasts, the other Prophets[as] who follow do not bring a new law. They are recipients of Prophetic revelation and they perform other functions on behalf of God, such as the strengthening of faith in Him and the reformation of society.

According to the Quran, worship of God, performing the prescribed prayers, and spending in a good cause are the three fundamental teachings common to all religions:

وَمَآ أُمِرُوٓا إِلَّا لِيَعۡبُدُوا اللَّهَ مُخۡلِصِيۡنَ لَهُ الدِّيۡنَ ۙ حُنَفَآءَ وَ يُقِيۡمُوا الصَّلَوٰةَ وَ يُؤۡتُوا الزَّكَوٰةَ وَ ذٰلِكَ دِيۡنُ الۡقَيِّمَةِ ۞

And they were not commanded but to serve Allah, being sincere to Him in obedience, *and* being upright, and to observe Prayer, and pay the Zakat. And that is

the religion *of the people* of the right path.
(Sūrah al-Bayyinah; Ch.98: V.6)

The Paradise of Adam[as]

The Divine law vouchsafed to Adam[as] could not be
any different from this universal principle. The above
verse describes the relationship between man and
God. As for the relationship between man and man,
the principles governing this relationship, i.e. the law
bestowed to Adam[as], are described in the Holy Quran
in two verses. The first of these verses, although
widely quoted, is as widely misunderstood. It deals
with the injunction of God to Adam[as] regarding the
two types of trees of paradise. In relation to one type,
Allah permitted Adam[as] and Eve to eat the fruit
thereof as they pleased without inhibition. But
regarding the other type, God warned Adam[as] to keep
his distance from that tree. This is mentioned as the
evil tree. Ordinarily people think in material terms and
consider them to be fruit-bearing trees as we know
them here on earth. As this description is very similar
to that found in the Old Testament, an attempt has
been made by scholars in Islam, Judaism, and
Christianity to understand the underlying meaning of
this metaphoric expression.

I do not want to go into a detailed account of what
different scholars have inferred from this, but without
doubt these two trees refer to the teaching of the
Divine law given to Adam[as] comprising do's and

don'ts. The evil tree mentioned has to be understood with respect to that part of the teaching in which religious society is forbidden by God to transgress the dictates of common morality and justice in relation to each other. However, this is not left to be defined by man, who may differ with his fellow human beings in his concept of justice and fair play, etc. To prevent this from happening, the teaching bestowed upon Prophets[as] is very clear and concise.

The other tree is the one which bears wholesome fruit, and Adam[as] and Eve are permitted to freely eat thereof as they desire. This evidently refers to the positive injunctions of Adam's[as] Divine law.

Although there are no details mentioned in this verse indicating the basic structure of the code of conduct prescribed, it can be safely inferred from this that Adam[as] and his society were forbidden from violating each other's fundamental rights—the practice which always leads to the disturbance of peace and resultant misery.

Another verse on the same subject seems to lay down the foundation for the code of economic justice suitable for that primitive society:

إِنَّ لَكَ أَلَّا تَجُوعَ فِيهَا وَلَا تَعْرَىٰ ۝ وَأَنَّكَ لَا تَظْمَؤُاْ فِيهَا وَلَا تَضْحَىٰ ۝

It is *provided* for you that you will not hunger therein, nor will you be naked. And that you will not thirst therein, nor will you be exposed to the sun.
(Sūrah Ṭā Hā; Ch.20: Vs.119, 120)

Hence, at the economic level, the teachings of Adam[as] comprise four fundamental rights granted to man at the very start of the making of society. They are:

1. Every man has the right to be properly fed; none will remain hungry.
2. Every man has the right to be adequately clothed.
3. Every man is guaranteed a supply of healthy water.
4. None will be left without shelter.

However, according to the orthodox scholars, the paradise mentioned in the story of Adam[as] is the same as is promised to true believers in the hereafter. If one considers such theories, one is astounded to see the vast difference between the description of the paradise of the other world, and the paradise as granted to Adam[as] and his followers. What manner of paradise was it, that which only guaranteed bare enough food to relieve hunger, plain water to drink, provision of some clothes, and a roof over one's head? No such paradise is described in the Holy Quran in relation to what is to be granted to pious people after death. Nor would anyone care to aspire to such a paradise at the cost of worldly happiness.

Even ordinary people at the lowest level in advanced societies enjoy a better paradise than the one from which Adam[as] was expelled! We seriously doubt that the orthodox clergy would ever desire to be rewarded with such a paradise. With one forlorn woman, one forlorn forbidden tree and a few trees laden with fruit of course, but plenty of snakes around! And the promise of proper clothing is broken, as Adam and Eve open their eyes and find themselves naked. No clothes to be had, no shelter to cover their heads. The nearest thing to clothing are nothing but a few fallen leaves of the tree of paradise. One really wonders as to whether any righteous person would ever crave to be admitted to this glorious paradise! Alas, they do not see! This certainly is not the paradise promised in the Quran to believers as a reward for their sacrifices.

This (the paradise of Adam[as] and Eve) is no more than an image of an economic society based on the philosophy of scientific socialism as presented by Karl Marx. This is the very first promise vouchsafed to man through the story of Adam[as] and Eve. This can be referred to as the first charter of fundamental human rights and even that is more advanced than the vision of paradise on earth of the scientific socialists. A closer study of socialist philosophy would fully support our view that Marxism/Leninism remains confined to only three fundamental rights and no more. What is beyond is optional, and may or may not be provided. All that is guaranteed by scientific socialism is the right to be fed, the right to be sheltered, and the right to be clothed.

In comparison, the most elementary concept of economic justice mentioned in the Quran is wider than the socialist ideal. In socialist societies water is not guaranteed, perhaps under the false notion that it is not important enough to be mentioned. The facts and figures as presented by the experts convey a completely different story. A very large number of human beings living in Africa and Asia barely survive on a meagre supply of water which, more often than not, is unhealthy and unfit for human consumption. Lately, the importance of water and the right to have access to a sufficient supply of healthy water is being taken seriously by the relevant organisations of the United Nations. Imagine, therefore, the excellence of this Quranic concept of Paradise, where at its very rudimentary level the importance of water is recognised and is not taken for granted.

The Development of the Institution of Prophethood

The institution of Prophethood continued after Adam[as] and it is likely that Prophets[as] appeared in this world after Adam[as] and before Noah[as]. These Prophets[as], however, are not mentioned in the Quran possibly for the reason that they were not Law-bearing Prophets[as]. Until the time of Noah[as], the law of Adam[as] remained in force.

Civilisation advanced considerably from the time of Adam[as] to the time of Noah[as]. If Noah[as] appeared in Mesopotamia, then history bears witness to the fact that that general area had become a well-developed trade centre, which attracted caravans from far and wide. Favourable weather conditions allowed the peoples of Mesopotamia to pass from being a rootless hunter-gatherer culture, to a culture based on agriculture and permanent settlements. Irrigation techniques, metal production, pottery and other crafts and building methods were developed to a high degree. The description in the Quran speaks of an affluent society similar to the one that existed in Pompeii, before the great earthquake and volcano eruption wiped it out of existence.

This advanced human society naturally required a more advanced Divine teaching in view of the changed circumstances and growing needs of society. But we find in the Holy Quran that the people of Noah[as] were guilty of all kinds of aggression against, and digression from, the right path, and are dubbed therein as a thoroughly sinful society. From this it can be safely inferred that the concept of sin had been made clear, because without a law the concept of sin cannot be entertained. It is the violation of Divine law which in religious terminology is referred to as sin.

The same is the case of other people addressed by various Prophets[as] of their time in different parts of the world. Their teachings, however, are only mentioned in the Quran in general terms, a detailed account being unnecessary. Abraham[as], Isaac[as], Ishmael[as], Jacob[as] and also Joseph[as] are mentioned as belonging to the same law, the one vouchsafed to Abraham[as]. The central theme of religion is referred to as worship of God with total dedication and to abide by the practices of Abraham[as] and the teachings he brought. The word *Millah* is used which covers this meaning. However, the details of the teachings are not described. One guiding principle mentioned is invariably applicable to all Divine laws revealed before the Quran, and that is that God always burdened people only with what they could take. He bound them to such practices as were in accordance with their requirements and their socio-economic moral environments.

This continued until we reach the time of Moses[as]. The Mosaic law is discussed in far greater detail than that of earlier Prophets[as]. In the course of elaborating some injunctions of that law, the Holy Quran throws light on the instructions regarding food with respect to the time of Jacob[as]. In the Quran, the Holy Founder[sa] of Islam is likened to Moses[as] in many respects. Again, we find mention of the similarity in the Old Testament (Deuteronomy 18:18), where Moses[as] is informed of a future Prophet[sa] who would be born from among his brothers and who would be likened unto him.

Why do we read such an elaborate account of the law of Moses[as] in the Holy Quran, as against almost complete silence regarding the teachings of Noah[as] who was himself a great Law-bearing Prophet[as]? In answer to this question one should keep in mind that, according to the Quran, the Sharia revealed to Prophet Muhammad[sa] was directly comparable to that revealed to Moses[as]. Both of the Prophets[as] were similar. Again, it is claimed that the Quranic law is the most perfect; so wherever there are differences between the two, this claim is also to be verified. Hence, among other reasons, the need for the preservation of all the important teachings of the Mosaic law for the sake of comparison. It is a very important landmark in the evolution of religion, which was designed and controlled under Divine command. The emphasis of the Mosaic law is obviously and strongly on justice. Forgiveness is mentioned indeed but only as a small alternative by way of exception. The general rule which runs through the law of Moses[as] is that of firm exercise of justice and revenge.

As we can well see, the provision of forgiveness is covered by the word *Iḥsān*. This indicates that although *Iḥsān* was not altogether denied, it had not yet acquired the significance that it has in Jesus's[as] teachings. Despite the fact that Jesus[as] categorically rejects the allegation that he had come to change the law (Matthew 5:17-18), he shifts the emphasis from the provision of revenge to the provision of forgiveness. It is a case of a shift of emphasis within the same Divine law from one injunction to another. But as religion evolved to its full maturity at the time of the last Law-bearing Prophet, Muhammad[sa], we find a highly developed, comprehensive and balanced teaching which firmly maintains a poise between *'Adl, Ihsān* and *Ītā'i Dhil-Qurbā*.

Returning to the discussion of Noah[as], many questions need to be answered regarding the teachings of justice. It is not difficult to deduce from the study of the Quran that Noah's[as] nation had become totally devoid of justice and that tyranny and oppression had spread to all walks of life. Can an unjust people be forgiven in accordance with the teachings of benevolence? Or, do the dictates of justice require that every transgressor be punished for his sins? These are two very important questions that need to be addressed.

Noah's[as] people mocked him relentlessly, they stubbornly rejected his teachings and left no stone unturned to frustrate his work. Yet in spite of all this, God knew that Noah[as] would be inclined towards clemency. So before the appointed time of their ruin, God dissuaded him from seeking forgiveness on their behalf by informing him that their case was beyond all hope of repair or reformation. After receiving this verdict from God, Noah[as] ultimately prayed against them rather than for them. In that prayer no exception was made. All who had not believed in him were included. Little did Noah[as] know that his own son would also be included in that prayer! The dramatic realisation only dawned upon Noah[as] at the time when he saw his own son about to drown. 'My son! My son!

My blood! My blood!' cried Noah[as], expressing his bewilderment at seeing his son being drowned alongside his tormentors.

It was the decree of God to establish an example which would serve as a great and noble lesson for generations to come. The lesson being that when absolute justice is the rule of the day, no other human relationship can be allowed to interfere with its operation. When God decides to punish one category of transgressor, every person belonging to that category is treated alike with no preference given to one over the other. In such a circumstance, even the close relatives of the Prophets[as] are not spared.

The people of Lot[as] were guilty of the crimes of sodomy, public display of shamelessness and highway robbery. God permitted Abraham[as] to pray on their behalf. But when they refused to take heed of Lot's[as] warnings and persisted in their abominations, it became God's decree to destroy them. After Abraham[as] and Lot[as] were warned of the impending ruin, the people of Sodom and Gomorah became the victims of a horrendous earthquake which wiped them out of existence. In this case, although the Prophets[as] prayed for benevolence, it was God's decree to punish the wrongdoers rather than to forgive them and this was perfectly consistent with the principles of absolute justice.

In contrast, the people of Jonah[as] were saved by God despite the prophecy of their early ruin. Jonah's[as] people rejected him totally and emphatically. At the last moment before the decree of their annihilation was about to pass, they repented and were forgiven by their Lord. This shows that such decrees from God as relate to punishment and His wrath are changeable even at the very last moment. If a people change their condition, then God's decree changes accordingly. Only when crime completely overwhelms society in terms of quantity and quality is the community destroyed. However, if the people repent, then they become beneficiaries of God's mercy. But if they persist in their crimes then not even the prayers of God's chosen Prophets[as] can save them from destruction.

Hence, the dictates of justice do not require that every transgressor be punished. Sometimes the door of forgiveness and mercy remains open. If brutality goes beyond all limits, benevolence can be of no avail. In that case even the most earnest supplications of the Prophets[as] cannot save such wrongdoing nations.

The Development of the Teaching of Absolute Justice

A study of the Prophets[as] through the ages would throw light on how the teaching of justice developed from a rudimentary level to the highly evolved teachings that form the basis of the Islamic law.

We discussed earlier the four basic principles of the law of Adam[as], in which every person was guaranteed food, water, shelter and clothing—the basic necessities of life. Moving on to the time of Noah[as], we find that in spite of worldly advancement and a highly developed civilisation, his people had become barren of all moral excellence. They rejected his teachings and transgressed all limits to the extent that it became God's decree to punish all wrongdoers without exception. No exception was made and no plea accepted. Those who rejected Noah[as] were destroyed, one and all. Noah's[as] plea on behalf of his son was in itself contrary to the principle of absolute justice. God would have nothing but justice, thus strengthening the foundation of *'Adl,* the only foundation on which further moral evolution could take place.

By the time of Joseph[as], the teachings of justice had become so concrete and so firmly entrenched in society, that even the most powerful of men dared not use his influence to contravene the dictates of justice. Hence, despite the fact that Joseph[as] held the high honour of being treasurer of the whole of Egypt—a position of great power—even he was not authorised to detain his own brother unlawfully.

The Mosaic law further emphasises the role of justice to such a high degree, that *Iḥsān* and forgiveness seem to retreat into insignificance. 'An eye for an eye and a tooth for a tooth' is how the Jews were taught to conduct their affairs with their fellow human beings. In contrast, we find Jesus[as] exhorting his followers to 'turn the other cheek.' So Moses[as] stressed the importance of justice and of exercising one's rights, whereas the teachings of Christianity went to the other extreme of benevolence and of sacrificing one's rights for the sake of others.

In some ages, justice is highly emphasised while in others the emphasis is on benevolence but not at the cost of justice. Whatever the teaching, the principle of justice is never violated. It should be remembered that self-sacrifice does not contradict justice. However, to trample on others' rights even for the sake of benevolence is inconceivable in religion. Christianity never permitted the usurpation of others' rights for the sake of forgiveness, or for showing favours.

The teachings always remained in perfect accordance with the requirements of the age. In the age of Moses[as], the specific requirements of the Children of Israel dictated the emphasis on justice and equitable revenge. The age of Jesus[as] cried out for a completely different remedy to cure the ailing society. In this comparison one can detect the thread of justice linking the two different ages.

9 Islam as the Ultimate Goal of Religious Teachings

Islam and the Advanced Era of Prophet Muhammad[sa]

We now turn our attention towards the age of the revelation of the Holy Quran. This is the time when, according to the Quran, the development of religion reached its pinnacle and the teachings reached perfection. The Quran says:

... اَلۡيَوۡمَ اَكۡمَلۡتُ لَكُمۡ دِيۡنَكُمۡ وَ اَتۡمَمۡتُ عَلَيۡكُمۡ نِعۡمَتِيۡ وَرَضِيۡتُ لَكُمُ الۡاِسۡلَامَ دِيۡنًا ...

...This day have I perfected your religion for you and completed My favour upon you and have chosen for you Islam as religion...
(Sūrah al-Māʾidah; Ch.5: V.4)

The Quran relates the subject of justice to all areas of human concern here. This makes a very interesting and vast study. It is not intended here to discuss each and every aspect of justice, but it is essential to discuss it in enough detail for the reader to comprehend the subject fully and for him to accept with confidence the Quranic claim of perfection.

137

Introducing the Holy Founder of Islam, Muhammad[sa], and the Quran in the context of justice, Allah says:

الْحَمْدُ لِلَّهِ الَّذِيٓ أَنزَلَ عَلَىٰ عَبْدِهِ الْكِتَٰبَ وَلَمْ يَجْعَل لَّهُۥ عِوَجَا ۜ □

All praise belongs to Allah Who has revealed to His servant a book in which he has placed no crookedness. (Sūrah al-Kahf; Ch.18: V.2)

None of the Quran's teachings are without purpose. In other words, if one were to study the Quran from A to Z, one would not detect even the slightest of deviations from the middle path in its teachings. It does not lean towards any particular nation or ideology. It is a perfectly balanced and well-poised book, with a character of universality that deals with humanity at large.

As the Arabic preposition *fī* (in) can be used in conjunction with *'Abd* or servant of God (i.e. Muhammad[sa]), the above verse can also be translated as 'All praise belongs to Allah who has revealed a book to His servant; a servant in whom there is no crookedness.'

Elaborating this further, Allah declares that Muhammad[sa] had been sent as a guide for the entire world. His light is not confined to any one people or to any geographical territory, but is intended for the illumination of the whole of mankind:

اَللّٰهُ نُوۡرُ السَّمٰوٰتِ وَالۡاَرۡضِ ، مَثَلُ نُوۡرِهٖ كَمِشۡكٰوةٍ فِيۡهَا مِصۡبَاحٌ ، الۡمِصۡبَاحُ فِيۡ زُجَاجَةٍ ، الزُّجَاجَةُ كَاَنَّهَا كَوۡكَبٌ دُرِّيٌّ يُّوۡقَدُ مِنۡ شَجَرَةٍ مُّبٰرَكَةٍ زَيۡتُوۡنَةٍ لَّا شَرۡقِيَّةٍ وَّلَا غَرۡبِيَّةٍ ، يَّكَادُ زَيۡتُهَا يُضِیٓءُ وَلَوۡ لَمۡ تَمۡسَسۡهُ نَارٌ ۔ ۔ ۔

Allah is the Light of the heavens and the earth. The similitude of His light is as a *lustrous* niche, wherein is a lamp. The lamp is in a glass. The glass is as it were a glittering star. It is lit from a blessed tree—an olive—neither of the east nor of the west, whose oil would well-nigh glow forth even though fire touched it not...
(Sūrah al-Nūr; Ch.24: V.36)

With this illustration of Allah's light starts the mention of the exalted attributes of the Holy Prophet[sa]. The description culminates in the phrase 'neither of the east nor of the west.' God created the sun as a source of light for the east and the west alike. Spiritually, Muhammad[sa] is the means for relaying God's light to all mankind. In this respect he holds a glorious status like unto the sun, which illuminates both the east and the west together.

The sun seems to be the ultimate source of light but if one ponders deeper, one will find that it owes its quality of light to the Creator. One can safely conclude therefore that the ultimate source of all light is God. In a like manner, Prophets[as] play the role of the sun in conveying the light of God to His servants.

There are so many sources of light in the heavenly bodies. Of them, the sun occupies a unique position in relation to the Earth. Its universal character stands out most conspicuously. Similarly the image of the Holy Prophet[sa] stands out as universal, illuminating the entire globe and making no discrimination between the orient and the occident.

The teachings of the Quran are perfectly reflected in the person of Muhammad[sa]. Both the teaching and the example of the Prophet[as] are in perfect harmony with each other. Thus when Ḥaḍrat 'Ā'ishah[ra], the wife of the Holy Prophet[sa], was requested to describe his character, the brief but most comprehensive answer given by her was:

$$كَانَ خُلُقُهُ الْقُرآنَ$$

He was the Quran personified. **8**

The teachings of Islam concur in each and every aspect with the nature of the Holy Prophet[sa]. Islamic teachings are perfectly well-balanced and based on the principles of justice, benevolence and kinship, as was the character of the Holy Prophet[sa].

The Middle Way

The nature of the Islamic umma as a people also concurs completely with the Prophet[sa] and his teachings:

140

وَكَذٰلِكَ جَعَلْنٰكُمْ اُمَّةً وَّسَطًا...

We have made you into a nation which adheres to the middle path...
(Sūrah al-Baqarah; Ch.2: V.144)

Just as the Founder[sa] of Islam and the Book revealed to him are free from one sidedness and both adhere to the middle path, so the umma of Muhammad[sa] is also described as adhering to the middle path without leaning to right or left. Incidentally, the so-called extremism as preached, followed and practised by some Muslim sects has nothing to do with Islam.

In addition to meaning 'the middle', the Arabic word *Wast* also has the connotation of excellence. So anybody who is described as *Wast* is a person who is well-poised and keeping to the middle as well as having a quality of excellence. Hence *Ummatan Wasatan* can also be interpreted as meaning the very best. If this becomes part of the basic character of a nation, and if that nation in all circumstances and trials adheres to the path of moderation, and its leanings are not one-sided, it becomes worthy of the trust and respect of other nations. A people with one-sided leanings can in no way hold the right to adjudicate between others. So it is quite justified that Islam is presented as a universal adjudicator possessing the potential to be the guardian over the whole of mankind. In a similar way, the Prophet[sa] of

Islam guards over the conduct of his umma, and ensures that they adhere to justice and fair play. He was entrusted with this task because he stood supreme among all the just. He enjoyed the full trust of his Supreme Master, the Lord of the universe. Not only is he described as guardian over Muslims, but in the following verse he is also described as guardian over all the Prophets[as]:

$$ فَكَيْفَ إِذَا جِئْنَا مِن كُلِّ أُمَّةٍ بِشَهِيدٍ وَّجِئْنَا بِكَ عَلَىٰ هَـٰؤُلَآءِ شَهِيدًا ۝ $$

And how *will it fare for them* when We shall bring forth a witness from every people, and shall bring you as a witness against these!
(Sūrah al-Nisā'; Ch.4: V.42)

The Straight Path

The way of life proposed by the Quran for Muslims is not only well-balanced and belonging to the middle path, but is also pronounced to be free from any apparent or hidden crookedness. The essence of Islam is that all its teachings are finely balanced and free of prejudice. Elaborating on this theme further, the Quran says:

قُلْ اِنَّنِيْ هَدٰىنِيْ رَبِّيٓ اِلٰى صِرَاطٍ مُّسْتَقِيْمٍ دِيْنًا قِيَمًا مِّلَّةَ اِبْرٰهِيْمَ حَنِيْفًا۪ وَمَا كَانَ مِنَ الْمُشْرِكِيْنَ ☐

Say, 'As for me, my Lord had guided me unto a straight path—a right religion, the religion of Abraham, the upright. And he was not of those who join gods *with God*.'
(Sūrah al-An'ām; Ch.6: V.162)

This verse throws new light on the meaning of *Ṣirāṭi Mustaqīm* or the straight path. Apart from being the middle path, it has the quality of steadfastness and perseverance. *Istaqāma Zaidun*, for example, means 'Zaid stood firm against all efforts to dislodge him and to throw him off balance', while *Qāma* merely means to stand upright. The infinitive of *Qāma* and *Istaqāma* are the same, but when *'ist'* is added in the beginning as a prefix a new connotation is added to its central meaning. The new connotation is one of perseverance in the face of all outside efforts to uproot, dislodge and throw off balance. In the case of human beings, it means perseverance, steadfastness and resolution to hold fast to one's beliefs—despite the odds being against it. Hence, Muslims are required to pray for the strength to stay on the *Ṣirāṭi Mustaqīm,* despite enemy attacks which are designed to deflect them from the same.

So *Ṣirāṭi Mustaqīm* is a straight path which others seek to twist and bend out of shape. In spite of such concerted efforts, God has ensured that all attempts to change the straight path will ultimately be frustrated. The promise of the restoration of the true teachings of Islam at least once every hundred years by a Divinely guided leader ensures that man-made changes and other signs of natural decay are repaired periodically.

In any event, the true meaning of *Wasaṭan* is that the Prophet[sa] of Islam is free from crookedness and one-sided leanings, as also are his umma and his teachings.

It should be borne in mind that the concept of the straight path was gradually expanded through the ages and was developed in stages alongside the progress of man. The term 'straight path' is also found in religions prior to Islam. For example, in the above mentioned verse, the Holy Prophet[sa] referring to his own religion as the straight path attributes the same to Abraham[as] and declares himself to be in line with his teachings. What was the difference between the straight path shown to Abraham[as] and the one shown to Muhammad[sa]? The difference was only one of degrees. Right from the inception of religion, man was guided on the right path. But prior to Islam all religions were revealed in accordance with the requirements of a particular age or nation. There was no universal religion. Hence the definition of the straight path was limited in keeping with the specific requirements of a particular time or nation. In the Quran, Allah states:

اَلَّذِیْنَ اٰمَنُوْا وَ لَمْ یَلْبِسُوْآ اِیْمَانَهُمْ بِظُلْمٍ اُولٰٓئِكَ لَهُمُ الْاَمْنُ وَهُمْ مُّهْتَدُوْنَ ۞ وَ تِلْكَ حُجَّتُنَآ اٰتَیْنٰهَآ اِبْرٰهِیْمَ عَلٰی قَوْمِهٖ ۚ نَرْفَعُ دَرَجٰتٍ مَّنْ نَّشَآءُ ؕ اِنَّ رَبَّكَ حَكِیْمٌ عَلِیْمٌ ۞ وَ وَهَبْنَا لَهٗٓ اِسْحٰقَ وَ یَعْقُوْبَ ؕ كُلًّا هَدَیْنَا ۚ وَ نُوْحًا هَدَیْنَا مِنْ قَبْلُ وَمِنْ ذُرِّیَّتِهٖ دَاوٗدَ وَ سُلَیْمٰنَ وَ اَیُّوْبَ وَ یُوْسُفَ وَ مُوْسٰی وَ هٰرُوْنَ ؕ وَكَذٰلِكَ نَجْزِی الْمُحْسِنِیْنَ ۞ وَ زَكَرِیَّا وَ یَحْیٰی وَ عِیْسٰی وَ اِلْیَاسَ ؕ كُلٌّ مِّنَ الصّٰلِحِیْنَ ۞ وَاِسْمٰعِیْلَ وَالْیَسَعَ وَ یُوْنُسَ وَ لُوْطًا ؕ وَكُلًّا فَضَّلْنَا عَلَی الْعٰلَمِیْنَ ۞ وَمِنْ اٰبَآئِهِمْ وَذُرِّیّٰتِهِمْ وَاِخْوَانِهِمْ ۚ وَ اجْتَبَیْنٰهُمْ وَ هَدَیْنٰهُمْ اِلٰی صِرَاطٍ مُّسْتَقِیْمٍ ۞

Those who believe and mix not up their belief with injustice—it is they who shall have peace, and who are rightly guided. And that is Our argument which We gave to Abraham against his people. We exalt in degrees of rank whomso We please. Your Lord is indeed Wise, All-Knowing. And We gave him Isaac and Jacob; each did We guide aright, and Noah did We guide aright aforetime, and of his progeny, David and Solomon and Job and Joseph and Moses and Aaron. Thus do We reward those who do good. And *We guided* Zachariah and John and Jesus and Elias; each *one of them* was of the virtuous. And *We also guided* Ishmael and Elisha and Jonah and Lot; and each one did We exalt above the people. And *We exalted* some of their fathers and their children and their brethren, and We chose them and We guided them in the straight path.
(Sūrah al-An'ām; Ch.6: Vs.83-88)

The 'right path' is not a monopoly of Islam. In fact all Prophets[as] prior to the inception of Islam had been given teachings of the right path, as asserted by the verses mentioned above. So when did a universal Prophet[sa] appear in the world? And when did the concept of the straight path gain a universal import? To answer these questions we need to study such verses of the Quran as deal with the subject of the universality of Islam, and the universality of the Holy Prophet[sa]. The Quran says:

وَمَآ أَرۡسَلۡنَٰكَ إِلَّا رَحۡمَةً لِّلۡعَٰلَمِينَ ۝

And We have sent you not but as a mercy for the entire world.
(Sūrah al-Anbiyā'; Ch.21: V.108)

And:

وَمَآ أَرۡسَلۡنَٰكَ إِلَّا كَآفَّةً لِّلنَّاسِ بَشِيرًا وَّنَذِيرًا وَّلَٰكِنَّ أَكۡثَرَ النَّاسِ لَا يَعۡلَمُونَ ۝

And We have not sent you but as a bearer of glad tidings and a Warner, for all mankind, but most men know not.
(Sūrah Sabā'; Ch.34: V.29)

It needs to be further emphasised here that up to the time of the revelation of the Quran, none of the Divine scriptures, apart from the Quran, had claimed to be universal in their message and their application. Nor did any Prophet[as] prior to Muhammad[sa] ever proclaim himself to be universal, addressing the whole of mankind without making any discrimination between nation and nation, and people and people. All other Prophets[as] addressed only their own people. At best they included neighbouring nations or those living as immigrants among the host nation. But apart from the Quran no Divine scripture is addressed to the whole of mankind collectively. Hence, for previous religions the straight path, as defined by them, must be understood to be limited to their specific needs and requirements.

Islam and the Nature of Man

Having established the fact that the Quran is the only Divine book which claims to be for all people and for all times, it follows that its teachings should be applicable to all human beings alike. Its teachings should not show deference or preference to any one section of society, nor should it be applicable to any one era alone. It must transcend all barriers and divisions of space and time, otherwise the claim of universality cannot be accepted.

When we examine the Quran from this angle, we find that its teachings fully support its claim of universality. The most important and basic argument put forward in this regard is that the religion of Islam is in perfect harmony with the nature of man. In other words, Islam was not designed with any particular age or nation in mind but was designed in perfect consistency with the human character. It goes without saying that human nature is uniform the world over and is not influenced by racial or ethnic divisions. Similarly the passage of time does not alter the basic traits of man. The relatively uncivilised man who lived ten thousand years ago had exactly the same nature as does the comparatively advanced and civilised man of today. The Quran says:

فِطْرَتَ اللّٰهِ الَّتِيْ فَطَرَ النَّاسَ عَلَيْهَا ۚ لَا تَبْدِيْلَ لِخَلْقِ اللّٰهِ ۚ ذٰلِكَ الدِّيْنُ الْقَيِّمُ ۙ وَلٰكِنَّ اَكْثَرَ النَّاسِ لَا يَعْلَمُوْنَ ۙ

The nature of Allah is one in accordance with which He has fashioned all humans. There is no altering the creation of Allah. That is the right religion. But most men know not.
(Sūrah al-Rūm; Ch.30: V.31)

The mould of man created by Allah is unchangeable. Everything created by God has a certain mould and stamp. This is true for every species, every order and every genre. No species, no order, no genre is exempt from this principle. As long as a species remains confined to its specific purpose of creation, it has no choice but to follow the pattern of life designed for it. When it begins to change its character, even then it does not violate the plan of nature. In fact, by this process of gradual change in certain characters, it is being prepared to be shifted from a species of a lower order to that of a higher order. This, too, is a part of nature and as such the scheme of things remains unchangeable. In that sense, as long as he falls into the category of Homosapien, man will possess the same genetically controlled characteristics his ancient forefathers held. Any religious teachings which take into account this unchangeable universal nature of man, consequently become unchangeable.

Hence, these religions, though not changed, were occasionally modified according to the requirements of a given era. Hence, it should be clearly understood that Islam does not monopolise truth to the exclusion of other religions. On the contrary, it explicitly speaks of a central core of Godliness commonly shared by all Divine religions. With the passage of time, the central stem grew in strength and volume, giving birth to many branches which worked as the secondary teaching of that religion. Thus the ratio of secondary teachings to the fundamentals became more voluminous as the religion progressed. The branches and foliage which grew out of this main stem kept changing without altering the basic design.

The Quran claims to have brought the religion that covers each of the essential features of human characteristics without sacrificing their fundamental nature. This is termed as *Dīni Qayyim* (30:31), meaning 'right religion', and having the connotation of being not only right in itself but also possessing the power of setting others right. Religion is the word of God as imprinted on human nature. It is Allah's nature which is stamped on all humans. The Holy Prophet[sa] observes the following in this regard:

$$مَامِنْ مَوْلُوْدٍ يُوْلَدُ إِلَّا عَلٰى فِطْرَةِ الْإِسْلَامِ$$

No child is born but in the mould of Islam.[9]

In another hadith, he further elaborates:

$$مَامِنْ مَوْلُوْدٍ إِلَّا يُوْلَدُ عَلَى الْفِطْرَةِ فَأَبَوَاهُ يُهَوِّدَانِهِ اَوْيُنَصِّرَانِهِ$$
$$اَوْيُمَجِّسَانِهِ$$

No child is born but in harmony with nature. It is his parents who turn him into a Jew or a Christian or a fire-worshipper. [10]

The logical conclusion to be drawn is that according to both the Quran and the Prophet[sa] of Islam, human nature and the religion of Islam are synonymous. However, it is the parents who mould their child into whichever shape they please.

Freud presented various twisted and unsavoury theories, many of which have since been proven false. He was opposed to religion in general and Islam in particular. In his attempts to discredit religion and disprove the existence of God, he put forward the view that a child's religion in itself holds no influence over his personality. Anyone could rear a child to become an aetheist or a religious person of any denomination. A child could also be raised in such a manner that he would have a strong conviction of being a Prophet of God, as he grew into adulthood.

Little did Freud realise that by building this argument against Islam and God, he was only supporting the Islamic concept of a child's birth and his subsequent development. Long before Freud was born, the Prophet[sa] of Islam had already informed us that every child is born in the nature of God but he can be moulded into anything else under the influence of his parents or that of those who are responsible for his upbringing.

Again, a pertinent question arises as to what is the nature of human conscience, if anything at all? Many renowned philosophers and scholars agree with the principle that man's nature has the imprint of a universal moral teaching—one which is not born out of any particular religious influence. The awareness of this innate moral teaching is what is termed as conscience.

Here it would be appropriate to mention the famous eighteenth century philosopher, Immanuel Kant. He refuted many an argument which various people had presented as proof of the existence of God. In particular, after studying Anselm's Ontological argument in favour of God, Kant strongly rebutted it. However, the only thing which bothered Kant's own conscience was the presence of a universal moral sense in every human. This could be the only entertainable argument in favour of God's existence, he conceded.[11]

This moral code forms part of the human subconscious, and not every person has the ability to comprehend it clearly. The Divine revelation vouchsafed to the last Law-bearing Prophet[sa] brought these teachings to light.

Kant's reasoning is a weighty one. His realisation of some imprint of the concept of God in every human being brings to mind a great Quranic revelation which speaks of the image of God being stamped onto man even before his creation. It formed part of the blueprint which was to govern and guide the course of human evolution. It says in the Quran:

وَ اِذۡ اَخَذَ رَبُّكَ مِنۡ بَنِیۡۤ اٰدَمَ مِنۡ ظُهُوۡرِهِمۡ ذُرِّیَّتَهُمۡ وَ اَشۡهَدَهُمۡ
عَلٰۤی اَنۡفُسِهِمۡ ۚ اَلَسۡتُ بِرَبِّكُمۡ ؕ قَالُوۡا بَلٰی ۚ شَهِدۡنَا ۚ اَنۡ تَقُوۡلُوۡا
یَوۡمَ الۡقِیٰمَةِ اِنَّا كُنَّا عَنۡ هٰذَا غٰفِلِیۡنَ ☐

And when your Lord brings forth from Adam's children, out of their loins—their offspring and makes them witnesses against their own selves *by saying:* 'Am I not your Lord?' They say, 'Yes, why not!' *This He does* lest you should say on the Day of Resurrection, 'We were surely unaware of this.'
(Sūrah al-Aʿrāf; Ch.7: V.173)

This verse is a metaphorical illustration of how the belief in God has gone into the very making of man.

Accountability and Inherited Sin

In Islam we find a teaching of perfect justice, not only between one man and another, but also between one age and the next. Examining the same principle as reflected by religious history, one can come to the conclusion that man of all ages has been treated with the same principle of justice by God. We read in the Quran:

تِلْكَ أُمَّـةٌ قَدْ خَلَتْ ۖ لَهَا مَا كَسَبَتْ وَلَكُمْ مَّا كَسَبْتُمْ ۖ وَلَا
تُسْئَلُونَ عَمَّا كَانُوا يَعْمَلُونَ ☐

Those are a people who have passed away; for them is what they earned, and for you shall be what you earn; and you shall not be questioned as to what they did.
(Sūrah al-Baqarah; Ch.2: V.135)

As far as the question of answerability is concerned, each generation is answerable for its deeds and each age will be held accountable for its conduct. This Quranic style further enlightens us on the issue of relative states of advancement of men of different ages. Thus accountability will be with reference to the capabilities of human beings at a certain period of their history. They will be judged in view of their aptitudes, as we shall be judged in view of ours. This aspect presents the Quranic teachings as being universal in both planes of space and time.

Human nature accepts such a just teaching to be Divine, and this is what becomes the criterion for distinguishing man's teaching from that of God. A study of the Christian dogma of hereditary sin is an interesting case in point. It could not have emanated from God's teaching endowed to Christ[as]. We are justified therefore in believing that it had to be a Pauline interpolation of Christ's[as] teaching, otherwise it would be a strange God who would continually punish the subsequent generations of Adam[as] till the end of time for a momentary, transient lapse on his part. This reflection is not aimed at censuring Christianity, but is only meant to highlight the role of the human hand and the havoc it plays with truth.

Without getting into an argument on the relative merits of the Christian doctrine of hereditary sin, let us see how the Quran in one stroke wipes out this notion. In the verse quoted above, Allah says, you will not be questioned about the wrongdoings of your ancestors. They will be answerable for what they did; you need only be concerned with what you do.

In this regard the Quran declares:

وَلَا تَزِرُ وَازِرَةٌ وِّزْرَ أُخْرَى ۖ وَإِن تَدْعُ مُثْقَلَةٌ إِلَىٰ حِمْلِهَا لَا يُحْمَلْ مِنْهُ شَيْءٌ ۚ وَلَوْ كَانَ ذَا قُرْبَىٰ ...

And no burdened *soul* can bear the burden of another; and if a heavily laden *soul* call another to *bear* its

load, naught of it shall be carried *by the other*, even
though he be a kinsman...
(Sūrah Fāṭir; Ch.35: V.19)

If a bearer of a burden seeks the help of another to
carry its burden, it will not be carried, even if the call
is made to the nearest of kin. This verse of the Quran
refutes the Christian doctrine of atonement, (i.e. that
Jesus[as] died on the cross to atone for the sins of
others), by declaring that no present or future
generation would be expected to bear the burden of
the sins of previous generations. The burden of an
individual's sins can in no way be transferred to
another, even if the other is willing to accept such a
load. In fact to punish one for the sins of another is
declared to be contrary to the minimum demands of
Divine justice.

If the question were that of justice only, then the
verse in the New Testament (Luke 9:23)[12] seems
similar to the above verse of the Holy Quran. It would
appear that the Prophet Jesus[as] had no hand in the
tales of atonement attributed to him by the future
generations. In fact, Jesus's[as] teaching was basically
the same as the simple and straightforward teaching of
the Quran, justice where justice is due, and mercy
where mercy is appropriate.

This unequivocal declaration of the Quran presents
an important aspect of the issue of crime and
punishment which is in exact keeping with human
nature. Another verse of the Quran presented above in

a different context effectively demolishes the concept of inherited sin. Not only does it exonerate man from the false stigma of him being a born sinner, but by declaring that his nature resembles the nature of God, it pays a great tribute to the honour and esteem of mankind. The verse is repeated below:

فِطْرَتَ اللّٰهِ الَّتِيْ فَطَرَ النَّاسَ عَلَيْهَا ۚ لَا تَبْدِيْلَ لِخَلْقِ اللّٰهِ ۚ ذٰلِكَ الدِّيْنُ الْقَيِّمُ ۚۖ وَلٰكِنَّ اَكْثَرَ النَّاسِ لَا يَعْلَمُوْنَ ☐

The nature of Allah is the one in accordance with which He has fashioned all humans. There is no altering the creation of Allah. That is the right religion. But most men know not.
(Sūrah al-Rūm; Ch.30: V.31)

As far as the past, present and future eras are concerned, the above verses paint a beautiful picture of the perfect balance that exists between the man of these three ages. Each generation is treated with uniformity, with no generation being exempt from accountability. Discussing the issue of justice between past, present and future ages, the Quran directs:

يٰٓاَيُّهَا الَّذِيْنَ اٰمَنُوا اتَّقُوا اللّٰهَ وَلْتَنْظُرْ نَفْسٌ مَّا قَدَّمَتْ لِغَدٍ ۚ ...

O ye who believe! fear Allah; and let *every* soul look to what it sends forth for the morrow...
(Sūrah al-Ḥashr; Ch.59: V.19)

The future generations will be held accountable for

their wrongdoings, just as the present and past generations will respectively be held accountable for theirs. In terms of God's wrath and punishment, each generation is isolated from the other. The sins of a previous age will not be transferred to the present age, nor will the sins of the present age be transferred to the next.

This beautiful definition of justice is not found in Pauline Christianity, as practised by many today. Whereas Jesus taught that each man would bear his own cross, Pauline Christians believe that each subsequent generation will be laden with the sins of all previous ones.

Allah also says in the Quran:

فَخَلَفَ مِنْۢ بَعْدِهِمْ خَلْفٌ اَضَاعُوا الصَّلٰوةَ وَ اتَّبَعُوا الشَّهَوٰتِ فَسَوْفَ يَلْقَوْنَ غَيًّا ☐

Then there came after them descendants who neglected Prayer, and followed their evil desires. So they will meet with destruction,
(Sūrah Maryam; Ch.19: V.60)

If the progeny of pious people choose to neglect their prayer and follow their evil desires, then the piety of their forefathers will avail them naught. Just as one generation will not be punished for the sins of previous generations, man of a subsequent era will not be rewarded for the good deeds of the people of the past.

A careful study of the Quran will show that its teachings are not accidental, nor are they disjointed. Rather they conform to a great and noble plan of things; which is the establishment of justice. All people are treated equally, regardless of wherever and whenever they were born. The basic rights of all are one and the same. The racial and generational distinctions that exist between man and man are based on justice. The ties that bind together the East and the West, the Black and the White, the Arab and the non-Arab, are all based on the universal principle of justice.

It is claimed by some that this great, noble, perfect and wondrous teaching was the creation of an unlettered Arab herdsman, who then chose to attribute it to God. Nothing could be farther from the truth. No scholar of any age has ever been able to concoct a religion which is even fractionally as well-balanced and well-poised as is the teaching of Islam. In fact, all the scriptures believed to be of Divine origin put together cannot boast such balance and poise as is displayed by Islam. How is it possible that, according to them, an unlettered man should have been the source of this fountain of profound and perfect wisdom?

It is towards these miraculous qualities of the Quran that our attention is repeatedly drawn:

قُلْ لَّئِنِ اجْتَمَعَتِ الْإِنْسُ وَ الْجِنُّ عَلَى أَن يَّأْتُوا بِمِثْلِ هَـذَا الْقُرْآنِ لَا يَأْتُونَ بِمِثْلِهِ وَلَوْ كَانَ بَعْضُهُمْ لِبَعْضٍ ظَهِـيْرًا ☐

Say, 'If mankind and the Jinn gathered together to produce the like of this Quran, they could not produce the like thereof, even though they should help one another.'
(Sūrah Banī Isrā'īl; Ch.17: V.89)

This challenge stands unaccepted even today!

Guidance for Mankind

Having discussed the notion of inherited sin, we now turn to a positive aspect of religion; and that is the concept of God's guidance for mankind. The world has witnessed many religions which were specific to a particular age or nation. Although they had a great role to play in the history of mankind, yet their blessings were confined to a small number of societies who themselves had a limited life span. Hence, the religions and the teachings of those bygone people were not intended to be applicable for all times. New and changing circumstances gave rise to the need for new teachings. When the old teachings lost their relevance, God would modify them and lay the foundation for a new religion. Once this happened, a new lease of life was given to the religion because for some time to come the teachings would remain applicable to the requirements of the age.

159

This philosophy of religions is simple and easy to comprehend, yet it is surprising to note that no mention of it is found in any Divine scripture other than the Quran. All other scriptures seem to be addressed to one people or one nation, to the exclusion of the rest of mankind. It is almost as if God chose to guide one nation alone, leaving all others bereft of His mercy and without any Divine messenger to guide them.

In no religion apart from Islam, do we find mention of other nations and other ages as being recipients of Divine guidance. Strange though this claim may seem, it is nonetheless true. Even today, a study of the Divine scriptures would leave us with no alternative but to accept this claim as being a true statement of fact. The Quran is the only book that speaks of a universal concern of God for His creatures, and of His communion with man of all the countries and all the ages. As far as different nations are concerned, the Quran says:

وَلِكُلِّ قَوْمٍ هَادٍ ۞

We have sent a guide to every people.
(Sūrah al-Ra'd; Ch.13: V.8)

Mankind is divided either by time, nationality or geographical regions, i.e. city-states. In the ancient times, political sovereignty was identified with reference to city-states rather than countries. The Quran declares that no nation and no region of the world was discriminated against.

160

وَ مَآ اَهۡلَكۡنَا مِنۡ قَرۡيَةٍ اِلَّا لَهَا مُنۡذِرُوۡنَ ۖ ذِكۡرٰی ۚ وَمَا
كُنَّا ظٰلِمِیۡنَ

And never did We destroy any township but it had
Warners. *This is* an admonition; and We are not
unjust.
(Sūrah al-Shuʻarāʾ; Ch.26: Vs.209-210)

Although in this translation the word *Dhikrā* has been
translated as 'admonition', this is a word which can
also be translated in its other connotations. *Dhikrā*
may mean a lesson for others and also the memory of
God personified. Thus the Prophets[as] are not shown as
mere warners but also as bearers of glad tidings, so
that people, by following their example, could be led
to God whose memory they personify. They were not
like the oracles of Greek mythology who bode ill for
the people, leaving them no chance to escape from the
calamities portended. Instead, they were admonishers
who drew lessons from history and who attempted to
persuade others to rectify their conduct in the light of
the history of earlier people. The warners did not
come only to close the doors of destruction, they also
came to open the gates of paradise.

References Part I

1. *Tafsīr Ḥaqqānī*, by Maulāna 'Abdul Ḥaq Ḥaqqānī, volum I, page 434, under the verse no. 65 of Surah al-Baqarah (chapter II).

2. See '*Out of My Later Years*' by Albert Einstein, Philosophical Library, New York and *The Encyclopedia of Religion*, Vol. 5, pp 71-72, Published by Macmillan Publishing Company, New York.

3. *Grolier Encyclopaedia*, Vol. 6.

4. *Op. cit.*

5. *Textbook of Medical Physiology*, Arthur C. Guyton, 5th Edition, Saunders, 1976, Chapter 78.

6. *Ṣaḥīḥ Muslim* Kitābul Ashriba, Bābun al-Mu'minu Y'akulu..., Ch. 34, Hadith 182, 184.

7. *Textbook of Medical Physiology*, Arthur C. Guyton, Chap. 79, 5th Edition, Saunders, 1976.

8. *Musnad Aḥmad bin Ḥambal, Musnadi 'Ā'ishah* Vol. 6, p.91.
   Note: With slight difference of words the Hadith referring to the same subject is found in *Ṣaḥīḥ Muslim,* Kitābu Ṣalāti Musāfirīna, Bābu Jām'iṣ Ṣalāti Laili Wa Man Nāma 'Anhu.

9. *Al-Mu'jamul Kabīr lil-Ḥāfiẓ Abul Qāsim Suleimān ibni Ahmad al-Ṭabrānī*, Vol.1, p.283.

10. *Ṣaḥīḥ Bukhāri*, Kitābul Janāi'z, Bābu Idha Aslamas Sabiyyu fa Māta...

11. a) *Critique of Pure Reason*, by Immanuel Kant, Translated by J.M.D. Meiklejohn, pp. 367-372, published by J.M.Dent & Sons Ltd, 1978.

    b) *Critique of Judgement*, by Immanuel Kant, Translated by James Creed Meredith, pp. 114-122, Oxford University Press, 1986.

12. 'and he said unto all, If any man would come after me, let him deny himself and take up his cross daily, and follow me.' (Luke ch. 9 Vs.23, [*The Holy Bible, The Revised Version with Marginal References*]. London: Cambridge University Press, 1898)

Absolute Justice, Kindness and Kinship

The Three Creative Principles

Ḥaḍrat Mirza Tahir Ahmad

Part II

Speech delivered at the Annual Convention
of the Ahmadiyyah Muslim Jama'at
in Rabwah, Pakistan on December 27, 1983

LIST OF CHAPTERS IN PART II

In the name of Allah, the Most Gracious, the Ever Merciful.

As has been shown in Part I, comprising the first speech, the principles of absolute justice, fair-play and kinship (*'Adl, Iḥsān* and *Ītā'i Dhil-Qurbā*) apply not only to the creation of the universe but they also apply equally to the creation of life on planet Earth. The entire course of evolution is strictly governed by these principles, man being no exception.

10 Freedom of Conscience in Matters of Faith

The verse mentioned below deals with a completely new aspect of the same aforementioned principles. According to this verse, all matters pertaining to the area of human faith are likewise governed by these principles. Moreover, they are not confined to the faith of humans of any one era; in fact they are related to all humans of every age, individually and collectively. The verse is as follows:

اِنَّ الَّذِيْنَ اٰمَنُوْا وَ الَّذِيْنَ هَادُوْا وَ النَّصٰرٰى وَ الصَّابِئِيْنَ مَنْ اٰمَنَ بِاللّٰهِ وَ الْيَوْمِ الْاٰخِرِ وَ عَمِلَ صَالِحًا فَلَهُمْ اَجْرُهُمْ عِنْدَ رَبِّهِمْ وَلَا خَوْفٌ عَلَيْهِمْ وَلَا هُمْ يَحْزَنُوْنَ ☐

Surely, the Believers, and the Jews, and the Christians and the Sabians—whichever party *from among these truly* believes in Allah and the Last Day and does good deeds—shall have their reward with their Lord, and no fear *shall come* upon them, nor shall they grieve.
(Sūrah al-Baqarah; Ch.2: V.63)

Muslim commentators have presented various interpretations of this verse which mostly show their lack of full comprehension, whereas the non-Muslims treat this verse completely out of context and their interpretations are mostly prejudiced and hostile. Some have gone so far in their arrogance as to make it a special target of their negative criticism. They believe that it liberates mankind from the obligation of accepting Islam. According to their interpretation, the only conditions for salvation are that you believe in Allah and the Last Day and that you do good works; it does not matter whether you are a Jew, a Christian or a Sabian—a Sabian is defined as a believer in God who may follow any of the Divine books revealed earlier in any part of the world.

In other words they claim that, according to this verse, Islam is not at all essential for the salvation of mankind; whichever faith man chooses to follow will lead him to salvation. They fail to realise that this verse encompasses a wide subject of great depth and universal application. To understand its import, one must study it in the light of other similar verses of the Quran and derive an inference which is fully in line with them.

In its flexibility this verse is generally applicable to many different situations without creating any internal contradiction. None of its genuine interpretations can ever be found in conflict with each other or even with any other verse related to the same subject. But to understand this point clearly, a more detailed study of this verse is required from different points of view.

First, in application to the time span prior to Islam,

166

this verse provides us with an excellent example of how the Holy Quran treats every other religion with absolute justice in a manner which is totally unrivalled in any other Scripture. This verse promises people of all ages, prior to the revelation of the Quran, that regardless of the religion they subscribed to, or by whatever name it was called, as long as they believed in Allah and the Last Day and performed good deeds as their religion required of them, Allah assures them peace and salvation. He promises that they will fear not, nor will they ever grieve.

So far as all earlier faiths are concerned, this verse gives glad tidings of salvation to all people belonging to them, provided they sincerely act upon their teachings and also believe in the inevitability of the Day of Judgement.

The second aspect of this verse applies to all those people who, despite living at the same time as the Holy Prophet[sa], did not receive the message of Islam. In this respect they are placed in the same category as the people of earlier eras. For them the message becomes: *All humans, wherever they reside in the world, should rest assured that as long as the message of Islam has not reached them, or is not conveyed to them in a convincing manner such as leaves no room for rejection, Allah will not deal with them unjustly. They will be judged by the standards of their respective religions.* As we find in Sūrah al-Baqarah:

لَا يُكَلِّفُ اللّٰهُ نَفْسًا اِلَّا وُسْعَهَا ...

Allah burdens not any soul beyond its capacity...
(Sūrah al-Baqarah; Ch.2: V.287)

i.e. He will safeguard them and judge them by the measure of their own religions.

Similarly, a third application of the same verse addresses those people who were contemporaries of the Holy Prophet[sa] but were adherents of other religions. If they were true to their principles and steadfast in their faith and good works, this verse gives them glad tidings that Allah will not deprive them of their reward.

In this respect, we find from the Holy Quran that good works are rewarded in two ways; one being here on earth, the other being attained in the life after death. As far as the former category is concerned, it means that as a result of their good works and sincere faith, as soon as the message of Islam reaches these people, they are expected to accept it. Thus in the expression 'Falahum Ajruhum', one meaning of the *ajr* (reward) is their being led to Islam as a reward for their good deeds. This interpretation is fully supported by the Holy Founder[sa] of Islam himself. Ḥaḍrat Ḥakīm bin Ḥizām[ra] narrates:

> Before accepting Islam I undertook many good works. I served the poor, I fed the hungry and helped the distressed. After accepting Islam, I asked the Holy

Prophet[sa], 'O Prophet of Allah! What will become of
the good deeds I performed before I accepted Islam?
Will they be rewarded?' Muhammad[sa] replied, 'Your
Islam is your reward.'[13]

Having examined one aspect of the principle of
Freedom of Consceience, we now turn to another
aspect of the same which concerns the prohibition of
converting others to a different religion by the
application of force.

The Quran is the one and the only book which
upholds complete and unconditional freedom in
matters of faith in unequivocal terms. It categorically
refutes the age-old allegation, levelled against religion
by the non-religious, that all religions promote
coercion.

لَآ إِكْرَاهَ فِى الدِّيْنِ ۛ قَدْ تَّبَيَّنَ الرُّشْدُ مِنَ الْغَيِّ ۚ فَمَنْ يَّكْفُرْ
بِالطَّاغُوْتِ وَ يُؤْمِنْ بِاللّٰهِ فَقَدِ اسْتَمْسَكَ بِالْعُرْوَةِ الْوُثْقٰى
لَا انْفِصَامَ لَهَا ۛ وَاللّٰهُ سَمِيْعٌ عَلِيْمٌ □

There should be no compulsion in matters of faith.
Surely, right has become distinct from wrong; so
whosoever refuses to be led by those who transgress,
and believes in Allah, has surely grasped a strong
handle which knows no breaking. And Allah is All-
Hearing, All-Knowing.
(Sūrah al-Baqarah; Ch.2: V.257)

In matters of faith there is no compulsion, every
person has complete freedom. No religion is given

169

permission to convert anyone forcibly and no person renouncing a religion can be prevented by force. In addition, the proclamation *'Lā Ikrāha Fiddīni'* alludes to an unalterable principle of human nature, that is, even if force is used it is ineffective in matters of religion because it cannot cause a change in an attitude of mind and heart. To try and do this by compulsion is a futile exercise which achieves nothing but oppression.

In this verse, the right to use force is denied to all religions, since the use of the word *dīn* is general and is applicable to all religions and not solely to Islam. Apparently, some other religions also disclaim the use of force, but the question is: do their Divine Scriptures present this teaching with such clarity? I believe, that in principle, a similar teaching may be found in all Divine books. Albeit, it may not be so comprehensive, it may be comparatively rudimentary and it may even have been doctored by later followers to suit their own personal objectives, but that is a separate issue.

As far as the Holy Quran is concerned, it does not stop at stating this basic principle but exonerates all religions from the accusation that they used force to propagate their teachings. It names previous Prophets[as] and their teachings and declares them to be the upholders of freedom of conscience. As against them, it is always the opponents of truth who attempt to suppress it with the help of coercion. The same verse speaks of the futility of their exercise. The message is loud and clear that the area of faith lies outside the domain of coercion.

With regard to the history of religion as portrayed in the Holy Quran, it has been clearly explained that ever since Allah established the institution of Prophethood for the guidance of man, there has ensued a continuous struggle between two diametrically opposed views. On the one hand are God's Prophets and Messengers who receive guidance through Divine revelation and invite their respective nations towards the same, whilst giving them a free choice to either accept or reject the message. They proclaim that neither do they have the authority to enforce their teachings upon anybody, nor do they believe in doing so. On the other hand, there are their opponents who always, without fail, not only declare their belief in the use of coercion but also in practice use force to prevent others from propagating their faith. They proclaim *if you do not desist from attempting to change our religion through arguments, you will be severely punished. And whosoever from among our people discards our own religion to adopt a new one will be treated with such cruelty as will become a warning to all others.*

Hence, according to the Holy Quran, every true Prophet proclaimed freedom of conscience, while every false opponent stood for coercion and force to prevent the spread of truth. Out of many examples, the Holy Quran mentions Ḥaḍrat Shuʻaib[as]:

قَالَ الْمَلَأُ الَّذِينَ اسْتَكْبَرُوْا مِنْ قَوْمِهٖ لَنُخْرِجَنَّكَ يٰشُعَيْبُ
وَ الَّذِيْنَ اٰمَنُوْا مَعَكَ مِنْ قَرْيَتِنَآ اَوْ لَتَعُوْدُنَّ فِيْ مِلَّتِنَا ؕ
قَالَ اَوَ لَوْ كُنَّا كَارِهِيْنَ ۚ

The chiefs among his people who were arrogant said,
'Assuredly we will drive you out, O Shu'aib, and the
believers *that are* with you, from our town, or you
shall have to return to our religion.' He said: 'Even
though we be unwilling?'
(Sūrah al-A'rāf; Ch.7: V.89)

In other words Ḥaḍrat Shu'aib[as] was told: *If you
renounce our religion then we will not allow you to
remain in our country.* On hearing this, he simply
said, 'Even though we be unwilling?' This pithy
statement of Ḥaḍrat Shu'aib[as] was the most wise and
incisive reply to his opponents' challenge.

It is obvious that if one's heart becomes averse to a
particular religion, then using threats of banishment
cannot bring one back into the fold. Threats can at
best turn people into hypocrites, but they cannot bring
about a change in their inner beliefs. People cannot be
forced into a religion. The only way to entice them
back (to the old religion) is by removing, through
logic and reason, the causes behind their rejection.
Physical force does not have the strength to change
people's beliefs.

The Holy Quran also mentions other Prophets[as]
who received similar treatment at the hands of their
opponents. In each case the basic story is the same.

Some of the Prophets[as] mentioned in this regard include Ḥaḍrat Nūḥ (Noah)[as], Ḥaḍrat Ibrāhīm (Abraham)[as], Ḥaḍrat Lūṭ (Lot)[as], Ḥaḍrat Hūd[as] and Ḥaḍrat Ṣāliḥ[as]. But this list is far from being exhausted. In fact, while on the subject, the Holy Quran refers to all the Prophets[as] generally without specifically mentioning their names. It clearly states that no Prophets[as], born at different epochs of history, ever permitted compulsion in matters of faith. In spite of tremendous suffering, all the Prophets[as] always held fast to the basic principle of freedom of conscience. If a tyrant ever attempted to coerce others into changing their faith, he found, and will find them always ready to defend their fundamental rights, even at the cost of immense sacrifices.

The same goes for the crime of apostasy. The following far-reaching Quranic verse is worthy of note:

وَ قَالَ الَّذِيْنَ كَفَرُوْا لِرُسُلِهِمْ لَنُخْرِجَنَّكُمْ مِّنْ اَرْضِنَآ اَوْ
لَتَعُوْدُنَّ فِيْ مِلَّتِنَا ۚ فَاَوْحٰۤى اِلَيْهِمْ رَبُّهُمْ لَنُهْلِكَنَّ الظّٰلِمِيْنَ ☐

And those who disbelieved said to their Messengers, 'We will, surely, expel you from our land unless you return to our religion.' Then their Lord sent unto them the revelation: 'We will, surely, destroy the wrongdoers.'
(Sūrah Ibrāhīm; Ch.14: V.14)

In addition to banishment from the homeland, other

173

severe punishments were meted out to the followers of the new religion for their so-called crime of 'apostacy'. Ḥaḍrat Abraham's[as] enemies not only proposed the death sentence for this 'crime', but also proposed that the sentence be carried out in a most brutal manner: they decided to burn Ḥaḍrat Abraham[as] alive. Allah says:

قَالُوْا حَرِّقُوْهُ وَ انْصُرُوْٓا اٰلِهَتَكُمْ اِنْ كُنْتُمْ فٰعِلِيْنَ ☐

They said, 'Burn him and help your gods, if *at all* you *mean to* do *anything*.
(Sūrah al-Ambiyā'; Ch.21: V.69)

Pharaoh devised various tortuous punishments for the people who turned away from his religion. He threatened those who accepted the religion of Moses[as] with punishments as follows:

قَالَ اٰمَنْتُمْ لَهُ قَبْلَ اَنْ اٰذَنَ لَكُمْ ۚ اِنَّهُ لَكَبِيْرُكُمُ الَّذِيْ عَلَّمَكُمُ السِّحْرَ ۚ فَلَاُقَطِّعَنَّ اَيْدِيَكُمْ وَ اَرْجُلَكُمْ مِّنْ خِلَافٍ وَّ لَاُوصَلِّبَنَّكُمْ فِيْ جُذُوْعِ النَّخْلِ ۫ وَلَتَعْلَمُنَّ اَيُّنَا آ اَشَدُّ عَذَابًا وَّ اَبْقٰى ☐

Pharaoh said, 'Do you believe in him before I give you leave? He must be your chief who has taught you magic. I will therefore surely cut off your hands and your feet on alternate sides, and I will surely crucify you on the trunks of palm-trees; and you shall know which of us is severer and more abiding in punishment.'
(Sūrah Ṭā Hā; Ch.20: V.72)

The Quranic ideal of absolute justice applies equally well to every situation. Having demolished the false notion that force is permissible in religious affairs, it absolves all Prophets[as] of the allegation that they coerced people into their religion and, in doing so, extends them (the people) the same right of being treated with justice.

The most potent argument the Quran builds is with respect to God Almighty, the Creator. If He had decided to coerce people to accept the truth, He could easily have done it without creating any fuss regarding the choice between right and wrong. The very existence of right and wrong, and the option given to man to choose between the two, presents incontrovertible proof that coercion is not a part of God's scheme of things.

As God says in the Holy Quran:

$$\text{وَلَوْ شَآءَ رَبُّكَ لَآمَنَ مَنْ فِي الْأَرْضِ كُلُّهُمْ جَمِيْعًا ۚ أَفَأَنْتَ تُكْرِهُ}$$
$$\text{النَّاسَ حَتّٰى يَكُوْنُوْا مُؤْمِنِيْنَ ◻}$$

And if your Lord had *enforced* His will, surely, all who are on the earth would have believed together. Will you, then, force men to become believers? (Sūrah Yūnus; Ch.10: V.100)

Some Muslim theologians maintain that although no Prophet[as] before the Holy Prophet[sa] of Islam was granted coercion in matters of faith, the Holy Prophet[sa] of Islam was granted this power to prove his excellence and superiority over all the other Prophets[as]. Evidently this argument is counter-productive. If lesser Prophets[as] than he upheld the torch of freedom of conscience, sanity would require that the Holy Prophet[sa] should have upheld this torch more loftily than any other Prophet[as] before him. For the very best of Prophets[sa] to have come to dash the freedom of human choice is a senseless allegation and is extremely blasphemous to the unblemished character of the Holy Prophet[sa]. This is exactly the power the Holy Quran denies the Holy Prophet[sa] when it declares:

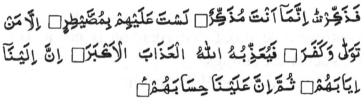

Admonish, therefore, for you are but an admonisher;
You are not a warden over them.
But whoever turns away and disbelieves,
Allah will punish him with the greatest punishment.
Unto Us surely is their return,
Then surely, it is for Us to call them to account.
(Sūrah al-Ghāshiyah; Ch.88: Vs.22-27)

In keeping with this inviolable principle, no Prophet[as] ever acquired the role of coercing people to righteousness. All who dared to violate this principle in the name of God, or in the name of righteousness, must be rejected as pseudo-gods, who acquired for themselves a role which was never acquired by any humble servant of God.

No true religion can be held accountable for the crimes committed in its name against human conscience. Those responsible are the so-called religious priesthood who unjustly distort the Divine teachings only to suit their own purpose at the cost of the purpose of God. They even acquire for themselves the license to kill life which is created by God. It is the Quran which comes to the defence of all such religions and exonerates them from the false allegations of their own depraved priesthood of later ages.

11 Islamic Jihad Misunderstood

Having examined the clear and unequivocal Islamic pronouncements as regards freedom of conscience, we must now resolve the apparent conflict between this and the teachings of Islamic Jihad. What kind of justice would it be if, on the one hand freedom of conscience is upheld unconditionally, while on the other, Muslims are required to take up the sword in the name of what they consider to be right, as against the other religions and the peoples of the world?

To understand this issue we bring the readers' attention to the following verse of the Quran:

أُذِنَ لِلَّذِينَ يُقْتَلُونَ بِأَنَّهُمْ ظُلِمُوا ۚ وَإِنَّ اللَّهَ عَلَى نَصْرِهِمْ لَقَدِيرٌ ۞ إِلَّذِينَ أُخْرِجُوا مِنْ دِيَارِهِمْ بِغَيْرِ حَقٍّ إِلَّا أَنْ يَّقُولُوا رَبُّنَا اللَّهُ ۗ وَلَوْلَا دَفْعُ اللَّهِ النَّاسَ بَعْضَهُمْ بِبَعْضٍ لَّهُدِّمَتْ صَوَامِعُ وَبِيَعٌ وَّ صَلَوَاتٌ وَّمَسَاجِدُ يُذْكَرُ فِيهَا اسْمُ اللَّهِ كَثِيرًا ۗ وَلَيَنْصُرَنَّ اللَّهُ مَنْ يَّنْصُرُهُ ۗ إِنَّ اللَّهَ لَقَوِيٌّ عَزِيزٌ ۞

Permission *to fight* is given to those against whom war is made, because they have been wronged—and Allah indeed has the power to help them—
Those who have been driven out from their homes unjustly only because they said, 'Our Lord is Allah'—
—And if Allah did not repel some men by means of

179

others, there would surely have been pulled down cloisters and churches and synagogues and mosques, wherein the name of Allah is oft commemorated. And Allah will surely help one who helps Him. Allah is indeed Powerful, Mighty.
(Sūrah al-Ḥajj; Ch. 22: Vs. 40-41)

These verses form the cornerstone of the Islamic injunctions regarding Jihad of the sword. It was upon the revelation of these verses that Muslims were allowed to take up the sword for the first time. These verses clearly lay down the necessary pre-conditions under which Muslims are not only permitted but are actually commanded to undertake Jihad of the sword. Even a cursory study of these verses will prove that the sword is only permitted in defence and never as a weapon of offense.

Primarily, the word Jihad does not mean an armed struggle. In the verses quoted above, even the defensive struggle is referred to as *Qitāl* and not Jihad. *Qitāl* is a term applicable to a situation where two parties are locked in battle.

Muslims are only permitted to defend themselves with the same weapons which are used against them to suppress their rights of existence. The verses declare them to already be the target of aggression, so much so that they had been turned out of their homes and were long subjected to an offensive warfare, while they had never offered any cause for offence to the enemy, except their claim that God was their

Provident. Any sensible man can see that when their right to defend themselves is finally granted, it cannot be dubbed as an aggression on their part.

The wisdom in authorising a defensive war does not apply only to the case of Muslims, it is granted to all religions whose message has ever been attempted to be suppressed by sword. It highlights this aspect and categorically declares that this fundamental right is granted to all religions.

Hence, had Allah not allowed some people to take up arms in defence of their places of worship, not only the mosques but also the churches and synagogues etc. would have been demolished.

In the light of the foregoing verses, one can conclude, without fear of contradiction, that Islam only defends the fundamental human right of freedom of conscience. Call it Jihad or *Qitāl* but it cannot be dubbed as an exclusive Muslim right. If any warning is given in this verse, it is given to the Muslims that they would not be granted most favoured treatment by God unless they show respect to the places of other people's worship. If they do not, they would forego the right for their places of worship to be treated respectfully. They must earn this right by showing the same respect for others.

These verses which have just been quoted do not only uphold the value of absolute justice but also enter the realm of *Iḥsān*, which means to go beyond the requirements of justice and to add the grace of benevolence in treatment to others. This means that even when worship is carried out in a manner as to cause offence, a true Muslim should not only treat the worshipper with respect, but should also be ready to defend their places of worship when attacked. This aspect is highlighted by the following writing of the Holy Prophet^{sa} of Islam which is still preserved in St. Catherine's Monastry in Mount Sinai:

> It is obligatory upon Muslims to defend Christian churches, monastries and shrines from enemy attacks. Whosoever fails to do so is disobedient to, and transgresses against, the commands of God. And he will give his religion (i.e. Islam) a bad name.[14]

The Holy Prophet^{sa} requires Muslims to go a step further than *Iḥsān*, and treat other religions with such grace as though they were your own kith and kin. The Prophet Muhammad's^{sa} love for mankind surpassed the love of a mother for her child. He not only engaged in a great Jihad to uphold the basic human rights of mankind, he went further and showed them more love and mercy than they had earned.

Under no circumstances is a Muslim permitted to transgress against others. It is preferable that a guilty man be shown clemency than an innocent man be punished.

Amazingly, the Founder of Islam^{sa} even rejected help from a renowned warrior when it was direly needed by Muslims during the Battle of Badr—a time when the Muslims' strength was at its lowest ebb. According to this incident at that time, one of the most famous infidel warriors expressed the wish to join the side of the Muslims. The Companions were overjoyed at this, but Prophet Muhammad[sa] rejected the request saying he would not accept help from an infidel in the cause of God. At this rejection the person immediately testified to the Unity of God, evidently because he wanted to join the battle. At this, the Holy Prophet[sa] accepted his claim without challenging his intention, despite the fact that he (the Holy Prophet[sa]) was well aware that the man in question only wanted to side with the Muslims to satisfy his personal grudge against the invaders from Mecca. The Prophet[sa] of Islam accepted him into the fold of Islam because he was evidently motivated by the unshakeable principle that only God knows what passes within a human heart. So he extended him this fundamental right to profess whatever faith he may.

The same principle applies to any hypocrite under all circumstances. This is fully elaborated in the opening three verses of Surah al-Munāfiqūn which run as follows:

بِسْمِ اللهِ الرَّحْمٰنِ الرَّحِيْمِ ۞ اِذَا جَآءَكَ الْمُنٰفِقُوْنَ قَالُوْا نَشْهَدُ اِنَّكَ لَرَسُوْلُ اللهِ ۗ وَاللهُ يَعْلَمُ اِنَّكَ لَرَسُوْلُهٗ ۭ وَاللهُ يَشْهَدُ اِنَّ الْمُنٰفِقِيْنَ لَكٰذِبُوْنَ ۞ اِتَّخَذُوْٓا اَيْمَانَهُمْ جُنَّةً فَصَدُّوْا عَنْ سَبِيْلِ اللهِ ۭ اِنَّهُمْ سَآءَ مَا كَانُوْا يَعْمَلُوْنَ ۞

In the name of Allah, the Gracious, the Merciful. When the hypocrites come to you, they say, 'We bear witness that you are indeed the Messenger of Allah.' And Allah knows that you are indeed His Messenger, but Allah bears witness that the hypocrites are surely liars.

They have made their oaths a shield; thus they turn *men* away from the way of Allah. Evil surely is that which they have been doing.

(Sūrah al-Munāfiqūn; Ch.63, Vs.1-3)

This means that they sought shelter under their profession to fulfil their twofold ill intentions. First, to save themselves from the Muslims while they were in a state of war. Second, under the cover of Islam they could mislead the innocent Muslim common folk while posing to be Muslims themselves. Despite this, the Holy Prophet[sa] is not permitted to deprive them of their fundemental right to profess with their mouths what did not lie in their hearts, and they are still extended the right to call themselves Muslims.

What a paradox we witness today in the various Muslim countries of the world, where coercion in religion is not only preached but is also most tenaciously practised. The mullahs see someone who calls himself a Muslim, who recites the *Kalima*, who performs prayer like other Muslims and who faces the Holy Kaaba while praying, yet they deny him the right of association with Islam. To them, forcing a person to recant his faith is a service to God, while actually it is tantamount to an open rebellion against the unequivocal teachings of the Quran and the noble practice of the Prophet Muhammad[sa]. Yet what do they care? How will these people face God on the Day of Judgement? They may not care, but God certainly will.

To further support this claim we quote the following tradition.

Ḥaḍrat Usāmah bin Zaid[ra] narrates:

> The Holy Prophet[sa] sent us to a battle. On the way we encountered an infidel who would hide himself in the jungle and then whenever he came across a lone Muslim he would attack and kill him. Eventually when he came into my grasp I declared my intention to kill him. In reply he recited the *Kalima-e-Tauḥīd: There is no God but Allah, and Muhammad is His Messenger.* In other words he pronounced himself to be a Muslim. However, I rejected his declaration and went ahead and killed him. When I related this story to the Holy Prophet[sa] he asked in great surprise: 'Did you really kill him, inspite of the fact that he recited the *Kalima?*' I said, 'Yes, O Prophet of Allah.' The Holy Prophet[sa] then said, 'How will you fare on the Day of Judgment when the *Kalima* will stand witness against you?' I repeatedly submitted to the Holy Prophet[sa], 'O Prophet of Allah, he only feigned belief out of fear.' Each time the Holy Prophet[sa] responded by saying, 'Did you open his heart that you know he was lying?' And then he kept saying, 'How are you going to reply to Allah when the *Kalima* of the deceased stands witness against you?' Ḥaḍrat Usāma bin Zaid[ra] says, 'I fervently wished that I had not been

a Muslim prior to that day, and that I had not committed such an act.'[15]

'There shall be no compulsion in matters of faith'— this Quranic declaration, though concise, is yet so comprehensive in its meaning, and so far-reaching in its application, that a close analysis of the same leaves one astounded.

It could be interpreted as meaning that no individual is allowed to use force against others, but at the same time it does not permit the individual, against whom force is applied, to submit to that force. The highest order of faith would not permit a person to surrender no matter how much torture and pain he has to endure for the sake of freedom of his conscience. Yet we cannot ignore the fact that not all people have the same level of faith and sincerity, nor do they have the same threshold to tolerate pain. Strangely, the same verse comes to their help, and with a slight turn of emphasis the message will become: *no one is required to tolerate pain beyond his capacity.* Thereby all weak persons are exonerated and are reassured that whatever was extracted from them under pressure does not mean anything because no coercion in religion is permissible. Hence the outcome of an unlawful act becomes null and void.

The same message of relief for the weak is more clearly delivered in the following verse:

مَنْ كَفَرَ بِاللَّهِ مِنْ بَعْدِ إِيمَانِهَ إِلَّا مَنْ أُكْرِهَ وَ قَلْبُهُ مُطْمَئِنٌّ
بِالْإِيمَانِ وَلَكِنْ مَّنْ شَرَحَ بِالْكُفْرِ صَدْرًا فَعَلَيْهِمْ
غَضَبٌ مِّنَ اللَّهِ ۚ وَلَهُمْ عَذَابٌ عَظِيمٌ ☐

Whoso disbelieves in Allah after he has believed—
save him who is coerced beyond the limits of his
tolerance while his heart remains firm in faith. But
those whose hearts are content with rejection, upon
them will fall the wrath of Allah; and for them shall
be a great chastisement.
(Sūrah al-Naḥl; Ch.16: V.107)

Now let us consider the case of those believers who
refuse to recant the truth despite being subjected to the
most extreme forms of punishment and torture; they
not only sacrifice their wealth and their worldly
possessions in the cause of truth, they go further and
sacrifice even their very lives. These are the ones who
have progressed through the stage of justice and
entered into the realm of benevolence. They are the
ones who have beautified their faith.

But there is another stage beyond the stage of
benevolence and that is the one of *Ītā'i Dhil-Qurbā*. Is
it possible that those who fight in defence of their
faith can be more than benevolent? Can they, as far as
their sacrifices are concerned, enter the stage of *Ītā'i
Dhil-Qurbā* in their relationship with God? Most
certainly they can and do. Unless they consider the
cause of God as actually their own, they could not
have sacrificed everything they held. The only

motivating factor in their case is their love of God and their extreme desire for it to be responded to by Him. The sacrifice is far more than real blood relations can make for the sake of their next of kin. When put to the trial of torture it is not rare that some mothers would let their child be taken away and tortured instead, but these lovers of God would dare anything and everything in their strife to hold fast to God. It is quite possible that they too have varying degrees of faith. There are some who sacrifice their lives but would be quite happy to avoid such a sacrifice if at all possible. Then there are others who fervently desire that they be martyred for the cause of faith. Many of the Companions of the Holy Prophet^{sa}, rather than backing down in the face of danger, actually requested him to pray for their martyrdom. The Battle of Uḥad provides us with an outstanding example of such zeal.

There was one Companion who, time and time again, put himself at the forefront of battle, yet each time he returned unscathed. He eventually requested the Holy Prophet^{sa} to pray for his martyrdom.

Then there were some who were not content with being martyred just once. It was their heartfelt desire that they be brought back to life many times so that each time they could sacrifice themselves in the cause of truth and not bow down to the tyrants. These people, surely, are the ones who have reached the stage of *Ītā'i Dhil-Qurbā* and beyond.

It is reported that the Prophet Muhammad[sa] once found his Companion Ḥaḍrat Jābir bin 'Abdullāh[ra] looking very downcast. Ḥaḍrat Jābir's father had been martyred in the Battle of Uḥud. Seeing him in such an unhappy state, the Prophet Muhammad[sa] said to him:

> "'Shall I give you some glad tidings?' Ḥaḍrat Jābir[ra] replied, 'Yes O Prophet of Allah'. The Holy Prophet[sa] then told him, 'When your father was martyred, Allah, the Almighty, addressed him without any formality and said, 'Ask of Me whatever you wish'. Your father replied, 'O my Allah! What blessing have you not bestowed on me? I do have one lingering desire, however, which is that I be sent back to earth to confront Your enemies and that once again I be killed in Your cause. And I would like this to happen again and again and again, a hundred times over'. Allah said, 'I would have fulfilled your desire, had I not already decreed that whoever comes to Me once will not be returned'."[16]

The subject of death in the cause of faith is discussed in great detail in the Quran. It mentions the rudimentary stages of faith and promises to treat the weak with justice. It mentions the benevolent and the manner in which they will be rewarded for their benevolence. It then goes on to mention the vanguard of believers, the ones who love the truth more than a mother loves her child. They do not look for any reward for their sacrifices, but find personal happiness in sacrificing themselves for the truth.

12 Justice ('Adl), Benevolence (Iḥsān) & Kinship (Ītā'i Dhil-Qurbā) in Worship.

Prayer is the cornerstone of all other forms of worship and it is also modelled according to the three principles of absolute justice, benevolence and kinship. Justice is found in the following Quranic teaching:

وَ اِذَا سَاَلَكَ عِبَادِ يْ عَنِّيْ فَاِنِّيْ قَرِيْبٌ ۚ اُجِيْبُ دَعْوَةَ الـدَّاعِ اِذَا دَعَانِ ۙ فَلْيَسْتَجِيْبُوْا لِيْ ۙ وَلْيُؤْمِنُوْا بِيْ لَعَلَّهُمْ يَرْشُدُوْنَ ▢

And when My servants ask you about Me, *say:* 'I am near. I answer the prayer of the supplicant when he prays to Me. So they should hearken to Me and believe in Me, that they may follow the right way.'
(Sūrah al-Baqarah; Ch.2: V.187)

Along with the glad tidings (that Allah is near the sincere worshipper) the Quran mentions the relationship of justice that is established between God and man. Prayer is not a one way street. The worshipper cannot treat God like a slave who stands ever ready to obey his master! Rather, the worshipper should also himself submit to God and obey His

191

commands.

This is the fundamental principle of the acceptance of prayer. In this verse, God addresses the whole of mankind and conveys to them the glad tidings that two way communication between God and man is not a mere myth, but is a living reality which can be attained. God does not ignore the rights of any of His servants, but He does require them to do their duty to Him as well. It is the prayers of such people that God promises to accept—the ones who are ever obedient to His commands.

This teaching of justice is essential in the guidance of mankind. However, the God that the Quran presents is more than Just, He is Benevolent too. So His servants have every right to hope for more than justice from Him. The Quran verifies this in the verse:

أَمَّن يُجِيبُ الْمُضْطَرَّ إِذَا دَعَاهُ وَيَكْشِفُ السُّوٓءَ وَيَجْعَلُكُمْ خُلَفَآءَ الْأَرْضِ ۗ ءَإِلَٰهٌ مَّعَ اللَّهِ ۚ قَلِيلًا مَّا تَذَكَّرُونَ ☐

Or, Who answers the distressed person when he calls upon Him, and removes the evil, and makes you successors in the earth? Is there a God besides Allah? Little is it that you reflect.
(Sūrah al-Naml; Ch.27: V.63)

Here 'distressed' means those who are fraught with misery and grief. Sometimes their unhappiness is so great that it seems as if their hearts would break. On such occasions, God does not stop short at justice, but cares for His servants with benevolence even if they have not earned it through good deeds. The distressed person may not have been a believer in God at all, yet it has to be admitted that after all, he is God's creation. As such, God treats him far beyond the dictates of justice and responds to his call in distress with benevolence. These cries of anguish are heard and responded to regardless of his previous deeds or misdeeds.

The world over, incidents occur where infidels call on God at times of extreme grief and God responds with His succour. This is the teaching of benevolence in prayer.

Among the distressed are the powerless, the dispossessed and the downtrodden. The Holy Prophet[sa] says of these people:

اِتَّقُوا دَعْوَةَ المَظْلُومِ وَاِنْ كَانَ كَافِرًا فَإِنَّهُ لَيْسَ دُوْنَهَا حِجَابٌ

Beware! Fear the malediction of the wronged one. Even though he may be an infidel, there is no distance between his prayer and God.[17]

The relationship between God and man can also enter into the realm of *Ītā'i Dhil Qurbā*. This stage is reached when one becomes totally devoted to God and there is no duplicity left in the relationship between man and Him. It is as though one is under the protection of God's dominion. Because such people give themselves over to God completely, He apparently shares what is His with them.

This is what the Prophets[as] and saints enjoy, and of those who enjoy nearness to God, the Holy Founder[sa] of Islam had the highest rank. Everything that was his, he handed over to God, apparently leaving himself nothing. The Quran says:

$$\text{قُلْ اِنَّ صَلَاتِيْ وَ نُسُكِيْ وَ مَحْيَايَ وَ مَمَاتِيْ لِلّٰهِ رَبِّ الْعٰلَمِيْنَ}$$

Say, 'My Prayer and my sacrifice and my life and my death are *all* for Allah, the Lord of all the worlds.' (Sūrah al-An'ām; Ch.6: V.163)

It should be remembered that each individual will be at a different rank and therefore each will be treated differently. When we talk of a particular category of achievement, not all people in that category will be of equal status. Each stage is further divided into sub-stages. Hence it is not only Prophets[as] who can enjoy a relationship of *Ītā'i Dhil-Qurbā* with God; others, too, can share the same with Him to a degree. The Holy Prophet[sa] says:

$$\text{رُبَّ اَشْعَثَ اَغْبَرَ ..... لَوْا اَقْسَمَ عَلَى اللّٰهِ لَاَبَرَّهُ}$$

That is to say, there are certain people who, in the eyes of the world, appear desolate and downtrodden. Yet it is these very people who enjoy an immensely close relationship with God; so much so that if they were to predict that God would cause a certain event to happen, then out of consideration for them God would make their predictions come true.[18]

It is similar to the case where a loving and beloved child has certain expectations of his parents and vice versa; because of the close mutual relationship that exists between parents and child, each tries to live up to the expectations of the other. We cannot term this as prayer, but it does bear some resemblance to the concept of prayer. For example, let us consider the case of a child who was accustomed to taking his meals out and not eating with the family. The family may not have known what he intended, or that outside in the street some very poor children were waiting for him. He would distribute all his meals to the poor children and retire by himself to a corner of the nearby mosque to eat some grains he had in his pocket, and some raw sugar lumps called *Gurr* (raw sugar produced from sugarcane) in the Punjabi language. Thereby he would relieve his hunger. This is a case which certainly extends the limits of *Ihsān* and enters the realm of *Ītā'i Dhil-Qurbā*. It is seldom that even a mother would make such sacrifices for her children.

This is not an imaginary case, it happened almost day in and day out to the Founder of the Ahmadiyya Community, Hadrat Mirza Ghulam Ahmad[as], when he was a small child.

Intercession by Prophets[as] (on behalf of their followers) is actually a sublime facet of prayer and a manifestation of *Ītā'i Dhil-Qurbā*. From this angle, it becomes easy to understand why the Holy Prophet[sa] was promised a much higher status among all intercessors.

God today is the same benevolent God as showed His special favours to the Holy Prophet[sa] and other pious servants of his time. In ordinary circumstances the laws of nature are permitted to take their course. It so happens that when God permits someone to intercede, some hidden laws take over and the ordinary course of laws is dominated by them. This happened many times in the time of the Holy Prophet[sa] but even in this age we have witnessed the same in the case of the Founder of the Ahmadiyya Muslim Community, Ḥaḍrat Mirza Ghulam Ahmad[as]. But it should be remembered that it was not a new blessing of this nature shown specifically to him; it was the continuation of the blessings of the Holy Prophet[sa], which manifest themselves in this age through him. One such instance is presented here for the sake of illustration.

Ḥaḍrat Munshī Ẓafar Aḥmad[ra] narrates the incident of a student named Muhammad Ḥayāt who was suffering from plague. The Promised Messiah[as] sent one of his close followers, Ḥaḍrat Maulawī Nūr-ud-Dīn[ra] to examine the patient. Upon examination, he found all the symptoms of plague to be present. Muhammad Ḥayāt had a soaring fever, six lumps were visible on his body, and blood was being passed in his urine. When he reported back to the Promised Messiah[as], he indicated that there was a greater likelihood of the patient dying than living. Ḥaḍrat Hakim Maulawī Nūr-ud-Dīn[ra] was always cautious in his choice of words. Worldly doctors and hakims show no hestitation in pronouncing their verdicts and in this particular case they would have declared that the patient would meet with certain death. Maulawī Sahib knew that until God's decree came to pass it would be incorrect to pronounce the verdict of death. So he stated that the probability that the patient would die was much greater than the likelihood of his survival.

Munshī Ṣāhib goes on to say that he requested the Promised Messiah[as] to pray for Muhammad Ḥayāt, and he readily agreed to do so. Munshī Sahib, greatly agitated, said to the Promised Messiah[as], 'Huḍūr, the time is not for prayer but for intercession'. Such was the grave condition of the boy. At this, the Promised Messiah[as] went into his home and dedicated himself entirely to pray for him piteously.

"At about two o'clock in the morning the Promised Messiah[as] came up to the roof and inquired after Muhammad Ḥayāt's health. One of us exclaimed, 'Perhaps he has died'. The Promised Messiah[as] instructed us to go and look for him. When we went downstairs we found him strolling on the lawn reading the Holy Quran. He said, 'You can come close to me; there is no need to fear. The lumps and the fever have vanished and I am perfectly alright.' We went back to the Promised Messiah[as] and reported that Muhammad Ḥayāt had made a complete recovery. He responded by saying, 'So why didn't you bring him with you?' Earlier, Muhammad Ḥayāt's father had been informed by telegram that there was no chance of his son surviving. It was now thought imperative that he should be informed of this great miracle so that his mind is set at ease. We took leave of the Promised Messiah[as] and were on our way to send him another telegram from Batala, a town twelve miles west of Qadian, which provided telegraphic facilities. But to our surprise we found Ḥayāt sitting in a horse carriage, coming towards Qadian at the canal two miles to the west of Qadian. He asked us, 'How is Ḥayāt Khān?' We narrated the above miracle to him. On hearing the good news he fainted. When he finally came around, he performed the ablution and began to offer supererogatory prayers. At this point we left him and returned home."[19]

The Philosophy of Prayer

Let us now turn to the manner of prayer and learn how it should be begged. Discussing the philosophy of prayer, Allah says clearly in the Quran that people who pray only for worldly things are granted just that; but God's servants are not satisfied with asking for minor things. So the Quran exhorts the true believers to offer the following prayer:

$$\text{...رَبَّنَآ اٰتِنَا فِى الدُّنْيَا حَسَنَةً وَّفِى الْاٰخِرَةِ حَسَنَةً وَّقِنَا عَذَابَ النَّارِ}$$

...'Our Lord, grant us good in this world as well as good in the world to come, and protect us from the torment of the Fire.'
(Sūrah al-Baqarah; Ch.2: V.202)

We learn from various *Ahādīth* that the Holy Prophet[sa] personally instructed one of his Companions about this prayer. It is narrated that one of his Companions fell ill and became extremely weak and emaciated. His appearance was described by one person as resembling a small bird whose wings had been plucked. The Holy Prophet[sa] went to visit him on his sick bed and put to him a question which could only have come to his mind as a result of a deep understanding of his Companion's nature. The Holy Prophet[sa] asked him, 'When you pray to Allah, do you ask Him to save your reward for your good deeds till the hereafter and give you no reward at all in this life?' The Companion replied, 'Yes, O Prophet of Allah, this is exactly what I have been doing. I request Allah to punish me for all my sins in this life and that I be saved from the punishment of the fire in the hereafter.' The Holy Prophet[sa] said, 'Holy is Allah! You have not the strength to bear His wrath. You should have prayed that Allah grant you the good of this life and save you from punishment in the hereafter.' It is narrated that the Holy Prophet[sa] so prayed for his Companion and then his condition took a turn for the better and he was thus saved from the clutches of death.[20]

This interesting incident encompasses *Ihsān* and *Ītā'i Dhil-Qurbā* as well as *'Adl*. If a person prays merely for justice then he will be treated with justice, but the Holy Prophet[sa] instructs us to pray for benevolence rather than justice. As far as the above incident is concerned, the patient was delivered from death as a result of the Holy Prophet's prayer and this in fact is a manifestation of *Ītā'i Dhil-Qurbā*, for otherwise there was apparently no way he could have survived such a severe illness.

While on the subject of prayer, we will now examine how *'Adl*, *Ihsān* and *Ītā'i Dhil-Qurbā* play their role in some other cases of worship. The Founder of the Ahmadiyya Movement, Hadrat Mirza Ghulam Ahmad[as], has dealt with all three topics individually in relation to this subject. A few extracts from his writings are presented here. He says:

> 'Those who abide by Divine Guidance belong to three categories. To the first category belong those who view the Almighty through the veil of reasons and causes and are thus prevented from appreciating the benevolence of Allah. They do not experience the stir of love in their hearts, which can only be experienced if they virtually see the hand of their Benefactor who shows His care for them with the minutest detail.'

In his everyday life man is dependent on the beneficence of Allah. Morning, evening, in sleep and while awake—every single moment of the day or night, man is recipient of God's blessings. Some people spend their life in oblivion and they remain unaware that Allah is constantly showering them with His blessings.

Hadrat Mirza Ghulam Ahmad[as] goes on to say:

'Because God does not burden any person beyond his intellectual capacity, such people remain in that state of oblivion. At this stage, He only expects them to be grateful to Him in accordance with their limited understanding. As long as this state of their mind does not change, whatever gratitude they could express is accepted by God as the best they could offer.'

He also declares that in the verse:

$$ إِنَّ اللّٰهَ يَأْمُرُ بِالْعَدْلِ $$

Allah enjoins adherence to absolute justice. This is exactly the justice which in turn is meted out to them. They are not treated beyond their capacity.

People who do not find pleasure in performing their prayers and do not find themselves submitting humbly to Allah, can take some comfort from this verse as it conveys the message that God will deal with each person in accordance with his potential. From this angle, God's justice actually becomes His benevolence. He is well aware of the shortcomings of His servants. He accepts even their imperfect worship and overlooks its flaws. But this should not be misconstrued to mean that one should be satisfied with one's state of imperfection. People at this level live in constant danger because with the slightest stumble they will rapidly descend into an abyss of destruction. So one should constantly strive to do justice in one's worship and to fulfil its elementary requirements.

The Promised Messiah[as] then says:

'Whereas God does not require man to strive beyond the limits of his understanding, so, as long as people observe this He only expects them to thank Him according to what they realise they owe Him. This is the true import of the verse:

$$\text{إِنَّ اللّٰهَ يَأْمُرُ بِالْعَدْلِ}^{21}$$

[Verily Allah enjoins justice.]

Here, the dictates of justice take into view the shortcomings of the worshipper and require God to grant him a handicap for his defects. In the process, he is expected to redress his shortcomings gradually to make him move from a lower to a higher stage.

The Promised Messiah[as] further directs:

'...But there is a yet higher stage of man's cognizance. As we have just mentioned, man's vision becomes purged of reasons and causes and at this stage he emerges from behind the veils of reason and causes. To him it becomes worthless and dishonest to say, 'I watered my fields well and that is why these healthy crops grew', or, 'My success is solely due to my hard work', or, 'Zaid helped me and that is why I achieved my purpose', or, 'Bakr's timely warning saved me from destruction'. At this stage man sees only One Being, only One Creator, only One Benefactor, only One Hand. He clearly sees God's benevolence and his vision is not blurred by even the slightest mist of reasons and causes. His vision becomes so clear that at the time of worship the benefactor seems to manifest Himself to the worshipper and does not remain hidden to him. In the Quran and in the Hadith this type of worship has been termed as *Iḥsān*.'[22]

This is how one progresses from the stage of justice to the stage of benevolence. When we become engrossed in the remembrance of Allah, His benevolence infiltrates every fibre of our life with His love. Thus an appreciation of His benevolence does not remain a mere interesting intellectual exercise, but becomes a natural part of one's emotional complex. Consequently, one begins to love God with a burning passion. Any person who performs his worship in the manner suggested here would notice that as a result it becomes impossible for him to return to his earlier state of oblivion and not to feel that yearning for Him constantly without cessation. The Promised Messiah[as] continues to build this theme as follows:

'After this comes another stage, which is called *Ītā'i Dhil-Qurbā*. This means that when man witnesses the favours of God without interruption and worships Him as One who is always present and bestows His favours directly upon him, as a result of this visualization and portrayal of Him, he will finally begin to entertain a very personal and intimate love for Him. It so happens because witnessing perpetual unending favours inevitably creates such effect upon the heart, that he is filled to the brim with the love of Him whose countless favours have engulfed him. In this state he (the worshipper) no longer loves Him with reference to His favours but he loves Him as a child loves his mother. Having reached this stage he does not merely see Him, but like all true lovers receives immense pleasure from the very sight of Him. Then no selfish motives exist any longer; what remains is only a personal love. This is the state which God refers to as *Ītā'i Dhil-Qurbā*, and it is to this same state the following verse refers:

$$\text{فَاذْكُرُوا اللّٰهَ كَذِكْرِكُمْ اٰبَآءَكُمْ اَوْ اَشَدَّ ذِكْرًا}^{23}$$

...Remember Allah like you remember your fathers or with a remembrance, even more intense....'
(Sūrah al-Baqarah; Ch.2: V.201)

What an amazing piece of writing! The Promised Messiah[as] does not omit even the subtlest shades of Divine love but unveils it with singular intimacy. He further observes:

This is the stage where all selfish desires are annihilated and one's heart is filled with the love of God just as a vial is filled with perfume. This stage is further elaborated in the following verse of the Holy Quran:

وَمِنَ النَّاسِ مَن يَّشْرِيْ نَفْسَهُ ابْتِغَآءَ مَرْضَاتِ اللهِ ۚ

وَاللهُ رَءُوْفٌ بِالْعِبَادِ ☐

meaning that of men there are those who would sell themselves to seek the pleasure of Allah; and Allah is Compassionate to such servants. **24**
(Sūrah al-Baqarah; Ch.2: V.208)

In other words, such people do not worship God with any ulterior motive. They are not concerned with rewards and favours. That is to say, they do not care whether their good deeds are rewarded or not. If a person does good for Allah's sake, then Allah in turn rewards him with His favours. But what the Promised Messiah[as] is discussing goes beyond the philosophy of labour and reward. People at this elevated stage do good deeds not for the purpose of earning a place in paradise but do them simply to win the pleasure of Allah. Allah's pleasure becomes dearer to their hearts and to please Him becomes their paradise and the sole purpose of their lives.

In short, the Islamic system of worship is amazingly well-balanced and complete. Every intricate detail bears the stamp of *'Adl, Ihsān* and *Ītā'i Dhil-Qurbā.* Essentially, a man, as Prophet Muhammad[sa] was, could not have wrought the miracle of the Quran by himself. Most certainly it was the work of an All-Knowing, All-Powerful Allah.

The preceding discussion was concerned with the spirit of worship. We now turn to some of the visible supporting pillars of worship and investigate whether we find *'Adl, Iḥsān* and *Ītā'i Dhil-Qurbā* play any significant role in this area as well.

Justice encompasses every fundamental aspect of Islamic worship. Prayers are offered in the mosques and at home, in congregation and individually. Had Islam prescribed only congregational prayers, a large number of people may gradually have drifted away from performing prayers altogether. If Islam had not offered them any alternative for congregational prayers, the prayer may altogether have disappeared from their daily lives. The case of most non-church going Christians offers an apparent similarity.

Another important aspect of justice in prayer is that it also combines individual prayers with congregational prayers. Individual prayers are almost always performed along with every congregational prayer.

Also worth mentioning is the fact that congregational prayers are not made obligatory upon women like they are upon men. Had it been the case, women would have found themselves placed under a tremendous burden. This is because they (the women) are generally responsible for the supervision of home and the care of the children. Even a mother of a small baby who requires constant attention would be required to go to the mosque. It will be a cruelty to her as well as to the baby. This would have been contrary to the dictates of justice. This is a marvellous example of the balance that is found in Islamic teachings. In certain other circumstances, women are entirely excused from saying any prayers whether in congregation or individually. This applies to the time of their menstruation or their post-natal period of bleeding.

Another feature of worship lies in its choices of saying prayers loudly or quietly. Human moods change in accordance with the changes occurring from morning till evening and from nightfall to the break of dawn early next morning. Mornings and evenings and also the hours of the night promote an inclination to sing in most persons. The middle of the day from the decline of the sun till late afternoon is a period when even the birds cease to sing. This is the time for quietness and siesta. That is why three of the five daily prayers can be offered in a loud singing voice while the other two are said quietly. Similarly in some sections of each prayer chanting is permitted, while in other parts of the same prayer silence is required. Moods change not only from the change in the hour but they also change from person to person. Options are provided to suit all.

A uniquely different injunction applies to the *Tahajjud*, or the pre-dawn prayer. For this prayer neither chanting nor silence are compulsorily admonished. The choice lies between the following two options:

$$\ldots وَلَا تَجْهَرْ بِصَلَاتِكَ وَلَا تُخَافِتْ بِهَا وَابْتَغِ بَيْنَ ذٰلِكَ سَبِيْلًا ۝$$

...And utter not you prayer aloud, nor utter it *too* low,
but seek a way between.
(Sūrah Banī Isrā'īl; Ch.17: V.111)

The following tradition explains this verse further. Ḥaḍrat Abū Bakr Ṣiddīq[ra] used to offer his *Tahajjud* prayer in complete silence. A person standing next to him would not have heard even the slightest of sounds. In contrast with him it was Ḥaḍrat 'Umar's[ra] custom to say his *Tahajjud* prayer in a loud, audible voice. The Holy Prophet[sa] once asked Ḥaḍrat Abū Bakr[ra], 'Why do you say your prayers in your heart?' Ḥaḍrat Abū Bakr[ra] replied, 'O Prophet of Allah! My prayer reaches the One for whom it is intended, and that is sufficient.' The Holy Prophet[sa] said, 'There is no need to say it absolutely quietly so that you must confine it to your heart alone. Some voice should be added to your prayer, albeit a gentle one.' Ḥaḍrat 'Umar's[ra] temperament was different to that of Ḥaḍrat Abū Bakr's[ra]. When asked why he recited the *Tahajjud* prayer loudly, he replied, 'I banish Satan from my presence by singing verses from the Quran!' The Holy Prophet[sa] said to Ḥaḍrat Umar[ra], 'There is no need to chastise Satan in this manner. You should recite the prayer in a gentler voice.' He was warned that by chanting the *Tahajjud* prayer in a loud voice, he may, in all likelihood, disturb and annoy those around him, who are saying their prayers.[25]

According to another tradition, the loud recitation of the *Tahajjud* prayers by the Companions of the Holy Prophet^{sa} had resulted in their neighbouring non-Muslims being disturbed in their sleep. This annoyed them and they would complain and grumble. The Holy Prophet^{sa} was instructed by Allah that particular consideration should be shown for others and that they should not be disturbed in their sleep. However, it is not only for the sake of the next door neighbours that the voices are required to be lowered. Most Muslim houses may comprise people like small children who must not be disturbed during that hour. There may be some ailing persons or those women who are not required to get up at *Tahajjud* time. All of them require the subduing of a worshipper's voice during his *Tahujjad* prayer. The above verse clearly requires us to strike a balance between the two extremes so that those who do not wish to offer the *Tahajjud* prayer are not disturbed by those who do.

There was a time in many Muslim countries when the *Fajr Adhān* (call for the morning prayer) was not relayed over loudspeakers. The low voice would awaken those who really wanted to hear it and who had every intention of waking up early in the morning. Again, the sound of the *Adhāns* (plural of *Adhān*) was limited to the neighbourhood surrounding the mosque. Now the situation is completely different. The ego of the clergy is satiated only if his call for prayer is made at the top of his voice and through the most powerful public address systems. If it were only a matter of just one loudspeaker the situation would not have become as intolerable as it has become now. Now the people in the neighbourhood of mosque have to listen to a multitude of *Adhāns,* each starting one after the other, all being recited in different voices at different times and being transmitted loudly, thanks to the highly powerful loudspeakers, from distant parts of the city. Some Maulawīs start their *Adhān* before the break of dawn, others start long after. The result is a cacophony of seemingly never ending *Adhāns!*

And that is not all. Some of them sing their *Adhāns* and many just croak. Some Maulawīs indulge in practices which were never heard of during the time of the Holy Prophet[sa]. Many mullahs start to sing *Na'ts* and hymns long before the time for morning prayer begins. Then comes the turn of *Ādhān* itself. So from the time of *Tahajjud* till the first light of day, the citizens including non-Muslims are robbed of their sleep and nerves.

Some Maulawīs, who think their voices are enchantingly melodious, compliment themselves by believing that the whole town is eagerly awaiting for their chantings to begin. Little do they realise that it is stricken with terror instead. Alas they never cast their eyes over the following verse of the Holy Quran:

$$...\text{وَاغْضُضْ مِنْ صَوْتِكَ ۚ إِنَّ أَنْكَرَ الْأَصْوَاتِ لَصَوْتُ الْحَمِيْرِ ▢}$$

…and lower your voice; verily, the most disagreeable
of voices is the voice of the donkey.
(Sūrah Luqmān; Ch.31: V.20)

It is said that Ḥāfiẓ Saʻdī Shīrāzī, a prominent Muslim
sufi, once came across a man who was reciting the
Holy Quran loudly. Unfortunately he had the most
unpleasant voice. Saʻdī suggested to him that he
should recite the Quran in a gentler tone and low
voice. The man replied, 'I recite loudly for the sake of
Allah, who are you to interfere!' Saʻdī's response was,
'For the sake of Allah, do not recite loudly, or the
people will turn against Allah and His Holy Word!'

Islam proclaims to be universal. It follows,
therefore, that its mode of worship should evince a
universality of its Divine origin. It would have been
contrary to the requirement of justice if the new mode
of worship imposed on them should have totally
rejected their past traditions, so that they could not
find any similarity between their customary mode and
the one proposed by Islam.

In some religions we find that people remember
God while sitting with their legs folded beneath them.
In some other religions they prefer to kneel down
before Him. Practices vary from people to people.
There are those who keep standing with their arms
hanging by their sides, and there are those who fold
their arms before them while they stand in the
presence of their Lord. In some religions bowing

211

down becomes the central feature of worship while in others, complete prostration with the forehead touching the ground is the ultimate homage paid to God. In Islamic worship you cannot fail to notice that Islam combines all these features in its comprehensive style so that every religion is partially represented.

Every section of society and every condition of man is taken into consideration in the Islamic injunction of prayer. Healthy adult men, who live near a mosque, are required to attend the congregational prayers five times a day. Now the times fixed for each of these prayers are such that generally they do not interfere with one's daily life. The *Zuhr* prayer, for example, can be offered during the lunch break and if a mosque happens to be close by, it should not be difficult to attend it at the time of the congregational prayer. The remaining four prayers are offered at times when people are generally free from their worldly obligations. However, there are cases where a person's professional obligations prevent him from going to the mosque for each prayer. Farmers, for example, start work long before dawn and shepherds take their herd far out into the pastures. It would be difficult for such people to leave their work and go looking for nearby mosques. They are allowed, therefore, to offer their prayers in whichever location they encounter the prayer time. This permission does not comply only with the dictates of justice, it moves a step forward and enters the area of benevolence.

According to the following tradition, once a shepherd heard the Holy Prophet[sa] emphasize the superiority of congregational prayer over the individual prayer. The shepherd humbly informed him that he spent his time in the desert away from urban settlements at most prayer times then how could he attend the congregational prayers? The Holy Prophet[sa] replied, 'Give the call for prayer in the desert at the prayer time. If anyone happens to be in the vicinity, he will hear the call and join you. Your prayer will thus become congregational. If no one joins you, stand up for prayer and angels will descend from heaven to join you in prayer.'[26]

Various inferences can be drawn from this tradition:

1. A person is granted leave from attending the mosque for prayers if his obligations prevent him from doing so.

2. If he arranges for congregational prayers to be held at his convenience, his prayer will still be counted by Allah as though he had done it at a regular mosque.

3. If in spite of his desire, no one is available to him for prayer, God will accept it as though it had been said in congregation.

The above tradition seems to contain all three stages of Justice (*'Adl*), Benevolence (*Ihsān*) & Kinship (*Ītā'i Dhil-Qurbā*) simultaneously. Justice is done because it does not burden any person beyond his capacity.

Out of His benevolence, Allah deems any piece of land available to a person to say his prayer to be a mosque. The courtesy of *Ītā'i Dhil-Qurbā* (Kinship) is extended by commanding the angels to join him.

Another interesting feature of the Muslim system of worship relates to the direction in which Muslims should turn to during their prayer. In day to day practice they are required to face the Kaaba if they know its direction. However, if someone is on a journey and is not sure of the direction of the Kaaba, then whichever direction he prays in will be accepted as correct. Moreover, if a person is travelling (e.g. in a car, an aeroplane etc.) the requirement to face the Kaaba is entirely waived.

It should be borne in mind that according to Islam, the performance of worship has priority over all other things. Under no circumstances is man exempt from his obligation to worship. If water is not available for ablution, a prerequisite for every prayer, *Tayammum* becomes its substitute. Every person is required to perform his prayer in accordance with his ability. Even if he cannot follow any posture of the prayer, his prayer will be considered complete if he uses sign-language instead. A very ill patient for instance, can simulate the postures by even slightly moving his eyes. For him, a prayer such as this will be accepted as though it were perfect.

Apparently these are all minor issues, but no other religion goes into such details, nor shows such consideration for the needs and limitations of man. It proves that Islam is a universal and eternal religion, not confined by any geographical space or time. The passage of time does not necessitate any modification.

Justice rules supreme. Young and old, rich and poor, all array themselves behind the Imam. No one is allowed to reserve a place for himself. Whoever reaches the mosque ahead of others has the prior option to sit wherever he pleases. None has the right to remove others from the place that they occupy. All are commanded to stand shoulder to shoulder. A wealthy person in the most expensive attire is not permitted to create any distance between himself and his fellow worshipper who may be a pauper dressed in rags. So not only are worshippers required to offer their prayers assembled equally behind an Imam, they are also delivered the categoric message that their station with God does not relate to their physical appearance. Whoever is more God-fearing will be ranked higher in the sight of Allah.

It is decreed that the reward for each prayer will be granted in relation to the inner state of the worshipper. It is narrated that once the Holy Prophet[sa] observed, 'In appearance all of you offer the same prayer, but Abū Bakr's[ra] prayer is worth seventy prayers in comparison to ordinary prayers said by you.' Ḥaḍrat Abū Bakr[ra] was a very righteous man; he always prayed with deep dedication. It was in reference to this quality of his prayer that the Holy Prophet[sa] made the foregoing observation.

Ītā'i Dhil-Qurbā in worship can be best described by the conduct of the Holy Prophet[sa] and the reciprocal treatment of him by God. Describing his eternal state of remembrance he once observed:

$$ تَنَامُ عَيْنِى وَلَا يَنَامُ قَلْبِى $$

My eyes succumb to sleep but not my heart.[27]

This is certainly a higher stage than benevolence, which can only be described as *Ītā'i Dhil-Qurbā*. Extending the similarity, even in sleep some mothers are always occupied with their concern for their beloved children. This thought remains hovering in their mind even when they are apparently fast asleep.

The Universalities of Mosques

$$ وَّاَنَّ الْمَسْجِدَ لِلّٰهِ ... $$

And *all* places of worship belong to Allah;...
(Sūrah al-Jinn; Ch. 72: V.19)

Mosques are only for the worship of Allah. No one has the right to prevent a believer from entering a mosque. This was exactly the attitude of the Holy Prophet[sa] regarding all places of worship dedicated to the Unity of God.

What a contrast to the situation that prevailed in the so-called world of the Muslims a hundred years ago. Their mosques did not seem to be modelled after the mosque of the Holy Prophet[sa]. They were strictly divided into sectarian divisions. No person belonging to any one sect would dare to enter the mosque of his opponent. This reminds one of the segregated churches that once existed in America. At that time the churches of the Whites were kept strictly separate from those of the Black. It is said that a black person once tried to enter a white church, but was forcibly prevented from doing so. This incident hurt him deeply and while he sat sobbing on the steps of the church he fell asleep. In his dream he saw Jesus[as] who asked him why he was crying so bitterly. The man replied, 'Why should I not cry? While I tried to enter this church for the sake of worship I was thrown out.' Jesus[as] replied, 'O poor man just look at me. Ever since this church was built, even I could not dare to enter it.'

Moderation in Worship

Another beautiful feature of Islamic worship is that Muslims are forbidden to overdo worship in an attempt to please God. The Holy Prophet[sa] always discouraged rigidity and extremism. He said, 'Do not be cruel to yourselves. Nations before you were ruined because of their efforts to forcibly extract the pleasure of God by exercising overmuch hardship in their prayers.'[28]

Again he said, 'You shall never be able to tire Allah. Do not think that you can gain ascendancy over Him by being extreme in worship. So be patient and only offer that much prayer which you can easily perform.'[29]

Once, three of the Holy Prophet's[sa] Companions were discussing the philosophy behind the injunction against excessive worship. They came to the conclusion that the Prophet Muhammad[sa], being a Holy person, was guaranteed complete mercy by God. But sinners, as we are, they argued, could not be assured such mercy. The more they prayed the better chance of His forgiveness would they stand. After carrying out a discussion along these lines, one of them vowed to spend every night standing in worship for the remainder of his life. The second Companion vowed to fast every day for the rest of his life and the third made a vow of celibacy. Having heard of this, the Holy Prophet[sa] said, 'My fear of Allah is greater than yours. At night I pray but I also sleep; I fast but some days I do eat and I do not live a life of celibacy. Whomsoever does not follow my conduct does not belong to my people.'[30]

No other religion stipulates that virtue and justice go hand in hand. In other words, when doing good deeds, one should always strive for balance. There is no virtue in extremes. Likewise, alms-giving is a good deed, but it is an injustice to give all one's wealth to charities ignoring one's immediate family altogether.

Praying is good but it should not be done at the cost of others. The following tradition of the Holy Prophet^{sa} clearly illustrates this point: It is reported that on one occasion the Holy Prophet^{sa} offered his prayers as if in a great hurry and he finished it in a much shorter time than usual. After he finished the prayer he explained that he had heard a child cry and it was his concern for this distressed child that made him shorten his prayer.[31] According to another Hadith, the Holy Prophet^{sa} expressed displeasure at the habit of an Imam whose prayers were reported to be too lengthy.[32]

Categories of Prayer

The Islamic system of worship has another unique distinction. All its prayers are divided into three categories: fundamental, non-fundamental but highly essential, and optional. All the five daily prayers are sub-divided into these categories. Central to them is what is termed as *Fard*. *Fard* (فرض) is that fundamental part of each prayer which cannot be dropped under any circumstances. It is like the skeleton around which the infrastructure of every living body is built.

All spiritual life revolves around this kernel. To drop even a single fundamental part of the five daily prayers will nullify that prayer altogether. The essential and optional prayers are like the muscles, flesh and skin without which fundamental prayers become lacklustre. Beauty, colour, and fragrance of each prayer owe their presence to them.

Talking of the voluntary prayers the Holy Prophet[sa] once observed: 'There is one among them which stands out above all; that is the prayer which is offered in the thick of night after waking from a deep sleep.'[33] Obviously, this extraordinary effort will only be made by a person who enjoys an exceptionally close relationship with God. We do not need to discuss this in greater detail here, but everyone can realise that this prayer belongs to the realm of *Ītā'i Dhil-Qurbā*.

The Quran specifically highlights the exceptional quality of the *Tahajjud* prayer in the following verse:

تَتَجَافٰى جُنُوْبُهُمْ عَنِ الْمَضَاجِعِ يَدْعُوْنَ رَبَّهُمْ خَوْفًا وَّ طَمَعًا ۗ وَّ مِمَّا رَزَقْنٰهُمْ يُنْفِقُوْنَ ☐

Their sides separate from their beds; *and* they call upon their Lord in fear and hope, and spend out of what We have bestowed on them.
(Sūrah al-Sajdah; Ch.32: V.17)

The following verse of Surah Banī Isrā'īl specifically promises the Holy Prophet[sa] the greatest station of nearness to Allah which exceeds the ordinary concept of *Ītā'i Dhil-Qurbā*:

وَ مِنَ الَّيْلِ فَتَهَجَّدْ بِهٖ نَافِلَةً لَّكَ ۖ عَسٰى اَنْ يَّبْعَثَكَ رَبُّكَ مَقَامًا مَّحْمُوْدًا ☐

And wake for it (the Quran) in *the latter part of* the night as a supererogatory service for you. It may be that your Lord will raise you to an exalted station.
(Sūrah Banī-Isrā'īl; Ch.17: V.80)

13 Absolute Justice
May Never be Withheld

Now we turn to a completely different avenue of Quranic teachings which relates to the social relationship between individuals and other individuals on the one hand, and the individuals and the society on the other. The role of politics in human affairs is also fully covered by the same teaching. Of the many verses which throw further light on this subject from different angles, we have selected only the following few by way of illustration. The first of these verses deals with the most important issues of giving testimony. It must always be given as though given in the presence of God, fulfilling all the requirements of absolute justice.

يَا أَيُّهَا الَّذِينَ اٰمَنُوا كُوْنُوا قَوَّامِيْنَ لِلّٰهِ شُهَدَآءَ بِالْقِسْطِ وَلَا يَجْرِمَنَّكُمْ شَنَاٰنُ قَوْمٍ عَلَى أَلَّا تَعْدِلُوا اِعْدِلُوا هُوَ أَقْرَبُ لِلتَّقْوٰى وَاتَّقُوا اللّٰهَ اِنَّ اللّٰهَ خَبِيْرٌ بِمَا تَعْمَلُوْنَ ☐

O ye who believe! be steadfast in the cause of Allah, bearing witness in equity; and let not a people's enmity incite you to act otherwise than with justice. Be *always* just, that is nearer to righteousness. And fear Allah. Surely, Allah is aware of what you do.
(Sūrah al-Mā'idah; Ch.5: V.9)

□ وَإِنْ حَكَمْتَ فَاحْكُم بَيْنَهُم بِالْقِسْطِ إِنَّ اللَّهَ يُحِبُّ الْمُقْسِطِينَ □

...And if thou judge, judge between them with justice.
Surely, Allah loves those who are just.
(Sūrah al-Mā'idah; Ch.5: V.43)

The following verse also builds up the same theme with great emphasis on the nature of enmity. If the enmity on the part of the people you have now come to rule had prevented you previously from performing your fundamental religious rights, even the memory of such enmity may never deter you from treating them with absolute justice.

وَلَا يَجْرِمَنَّكُمْ شَنَآنُ قَوْمٍ أَن صَدُّوكُمْ عَنِ الْمَسْجِدِ الْحَرَامِ
أَن تَعْتَدُوا ...

...And let not the enmity of a people, that they hindered you from the Sacred Mosque, incite you to transgress...
(Sūrah al-Mā'idah; Ch.5: V.3)

In these verses, man's attention is drawn to the fact that under no circumstances should justice be abandoned. Whatever the nature of the external or internal pressures, one must always hold fast to justice.

14 Trust and Accountability

The word 'trust', as employed by the Quran, inevitably leads to the subject of accountability. It is so tragic that the worldly democratic institutions are completely negligent of this responsibility of their trust, which they must discharge towards the people who elect them. Likewise, they are accountable to God, Who lays His trust in them. The blame for injustice and oppression in democratic societies where trusts are betrayed, lies squarely on the shoulders of such institutions and individuals who are primarily responsible for their breach of trust both to man and to God. Whenever an elected organisation or an individual fails to hand over this trust to those deserving of it, the end result is the emergence of many ills in society. Instead of absolute justice, man ends up facing oppression and cruelty.

Thus, the Quran does not impose any single form of government upon the whole world. To do so would be against the very dictates of justice. However, mention is made of the democratic political system in preference over all other systems of government. At the same time, the Quran requires every type of government to discharge its responsibility with a sense of answerability to God.

The democratic slogan 'for the people' is an ambiguous expression. Nowhere has the Holy Quran used the phrase 'for the people' as applicable to democratically elected governments. In relation to their function the emphasis is on justice.

According to this principle, the legislative process of a democratic country cannot encroach upon the rights of their citizens, no matter which political party they belong to. They must be granted the dignity of equally sharing their civic rights with all other citizens. To hold political majority does not empower the legislature to legislate against the fundamental rights of even a single individual. The excuse of sticking to the majority will is no excuse at all. To conclude, we quote the following verse of the Holy Quran which most comprehensively deals with this profound topic:

اِنَّ اللّٰهَ يَأْمُرُكُمْ اَنْ تُؤَدُّوا الْاَمٰنٰتِ اِلٰٓى اَهْلِهَا ۙ وَاِذَا حَكَمْتُمْ بَيْنَ النَّاسِ اَنْ تَحْكُمُوْا بِالْعَدْلِ ؕ اِنَّ اللّٰهَ نِعِمَّا يَعِظُكُمْ بِهٖ ؕ اِنَّ اللّٰهَ كَانَ سَمِيْعًا بَصِيْرًا ۞

Verily Allah commands you to make over the trusts to those entitled to them, and that, when you judge between men, you judge with justice. And surely excellent is that with which Allah admonishes you! Allah is All-Hearing, All-Seeing.
(Sūrah al-Nisā'; Ch.4: V.59)

The persistent conduct of the Holy Prophet[sa] brings to

226

light the implied beauty of this verse in its finest shades. While admonishing those who believed in him, he once warned them of their responsibilities with reference to the fate of earlier people who had transgressed before them saying:

اِنَّمَا اَهْلَكَ الَّذِينَ قَبْلَكُمْ اَنَّهُمْ كَانُوا اِذَا سَرَقَ فِيهِمُ الشَّرِيفُ تَرَكُوهُ، وَاِذَا سَرَقَ فِيهِمُ الضَّعِيفُ اَقَامُوا عَلَيْهِ الْحَدَّ، وَاَيْمُ اللّٰهِ لَوْ اَنَّ فَاطِمَةَ بِنْتَ مُحَمَّدٍ صَلَّى اللّٰهُ عَلَيْهِ وَآلِهِ وَسَلَّمُ سَرَقَتْ لَقَطَعْتُ يَدَهَا

People before you were ruined because they exceeded the limits when punishing the poor and showed excessive compassion when pardoning the rich. I swear by Almighty Allah that if my own daughter, Fāṭimah, were to steal, I would have her hands cut off.[34]

The Quran leaves no ambiguity in this matter. No blood ties or personal relationship is allowed to interfere with the course of justice. The story of Ḥaḍrat Noah[as] and his son illustrates the point further. His son was drowned in the flood along with other disbelievers of Noah[as] because he too was a disbeliever of him.

There is a subtle difference, however, in the incident mentioned in the tradition quoted above and the story of Noah[as]. Ḥaḍrat Noah[as] prayed that his son be pardoned, despite his denial, but God rejected his request, while the Prophet Muhammad^{sa} himself mentioned his resolve not to forgive his own daughter, should she commit the crime of displeasing God.

Some non-believers may argue that the Prophet^{sa} was speaking only hypothetically. Had he been really faced with a situation where he had to choose between justice and leniency in application to his blood relations he may have opted for a different course. The following incident reported by the authentic books of *Aḥādīth* dispels all such conjectures. 'Abbās^{ra}, a beloved uncle of the Holy Prophet^{sa}, had not yet converted to Islam at the time of Hijra. Consequently he sided with the Quraish during the Battle of Badr and was taken captive after the defeat of the Quraish. He, along with other prisoners, was rather tightly tied to a pillar in the mosque. 'Abbās^{ra} began to groan with pain. On hearing his cries, the Holy Prophet^{sa} became very perturbed. He could not sleep and kept tossing from side to side; but he said nothing. When the warden in charge of the prisoners learnt that the Holy Prophet^{sa} was upset, he loosened the rope of 'Abbās^{ra}. When 'Abbās^{ra} suddenly ceased to groan, the Holy Prophet^{sa} became even more perturbed. His inquiry revealed that the rope of 'Abbās^{ra} was loosened out of consideration for the Holy Prophet^{sa}. He was profoundly displeased at hearing this and ordered that if 'Abbās's^{ra} rope is loosened, the ropes of all the prisoners must also be loosened. That is they had no right to single out 'Abbās[ra]. This was his clear verdict.[35]

In contrast to his treatment of close relatives, his treatment of committed enemies was no different in matters of justice. He was invariably guided by the following injunction of the Quran.

$$ ...وَلَا يَجْرِمَنَّكُمْ شَنَانُ قَوْمٍ عَلَىٰٓ أَلَّا تَعْدِلُوا... $$

...and let not a people's enmity incite you to act otherwise than with justice....
(Sūrah al-Mā'idah; Ch.5: V.9)

The age-old enmity between Jews and Muslims has always been unduly exaggerated by the enemies of Islam. Yet, the conduct of the Holy Prophet[sa] towards the Jews was always governed by this verse. He always settled disputes between Muslims and Jews with absolute justice.

The following incident provides us with a shining example of his conduct in such matters. Banū Naḍīr were one of the Jewish tribes of Medina. This tribe was earlier exiled from Medina for committing treachery and breach of trust against their Muslim allies during the Battle of the Ditch. Although the teaching of the Talmud would condemn them to death, without exception, for committing this grave crime, it was only the kindness of the Holy Prophet[sa] which changed the verdict of death to banishment

from Medina. They migrated from Medina to Khaibar
where they built a most formidable fort, by the name
of the Fort of Khaibar. Having gathered strength, they
renewed their insurgencies against Islam. There is no
need to go into details, but their belligerency was
finally brought to halt after the Battle of Khaibar.
Prior to this battle Muslim surveillance parties were
sent into the area from time to time. Once it so
happened that a Muslim surveillance party plundered
one of their settlements and destroyed the fruits in
their orchards. When the Holy Prophet[sa] heard of this,
he was extremely displeased. He admonished the
Muslims:

> 'Allah does not permit you to enter into the homes of
> the People of the Book without their consent.
> Similarly, it is unlawful to kill their women or to take
> fruit from their orchards.'**36**

In short, despite extreme religious enmity on the part
of the Jews, the Holy Prophet's[sa] verdict was always,
in keeping with the Quranic teachings, in accordance
with the demands of absolute justice.

Absolute justice during the act of testimony is
admonished, even against one's own kith and kin. The
Holy Quran observes:

يَاۤأَيُّهَا الَّذِيْنَ اٰمَنُوْا كُوْنُوْا قَوَّامِيْنَ بِالْقِسْطِ شُهَدَآءَ لِلّٰهِ وَلَوْ
عَلٰۤى أَنْفُسِكُمْ أَوِ الْوَالِدَيْنِ وَالْأَقْرَبِيْنَ ...

O ye who believe! be strict in observance of justice,
and be witnesses for Allah, even though it be against
yourselves or *against* parents and kindred. ...
(Surah al-Nisā'; Ch.4: V.136)

One cannot envisage a more excellent teaching of
justice and benevolence. As a result of this teaching
the Holy Prophet[sa] raised the standard of his
Companions to the highest degree. It became a routine
with them to disregard blood ties and personal
relationships when giving evidence. Numerous
incidents can be quoted to support this contention.
The influence of his teachings and conduct still exerts
itself without cessation, upon his true servants. Ḥaḍrat
Mirza Ghulam Ahmad[as], the Founder of the
Ahmadiyya Jamā'at in Islam, was most certainly one
of them.

In this context, the following incident will speak
for itself. Mirza Sulṭān Ahmad was the eldest son of
Ḥaḍrat Mirza Ghulam Ahmad[as]. He had an
independent outlook and did not embrace Ahmadiyyat
during the lifetime of his father, but took the oath of
allegiance at the hand of his younger brother much
later. It was Mirza Sulṭān Ahmad who used to
administer the matters of the family estate. On one
occasion he accused a Hindu inhabitant of Qadian of
taking unlawful possession of a piece of land and
erecting a building on it. Mirza Sulṭān Ahmad Ṣāḥib
requested the court to rule that the construction be
demolished. His case, however, had one small flaw in

it. The land did indeed belong to the family estate of the Promised Messiah[as], but when preparing the case, the plaintiff's lawyer entered a false plea in one small section. This was an attempt on the part of the prosecution to strengthen its case. If the defendant could prove that this one small part of the claim was untrue the whole case would be dismissed.

Ḥaḍrat Mirza Ghulam Ahmad[as] was called as a witness for the defence. The defendant knew for certain that he would never give false evidence, no matter how great the consequential loss. The lawyer acting for Mirza Sulṭān Ahmad approached Ḥaḍrat Mirza Ghulam Ahmad and inquired how he intended to testify. In response, he asserted that his evidence would be based only on the truth, no matter how great the loss to his brother and family estate. The lawyer decided that there was no point in pursuing the matter further, so he withdrew the case.[37]

Much earlier when he was about 25-30 years of age and was not yet the Founder of the Ahmadiyya Community, he used to work for the family estate at the command of his father. Once his father became involved in a dispute with some of his land tillers over the felling of a tree. Ḥaḍrat Mirza Ghulam Ahmad was sent by his father to Gurdaspur to represent his interest at court. He was accompanied by two other witnesses. Addressing his two companions he said, 'My father is needlessly making this an issue. Trees can be considered part of the farmland. The people who work the land are poor; if they cut down a tree, where is the harm? Thus, I cannot say with certainty that the tree was our property. It is however possible that we may have a share in it.' They (the land tillers) had great faith in his truthfulness and when questioned by the magistrate, they said without any hesitation, 'Why do you question us? Ask Ḥaḍrat Mirza Sahib. He would tell you the truth.' So the magistrate questioned him. His reply was, 'In my opinion, trees are part of the farmland. We have a share in the farmland and those who till it have also a rightful share'. At this, the magistrate decided in favour of the tillers. When Ḥaḍrat Mirza Ghulam Ahmad's father heard of this, he became extremely upset and cried, 'Mullah, Mullah. My son is a Mullah!' meaning that he was over-religious and must be punished for this folly. Consequently, he threw him out of his parental home. His mother used to secretly send food to the place where he had found shelter. Learning this, his father forbade his mother to do this. After suffering for a while at Qadian, Ḥaḍrat Mirza Sahib moved to Batala where he spent a couple of months with the meagre resources he could muster. Eventually his father relented and called him back to Qadian.[38]

Once a certain gentleman constructed a terrace on the land adjoining his house. The land actually belonged to the family, but over the years it had been used by the owner of the house and by virtue of long and uninterupted possession it was considered his. Ḥaḍrat Mirza Sahib's elder brother took legal action to have the property restored. In keeping with the tradition of such law-suits, he pressed a case which was not altogether true. He claimed that the owner of the house did not have long standing continuous possession of the land and had only recently taken control of it.

The owner of the house did not have means to prove his long standing possession. He had only one option to defend himself. His plea was, 'I do not wish to call on any witness. I only ask that the plaintiff's younger brother be examined. Whatever statement he makes will be acceptable to me.' So Ḥaḍrat Mirza Sahib was summoned to court and asked whether he knew of the defendant and his family using the disputed land for some years. His reply was in the affirmative. Consequently the court decided the case against his brother.[39]

The Ahmadiyya Community is greatly honoured that God has commissioned them for the task of reviving the moral excellency of Islam. Although it is not possible for each and every individual to attain the same spiritual heights, yet it is possible for the Community as a whole to become the flag-bearer of the spiritual and moral beauty of Islam.

When the Ahmadis talk of the revival of Islam, they do not mean that there were certain periods in the history of Islam when Islamic values had become totally extinct. They simply mean that every successive generation moved further away from the intrinsic beauty of the source following a downward spiralling path.

The prime purpose of Ahmadiyyat in Islam is to restore Muslims to the loftiness they once occupied. They must die for Islam, if they require it to live forever.

15 Testimony of Muslims against Non-Muslims and Vice Versa

There is one aspect of the subject of testimony which has assumed great importance these days, namely the relative merit of evidence of Muslims and non-Muslims, one against the other. Many modern Muslim scholars do grave injustice to the teachings of Islam by arguing that Islam does not accept the evidence of a non-Muslim against that of a Muslim, while the evidence of a Muslim must always be accepted against his non-Muslim opponent. They misinterpret certain verses of the Quran in support of their contention which can never be proved as valid in the light of the overall teachings of Islam and the conduct of its Holy Founder[sa]. Virtually they allege that according to Islam, justice is fine as long as it serves the purpose of Muslims alone. If this is their sense of justice then let justice die forever. Long live injustice! But the justice which the Quran admonishes will never die.

وَقُلْ اٰمَنْتُ بِمَآ اَنْزَلَ اللّٰهُ مِنْ كِتٰبٍ ۚ وَاُمِرْتُ لِاَعْدِلَ بَيْنَكُمْ ۗ اَللّٰهُ رَبُّنَا وَرَبُّكُمْ ۗ لَنَآ اَعْمَالُنَا وَلَكُمْ اَعْمَالُكُمْ ۗ لَا حُجَّةَ بَيْنَنَا وَبَيْنَكُمْ ۗ اَللّٰهُ يَجْمَعُ بَيْنَنَا ۚ وَاِلَيْهِ الْمَصِيْرُ ☐

> ...and say, 'I believe in whatever Book Allah has sent down, and I am commanded to judge justly between you. Allah is our Lord and your Lord. For us is the reward of our works, and for you the reward of your works. There is no quarrel between us and you. Allah will gather us together, and to Him is the return.'
> (Sūrah al-Shūrā; Ch.42: V.16)

It is clear that the above verse is addressed to the whole of mankind, not to Muslims alone. Those belonging to different religions are included in the address. It states that the Holy Prophet[sa] is so trustworthy that God has given him the authority to judge between people in the full confidence that he will never be unjust to anyone. On the one hand we have this authentic Islamic teaching. On the other the orthodox mullah misleads the world by maintaining that according to Islam when a non-Muslim testifies against a Muslim, his testimony must be rejected, while when a Muslim testifies against a non-Muslim his testimony should be accepted.

Unfortunately a large majority of Muslims today lack the strict criteria for a witness in Islam. Yet, according to the ulema, the testimony of a dishonest Muslim will have more credence than the testimony of an honest non-Muslim. They attempt to present various Quranic verses in support of their twisted ideology. I will now present these same verses to demolish their false argumentation.

The one verse they quote in their favour is verse 283 of Sūrah al-Baqarah, which includes the instruction 'from among your men'. This, the mullahs misinterpret by maintaining that it refers only to Muslim men.

It is amazing that the ulema fail to realise that this verse cannot be applicable to everyday occurrences such as criminal offences and accidents. In such cases, the witnesses just happen to be present on those occasions regardless of their faith or gender. Sometimes there will be no witness to the event, at others it may be that only one woman saw what happened. To generalise a rule which is laid down for a specific situation, without proper proofs and without using one's common sense, is an injustice to the Quran.

The same subject is taken up at another place:

وَأَشْهِدُوْا ذَوَيْ عَدْلٍ مِّنْكُمْ وَ أَقِيْمُوا الشَّهَادَةَ لِلّٰهِ...

...and call to witness two just persons from among you; and bear *true* witness for Allah.
(Sūrah al-Ṭalāq; Ch.65: V3)

This is another verse which the ulema present in favour of their belief that witnesses have to be from among the Muslims. They argue that 'from among you' refers to only Muslims because the verse addresses the Muslim society. If this deduction is correct, what do the ulema make of the following verse where it is said that if witnesses cannot be found from among the Muslims, they should be sought from among the non-Muslims?

يَآَيُّهَا الَّذِيْنَ اَمَنُوْا شَهَادَةُ بَيْنِكُمْ اِذَا حَضَرَاَحَدَكُمُ الْمَوْتُ حِيْنَ الْوَصِيَّةِ اثْنَانِ ذَوَا عَدْلٍ مِّنْكُمْ اَوْ اخَرَانِ مِنْ غَيْرِكُمْ اِنْ اَنْتُمْ ضَرَبْتُمْ فِى الْاَرْضِ فَاَصَابَتْكُمْ مُّصِيْبَةُ الْمَوْتِ ...

> O ye who believe! The *right* evidence among you,
> when death presents itself to one of you, at the time of
> making a bequest, is of two just men from among you;
> or of two others not from among you, if you be
> journeying in the land and the calamity of death
> befalls you. ...
> (Sūrah al-Mā'idah; Ch.5: V.107)

Even with a slight amount of deliberation, one should be able to realise that in principle the testimony of a Muslim is not considered more reliable than that of a non-Muslim. In a Muslim society, when deciding on internal affairs which require the presence of witnesses, it is only natural to seek out witnesses from among the Muslims. But if, for instance, one is on a journey, the testimony of a non-Muslim will hold the same credence as the testimony of a Muslim.

Both of the above verses are specifically concerned with financial settlements. There is no license to give them general application. They are not applicable to everyday accidents or crimes etc.

A fundamental principle that should also be borne in mind is that an interpretation of a Quranic verse is unacceptable if it contradicts another verse, or if it goes against the example set by the Holy Prophet Muhammad[sa].

The best and easiest way to resolve the controversy surrounding the testimony of a Muslim versus the testimony of a non-Muslim is to judge the whole issue by the yardstick of the Holy Prophet's[sa] character and conduct. Any interpretation of the Quran which coincides with the Holy Prophet's[sa] character and conduct can be accepted with confidence. Where there is a contradiction between the two one must investigate further before coming to any conclusion. Let us analyse the following incident, recorded in *Ṣaḥīḥ Bukhārī*, to determine how the Holy Prophet[sa] interpreted the matter under consideration. His conduct was precisely shaped in accordance with this Quranic admonition.

> 'Ash'ath narrates: I was in dispute with a Jew over a piece of land. Our case was presented to the Holy Prophet[sa] who asked for proof of my claim. I had none. The Holy Prophet[sa] then turned to the Jew and said, 'You are the defendant so you must take the oath. Do you say under oath that the land is yours?' I remonstrated, 'O Prophet of Allah! This man is a Jew; he will perjure himself and take possession of my property.' The Holy Prophet[sa] replied, 'Nonetheless, there is no other option. My decision will be a just one.' He told the Jew, 'Take the oath and fear God. If you swear that the land belongs to you I will decide in your favour.'[40]

The following incident presents even a clearer case of how the Holy Founder[sa] of Islam himself understood Islamic jurisprudence to be. During the course of their normal work, some Muslims travelled to Khaibar. In this journey they came across the corpse of a slain Muslim. The territory belonged exclusively to the Jews. As no Muslims resided in that region, it seemed a foregone conclusion that the murderer had to be a Jew. The party of Muslims thought it appropriate that the Jews of that area be collectively held responsible for the murder of that Muslim and held liable to pay blood money to the relatives of the deceased. When this case was presented to the Holy Prophet[sa], he said, 'This is a serious matter, but do you have any evidence to support your claim that the murderer was a Jew?'

The Muslims replied, 'O Prophet of Allah, there are no witnesses.' So the Holy Prophet[sa] decided that a sworn statement would be taken from the Jews instead. 'But they will lie under oath', remonstrated the Muslims. The Holy Prophet[sa] expressed displeasure at this objection. The sworn statement of the Jews was accepted by the Holy Prophet[sa] and no further interrogation was regarded necessary. The relatives of the deceased were still entitled to blood money, which the Holy Prophet[sa] paid from public funds.

The Holy Prophet[sa] had a natural affinity for justice as exemplified in his person. However, the remote possibility remained that his verdict, reached on the basis of available evidence, was only provisionally correct. An eloquent person could argue his case in a most convincing manner and a judge, while fulfilling all the demands of justice, could come to the wrong conclusion. In that case the responsibility for the miscarriage of justice would fall on the shoulders of the dishonest advocate and not on the shoulders of the judge. It was towards this eventuality that the Holy Prophet[sa] was alluding when he said:

اِنَّـمَا اَنَا بَشَرٌ وَّ اِنَّكُمْ تَخْتَصِمُوْنَ اِلَيَّ وَلَعَلَّ بَعْضَكُمْ اَنْ يَّكُوْنَ اَلْحَنَ بِحُجَّتِهِ مِنْ بَعْضٍ فَاَقْضِىَ عَلٰى نَحْوِمَا اَسْمَعُ فَمَنْ قَضَيْتُ لَهُ بِحَقِّ اَخِيْهِ شَيْئًافَلَايَاْ خُذْهُ فَاِنَّمَا اَقْطَعُ لَهُ قِطْعَةً مِّنَ النَّارِ

I am but human. You bring your disputes to my attention, and one disputant may present his case in a more persuasive manner than the other. It is possible that I reach my verdict based on the arguments presented to me. Remember, the beneficiary of that verdict should not take what is awarded to him, as it will be like a ball of fire for him. [41]

The point to note is that even if the Holy Prophet[sa] could be misled on the strength of advocacy and available evidence to give a decision in favour of the wrong party, the responsibility would shift entirely from him to this party. It knows full well that it is the usurper and as such the Holy Prophet^{sa} warned that if the usurped property is not returned to the rightful owner, despite his decision against him, the usurper will be held answerable before God for this crime. The following incident further supports this.

During the course of a journey, the Holy Prophet^{sa} and his followers had set up camp when the armament of a Muslim was stolen. Word got out and the Holy Prophet^{sa} ordered a search of the entire camp. The theft had actually been committed by a Muslim, but when the search began he placed the armaments with the belongings of a Jew. The Holy Prophet^{sa} was about to pronounce punishment on the Jew, when the following verse was revealed:

$$\text{وَلَا تَكُنْ لِّلْخَآئِنِيْنَ خَصِيْمًا}$$

And be you not a disputer for the faithless.
(Sūrah al-Nisā'; Ch.4: V.106)

The Holy Prophet^{sa} immediately realised the message that God was conveying to him, i.e. although the Jew appeared to be the culprit, in reality it was the Muslim who had committed the crime and not the Jew. The Holy Prophet^{sa} ordered a further investigation and the real culprit was eventually caught.[42]

The import of this verse clearly indicates that according to Islamic principles of evidence the religion of the witness is irrelevant, and it is also irrelevant whether a Muslim suffers in consequence or a non-Muslim does.

Alas! Alas again! How far the Muslim clergy of today have strayed from the path of justice! As far as justice in testimony is concerned, the Holy Prophet's[sa] faith and his character would always support a secular and non-partisan attitude. It is the twisted nature of the latter day ulema which attempts to twist the teachings of Islam in accordance with their own.

So I call on all Muslims, not only Ahmadis, to be charged with the spirit to fight, to stand up in this Holy War against every unholy attempt which dares to attack the holy teachings of Islam and its Holy Master[sa]. They should be determined to frustrate all such attempts even at the cost of their own honour, wealth and property. Today, it is not only the enemy which is attacking Islam, but such is the extent of cruelty that even the so-called Muslim clergy is also stabbing Islam in the back. We must brace ourselves to boldly take upon our breast each arrow that is shot at our Holy Master[sa]. Do so because there is no better death than the death earned in the cause of Allah.

In the end, I beg you to pray. It is a great blessing of Allah, His Favour and His Graciousness that in a charming atmosphere, guarding us from all mischief and disorder, He has granted us the opportunity to gather here to earn His favour. The lovers of the Holy

Prophet[sa] have gathered here from all the corners of the earth. While they were coming, their hearts kept singing the praises of Allah. Now, when they are about to return to their respective homes, they should return again singing the praises of Allah.

Now that you are leaving, my heart grieves at the thought of your departure. I pray that may God protect you in this journey, and I address you in the words of Ghālib:

وداع و وصل جداگانه لذّتے دارد

هزار بار برو صد هزار بار بيا

The poet pleads to his beloved: both parting and meeting have their own separate pleasures, you may part a thousand times but you must come back ten thousand times. Likewise, I plead with my beloved Ahmadis that they should also part a thousand times, only to return ten thousand times.

Repeatedly may we gather here to extol the name of Allah. Repeatedly may we kindle the lamps of His love and repeatedly may arise from our hearts blessings upon Ḥaḍrat Muhammad[sa]. May Allah that this state of love and endearment forever increase and spread and encompass the entire world—Āmīn.

References Part II

13. *Ṣaḥīḥ Bukhārī, Kitābul Buyū', Bābu Shirā'il Mamlūki Minal Ḥarbiyyi wa Hibatihī wa Itqihī wa Ahlil Ḥarbi.*
14. *Ṭabaqāt li Ibni Sa'd,* Vol. I, p. 266.
15. *Ṣaḥīḥ Muslim, Kitābul Īmān, Bābu Taḥrimi Qatlil Kāfiri Ba'da 'an Qāla Lā Ilāha Illallāhu.*
    Note: The quotation in the text combines three *Aḥādīth* (No. 4, 5, 6) of this Chapter.
16. *Sunan Tirmadhī, Abwābu Tafsīril-Quran, Bābu wa min Sūrati āl-e-'Imrān,* Hadith No. 3010.
17. *Musnad Aḥmad bin Hambal, Musnad Anas bin Mālik.*
18. *At-Targhīb wat-Tarhīb, Kitābut-Taubati waz-Zuhdi,* Hadith No. 4912.
    Note: The Hadith is also found in Muslim, but the wording is slightly different.
    See *Ṣaḥiḥ Muslim, Kitābul Birr waṣ Ṣilah, Bābu Faḍliḍu'afā'i wal Khāmilīna.*
19. *Aṣḥābi Aḥmad,* Vol.4, pp. 172-173.
20. *Tirmadhī, Kitābud Da'wāt, Bābu 'Aqdit Tasbīḥi Bil Yad.*
21. *Nūrul Quran, Rūḥānī Khazā'in,* Vol. 9, p. 437-438
22. ibid, pp. 438-439
23. ibid, pp. 439-440
24. ibid, p. 440
25. (a) *Jāmi' Tirmadhi, Kitābuṣ Ṣalāt, Bābu mā Jā'a Fil Qirā'ati Bil-Laili.*
    (b) *Sunan Abū Dāwūd, Kitābut Taṭawwu'i, Bābu Raf'iṣ Ṣauti bil Qirā'ati Fī Ṣalātil Laili.*
26. *Ṣaḥīḥ Bukhārī, Kitābul Adhān, Bābu Raf'iṣ Ṣauti Bin-Nidā'i.*
27. *Ṣaḥīḥ Bukhārī, Kitābul Manāqib, Bābu Kānan-Nabiyyu Tanāmu 'Ainohū wa lā Yanāmu Qalbuhū.*
28. *Sunan Abū Dāwūd, Kitābul Adab, Bābu Fil Ḥasadi.*
29. (a) *Ṣaḥīḥ Bukhārī, Kitābut Tahajjud, Bābu Mā Yukrahu Minat-Tashdīdi Fil 'Ibādati.*
    (b) *Mishkāt, Bābul Qaṣdi Fil 'Amali,* Hadith No. 1174.
30. *Ṣaḥīḥ Bukhārī, Kitābun-Nikāḥi, Bābut Taghrībi Fin Nikāḥi.*
31. *Ṣaḥīḥ Bukhārī, Kitābul Adhān, Bābu Man Akhaffaṣ Ṣalāta 'Inda Bukā'iṣ Ṣabīyyi.*
32. *Ṣaḥīḥ Bukhārī, Kitābul Jamā'ati wal Imāmati, Bābu Man Shakā Imāmahū Idhā Ṭawwala.*
33. *Ṣaḥīḥ Muslim, Kitābuṣ Ṣiyām Bābu Faḍli Ṣaumil Muḥarrami.*
34. (a) *Ṣaḥīḥ Muslim, Kitābul Ḥudūd, Bābu Qatlis Sāriqish-Sharīfi wa Ghairihī.*
    (b) *Ṣaḥīḥ Bukhārī, Kitābu Aḥādīthil Ambiyā, Bābu Ḥadīthil Ghāri.*
35. *Ṭabaqāt li Ibni Sa'd,* Vol.4, p.13. Published by Dāru Ṣādir, Bairut, 1985.
36. *Sunnan Abū Dāwūd, Kitābul Khirāji wal Imārati wal Fai'i, Bābu Fī Ta'shīri Ahliz Zimmati Idhakhtalafu Bit Tijārati.*
37. See *Ā'īna'-e-Kamālāt-e-Islām, Rūḥānī Khazā'in,* London 1984 edition, vol. 5, pp. 299-300.
38. *Tārīkh-i-Ahmadiyyat,* Vol. 1, p.74, with Reference to *Riwāyāt-e-Ṣaḥābah,* Part 9, p. 193.
39. ibid.
40. *Ṣaḥīḥ Bukhārī, Kitābush-Shahādati, Bābu Suwālil Ḥākimil Mudda'ī: Hal Laka Bayyinatun Qablal Yamīni?*
41. *Ṣaḥīḥ Bukhārī, Kitābul Aḥkāmi, Bābu Mau'iẓatil Imāmi Lil Khuṣūmi.*
42. *Aḥkāmul Quran lil Jaṣṣāṣ,* Vol. 2, p.340

Absolute Justice, Kindness and Kinship

The Three Creative Principles

Ḥaḍrat Mirza Tahir Ahmad

Part III

**Speech delivered at the Annual Convention
of the Ahmadiyyah Muslim Jamā'at UK
in Islamabad, Tilford, Surrey, United Kingdom
on August 2, 1987**

LIST OF CHAPTERS IN PART III

In the name of Allah, the Most Gracious, the Ever Merciful.

The Islamic system of evidence covers a very wide area. When we contemplate over it in the light of Quranic statements and sayings of the Holy Prophet[sa], we may not liken it to the system of evidence as prevails in the worldly courts. The Islamic system of evidence is in fact so wide that it covers not only the basics of justice but also comprises benevolence and kinship. Again, the expanse it covers is so wide that God considers justice binding even upon Himself and also treats His creation with benevolence and kinship wherever appropriate. Likewise, He presents a system of justice, benevolence and kinship, equally binding on His Prophets[as]. Similarly, God presents the same system of evidence as covering the people of the past and the people of the future. He also covers the Muslim's internal disputes and their disagreements with their non-Muslim fellow beings. In all such places, one can discern the manifestation of not only justice but also of benevolence and kinship.

16 Evidence in Financial Matters

As the subject of financial disputes has been previously discussed, we would like to pick up from the point where we left off.

In verse 283 of Sūrah al-Baqarah, the Holy Quran dictates:

يَآأَيُّهَا الَّذِينَ اٰمَنُوٓا إِذَا تَدَايَنْتُمْ بِدَيْنٍ اِلٰٓى اَجَلٍ مُّسَمًّى فَاكْتُبُوهُ ۖ وَلْيَكْتُبْ بَيْنَكُمْ كَاتِبٌ بِالْعَدْلِ ۚ وَلَا يَأْبَ كَاتِبٌ اَنْ يَّكْتُبَ كَمَا عَلَّمَهُ اللّٰهُ فَلْيَكْتُبْ ۚ وَلْيُمْلِلِ الَّذِى عَلَيْهِ الْحَقُّ وَلْيَتَّقِ اللّٰهَ رَبَّهُ وَلَا يَبْخَسْ مِنْهُ شَيْئًا ۚ فَاِنْ كَانَ الَّذِى عَلَيْهِ الْحَقُّ سَفِيهًا اَوْ ضَعِيفًا اَوْ لَا يَسْتَطِيعُ اَنْ يُّمِلَّ هُوَ فَلْيُمْلِلْ وَلِيُّهُ بِالْعَدْلِ ۚ وَاسْتَشْهِدُوا شَهِيدَيْنِ مِنْ رِّجَالِكُمْ ۚ فَاِنْ لَّمْ يَكُونَا رَجُلَيْنِ فَرَجُلٌ وَّامْرَاَتٰنِ مِمَّنْ تَرْضَوْنَ مِنَ الشُّهَدَآءِ اَنْ تَضِلَّ اِحْدٰىهُمَا فَتُذَكِّرَ اِحْدٰىهُمَا الْاُخْرٰى ۚ وَلَا يَأْبَ الشُّهَدَآءُ اِذَا مَا دُعُوا ۚ ....

O ye who believe! When you *are about to* borrow money for a definite period commit the transaction to writing and when it is dictated to a scribe it is binding upon the scribe to write with justice. And no scribe should refuse that he should write as God has taught him to write. He should dictate who owes money to the other and in doing so, he should entertain the fear of God and nothing from the other's right should be lessened. If the one who should dictate is of low understanding, or is too weak or incompetent to dictate himself, then his guardian representing him should dictate with justice *as his attorney. In addition to that* appoint two male witnesses from among you. However, if two male witnesses are not available then have one male and two females of such as you like for witnesses so that if one female forgets anything while registering her evidence, the other *sitting by her side*, should remind her *of what she might have omitted*. And the witness should not refuse when they are called. …

(Sūrah al-Baqarah Ch.2:V.283)

Here, it is especially noteworthy that in matters of financial transactions, it is clearly dictated that they must be committed to writing. For this to be included in the Islamic rule of conduct is an exceptional beauty of the Holy Quran. You may testify to it by reading the Divine Books of all religions. Nowhere among them will you find the obligatory injunction to commit all financial transactions to writing. Particularly worthy of note is the fact that during the age when the above-quoted Quranic revelation was made, as is evident from the verse itself, the custom of writing was very rare among the Arabs and men of letters were very few.

Such clear teaching in matters of financial transactions is amazing. Most financial disputes found among the Muslim society are because of their lack of observance of this injunction. In the beginning both parties to a transaction are fully satisfied with their verbal commitments but during the verbal discussion, all the conditions are not precisely laid out. This is despite the fact that almost everyone knows how to read and write: and to write is not a rare wonder. Again, even when the transaction is committed to writing, very often it is considered unnecessary to have it signed by witnesses. Hence, the lack of due respect to this perfect and comprehensive Quranic teaching results in the deprivation of both parties from its full benefit. An additional benefit of the Quranic instruction of having the contract signed by two witnesses is that during a dispute arising over the true meaning of the contract, such witnesses would be able to clarify the points of dispute because they would have known the background of this contract.

In this verse all the various possibilities are taken care of with such detail that it even mentions who should write or dictate the transaction contract. According to this verse, the one who owes the other party something is required to write or dictate. Anyone who commits himself to his obligations to the other is evidently much more cautious in his writing or dictation, so that his dues to the other stand in no danger of being even slightly exaggerated. If, on the contrary, the writing or dictation was left to the person who has claim upon the other, he could be tempted to twist his writing or dictation in such a manner that at the time of the dispute, the wording of the contract could be twisted in his favour.

There is also another danger that the claimant to be may be of low understanding and as such he may not be able to fully safeguard his own rights. In such a case the burden of writing or dictation is shifted from him to his patron who would work on his behalf as his attorney. As such, he would take every precaution that the spirit of the contract is moulded into appropriate wording.

This verse does not discriminate against women witnesses because it would not be two women standing together as witness. Only one woman will present the case and the second one will be there to remind her in case she forgets. Unfortunately, the orthodox mullah does not realise this difference and considers Islam to be actually presenting two female witnesses against one man.

This same verse points out that, on occasions, a woman may not fully grasp all the implications of a financial matter. Or she may be prone to forget some aspects of a financial settlements. It was to eliminate such possibilities that the Holy Quran introduced this convention. Nowhere in the Holy Quran do we find that the testimony of two women is considered equivalent to that of one man.

In the matter of transactions, the Holy Quran foresees such possibilities as may occur only very rarely. In verse 284 of the same chapter (Sūrah al-Baqarah) the Holy Quran says:

وَاِنْ كُنْتُمْ عَلٰى سَفَرٍ وَّلَمْ تَجِدُوْا كَاتِبًا فَرِهٰنٌ مَّقْبُوْضَةٌ ۭ

meaning that if someone is on a journey and unexpectedly requires some money with no scribe to commit this transaction to writing, he should pawn something as a guarantee against the money he borrows.

It goes on to say:

فَاِنْ اَمِنَ بَعْضُكُمْ بَعْضًا فَلْيُؤَدِّ الَّذِى اؤْتُمِنَ اَمَانَتَهٗ وَلْيَتَّقِ اللّٰهَ رَبَّهٗ ۭ

i.e. when anyone is entrusted with something and he is requested to return it, it is his duty to restore it to the owner in accordance with *Taqwā*. He should fear his Lord, Allah. وَلَا تَكْتُمُوا الشَّهَادَةَ and do not conceal testimony. وَمَنْ يَّكْتُمْهَا فَاِنَّهٗ اٰثِمٌ قَلْبُهٗ and whoever conceals evidence, his heart becomes sinful. وَاللّٰهُ بِمَا تَعْمَلُوْنَ عَلِيْمٌ Allah knows well what you do.

It is of interest to note that of all the religious Books in the world, it is the Holy Quran alone which for the first time discusses the possibility of a traveller requiring financial support. It is commonly observed that some people habitually beg for a loan with the plea of being on a journey, and many people loan them something out of pity which is seldom returned.

Around fourteen hundred years ago, the Holy Quran suggested measures for the safeguard of the rights of the future generations to such an extent. But unfortunately in this age when most travellers carry many valuable articles with them, which can easily be deposited as security against a loan, those who lend them money fall into trouble because they do not follow the Quranic injunction in this regard. Thus they sow the seeds of bitterness in the society. Another offshoot of this incautious conduct is that it encourages deceitful behaviour in monetary transacttions as well. So, these seemingly unnecessary details should not be lightly dismissed.

17 Evidence of the Existence of God

Having discussed these two aspects of financial dealings, I now turn to some features of testimony in Islam regarding the existence of God.

The Testimony of God, His Angels and Knowledgeable People

To begin with, the Holy Quran lays the utmost importance on the testimony of God Himself regarding His own existence. Does He or does He not exist? This is that fundamental upon which every religion is based. The question is, if God exists, who saw Him and who bore witness that he has as good as seen Him? It is vital that God Himself should speak of His own existence and present those witnesses who have heard His word. Incidentally, this is another matter which distinguishes the Holy Quran from other Divine books. Many such books fail to present a clear-cut claim made by God Himself that 'I Exist'. Some religious books have words to this effect but most do not. Those who do, do not support this claim with a series of witness after witness, to fulfil all the requirements of evidence.

The Holy Quran observes:

شَهِدَ اللهُ اَنَّهٗ لَا اِلٰهَ اِلَّا هُوَ ۙ وَالْمَلٰٓئِكَةُ وَاُولُوا الْعِلْمِ قَآئِمًا بِالْقِسْطِ ۚ لَا اِلٰهَ اِلَّا هُوَ الْعَزِيْزُ الْحَكِيْمُ □

Allah bears witness that there is no God but He—and *also do* the angels and those possessed of knowledge—Maintainer of justice; there is no God but He, the Mighty, the Wise.
(Sūrah āl-e-'Imrān; Ch.3: V.19)

Now, who has heard this claim from Allah and how should we know that He has made this claim? We can put this to the test from many angles. In the first place, no counterevidence exists. There is no claimant to godhead other than God Himself, who has ever made this claim that he also exists besides God. The only claim to this effect, that gods other than God exist, is made by humans. Hence, this lack of counterevidence is virtually a strong evidence in favour of Allah's claim. Had there been others they should have loudly counterclaimed 'we too exist, we too exist, we too exist', filling the universe with their noise, but this did not happen.

Thus, for those who believe in any concept of a single or plural godhead, the aforementioned lack of counterevidence should suffice. But as for those people who do not believe in God, for them the Holy Quran presents another type of evidence which we shall mention later.

For the time being, returning to the same verse quoted above, we hereby turn to the aspect of the evidence of the angels. From the mention of *Malā'ikah* ﷽ (Angels) spread all over the Holy Quran, we can safely conclude that they are such conscious beings as are created to control every law of nature. According to the in-depth wisdom of the Promised Messiah[as], the Founder of the Ahmadiyya Jamā'at, angels are masters of all natural laws, which continue to remain operational under their constant guidance. The entire world of science, divided into the branches of physics, chemistry, botany, zoology etc., is equally governed by these angels. Hence, if you see the laws of nature as if running by themselves, it would be a sad blunder. In this regard when you contemplate over the said testimony of angels, whether you believe in them or not, their testimony as manifested in nature would lead you to the same conclusion: if there is a God, He has to be one and only one. The concept of more than one Creator is shattered and scattered against this mighty evidence. The entire universe is pointing its finger to only one Creator.

Wherever religious people claim that angels descended on their hearts, they never attribute to them the message: do not worship one God, worship many gods because they also exist besides Him.

The third evidence presented in the same verse is that of knowledgeable people. They are bracketed with angels under God's attribute of *Qā'imam bil Qist* (قَآئِمًا بِالْقِسْطِ)—meaning that He is always the Maintainer of justice. Thus the same attribute is instilled into the evidence of angels and knowledgeable people. A truthful and knowledgeable person, who is known to be just by the entire society, would always bear witness, when you inquire from him, that he personally knows of no god other than God. He will give this witness regardless of whatever religion he follows. If the person does not believe in any God, He would still maintain the same. In answer to a direct question he might possibly say: no God has ever descended on my heart. But he would never say: more than one God descended on my heart.

The Evidence of the Existence of God for the Atheists

The Holy Quran also presents an argument which can be stated as the evidence of human nature. This argument has been mentioned in Surah al-A'rāf as follows:

وَإِذْ أَخَذَ رَبُّكَ مِنْ بَنِيْ اٰدَمَ مِنْ ظُهُوْرِهِمْ ذُرِّيَّتَهُمْ وَ
أَشْهَدَهُمْ عَلٰى أَنْفُسِهِمْ ۚ أَلَسْتُ بِرَبِّكُمْ ۖ قَالُوْا بَلٰى ۚ شَهِدْنَا ۚ
أَنْ تَقُوْلُوْا يَوْمَ الْقِيٰمَةِ إِنَّا كُنَّا عَنْ هٰذَا غٰفِلِيْنَ ☐

And when thy Lord brings forth from Adam's children—out of their loins—their offspring and makes them witnesses against their own selves *by saying*: 'Am I not your Lord?' they say, 'Yes, we do bear witness'. *This He does* lest you should say on the

Day of Resurrection, 'We were surely unaware of
this'.   (Sūrah al-A'rāf; Ch.7: V.173)

This means that all the progeny of Adam, born from
the seminary fluid springing forth from his loins,
whether born in the past or to be born in the future,
possess an internal evidence of the existence of God.
Most people do not realise consciously that the
combination of the sperm and ovum of which they are
born, carry chromosomes—a highly complicated
material built with incredibly minute genes. The genes
are very complex and well-ordered, bound in a long
chain of series, where each one is placed in its proper
number unalterable without destroying life. They,
despite being extremely minute, carry the entire blueprint determining the type, character, individual traits
etc. of the man or woman they carry in their
embryonic state. They contain such detail as to when
the organs of the yet unborn baby are to grow and
when they should stop growing. They also carry
written instructions regarding all the potentials of the
human body, its heart, future tendencies, its system of
resistance against disease, and all the changes to occur
at every stage of its future life and their limitations.

The entire sketch of life is imprinted within each
cell of the human body, indicating to those who
understand that such perfect organisation cannot exist
by itself. There has to be a Creator who has created
this matchless wonder, which man cannot fully

fathom, though generations of scientists are devoted to the understanding of the messages that genes contain. Although knowledgeable people can bear witness consciously that they could not have been born by themselves, even those who are completely ignorant of this fact have a deep unconscious realisation of the same. It is imprinted upon the essence of their life that when God inquired 'Am I not your Lord?', what sprang from the loins of their ancient forefathers answered in unspoken words, 'why not, why not?'

This subject is extremely vast. As I have mentioned earlier, even reading the information written by scientists would consume the lifetime of a reader. Just to preserve all the information in the form of written material, the scientists will have to work hard, generation after generation. All the outcome of the scientific investigation in this regard, if committed to writing, would result in the compilation of hundreds of voluminous books.

Thus in the first place, it is evident from the above verse, that the concept of God's existence is not internally possessed by one human generation alone, in any one age, but the progeny of Adam inherit this concept as a legacy. Even if the aetheists introspect themselves, they could discover many such testimonies within their own selves. Of course it does not follow that every human is conscious of God's existence. If this were intended the verse would not have contained the word '*alā* (عَلٰى) indicating that this written testimony would stand as witness against many among them.

In this regard there is another verse in the Holy Quran, contained in Sūrah Ḥā Mīm al-Sajdah, which draws man's attention to the same fact from two different angles:

سَنُرِيْهِمْ اٰيٰتِنَا فِى الْاٰفَاقِ وَفِىْٓ اَنْفُسِهِمْ حَتّٰى يَتَبَيَّنَ لَهُمْ اَنَّهُ الْحَقُّ ۗ اَوَلَمْ يَكْفِ بِرَبِّكَ اَنَّهُ عَلٰى كُلِّ شَيْءٍ شَهِيْدٌ ☐

Soon We will show them Our signs written in the horizons *of the earth* and also within themselves until it becomes manifest upon them that it, *the existence of God*, is the truth. Is it not enough that thy Lord is witness over all things?
(Sūrah Ḥā Mīm al-Sajdah; Ch.41: V.54)

This is a reminder that the evidence of God's existence can be seen scattered all over the earth. However, if someone is unable to indulge in this profound elaborate study, he should turn to his own heart and the intricacies of life. Then he would be able to listen to the testimony of His existence from within his own self. Is it not amazing that in every part of the world man has some sort of belief in God! Even among the Aborigines and the Native Americans, the same consciousness of the existence of God is present. Not only this, but among both, an unshakeable belief is common that He communicates with people regarding future fearful events or glad tidings.

Another evidence which the Holy Quran mentions so often is man's compulsion to admit that he came into being, despite having been nothing previously. Again, he knows that he is not the creator of himself. Hence his creation out of nothing, while he was not his own creator, requires an outside agency.

Yet another evidence etched upon human nature is man's fundamental realisation of morality found alike among people of every age. All somehow know evil to be evil and virtue to be virtue. Even the aetheist philosophers, who try and support aetheism by various arguments, stand bewildered and confused when they confront this universal testimony. They wonder why the concept of morality is found universally in all humans. If there is no God, a universal concept of morality cannot exist. This is the dilemma facing the communist philosophical world. They realise the presence of this internal evidence within themselves, yet they have to deny it. Otherwise the very first brick of the communist foundation could not have been laid by Marx, who proclaimed that man is an immoral animal.

According to the Holy Quran, the very existence of man depends on his morality. To support this contention the Holy Quran repeatedly presents the history of past people as evidence. They were destroyed only for the reason that they had become immoral in their mutual relationships. This is the essential basis of the rise and fall of all great nations in the past. However, Allah in His Grace, sent warners to them before their destruction. When they did not pay heed, they were allowed to be destroyed at their own hands.

Alas! every beginning, however great, has to be subject to decline and ultimate destruction. But the heights they had achieved cannot be denied by observing the fall. This destiny commands all things alike, both the animate and inanimate.

The Evidence of the Universe

The seed of the evidence is already described to have been sown in the evidence of the angels mentioned earlier. In addition, the Holy Quran draws our attention to God being One, without partners. This evidence is imprinted upon each particle of the universe. The following are the relevant verses:

اَمَّنْ خَلَقَ السَّمٰوٰتِ وَالْاَرْضَ وَاَنْزَلَ لَكُمْ مِّنَ السَّمَآءِ مَآءً ج فَاَنْبَتْنَا بِه حَدَآئِقَ ذَاتَ بَهْجَةٍ ج مَاكَانَ لَكُمْ اَنْ تُنْبِتُوْا شَجَرَهَا ءَاِلٰهٌ مَّعَ اللّٰهِ ؕ بَلْ هُمْ قَوْمٌ يَّعْدِلُوْنَ ☐ اَمَّنْ جَعَلَ الْاَرْضَ قَرَارًا وَّ جَعَلَ خِلٰلَهَآ اَنْهٰرًا وَّ جَعَلَ لَهَا رَوَاسِيَ وَ جَعَلَ بَيْنَ الْبَحْرَيْنِ حَاجِزًا ؕ ءَاِلٰهٌ مَّعَ اللّٰهِ ؕ بَلْ اَكْثَرُهُمْ لَا يَعْلَمُوْنَ ☐

Or, Who created the heavens and the earth, and Who sent down water for you from the sky wherewith We cause to grow beautiful orchards? You could not cause their trees to grow. Is there a God besides Allah? Nay, they are a people who deviate *from the right path.*

Or, Who made the earth a place to rest, and made rivers to flow amidst it and made upon it firm mountains, and put a barrier between the two waters? Is there a God besides Allah? Nay, most of them know not.

(Sūrah al-Naml; Ch.27: Vs.61-62)

Hence Allah's claim in the Holy Quran, that He alone has granted earth well-proportioned potentials to become a fit habitat for supporting life, could not have been true if there were other gods besides Him. If one ponders over the prerequisites necessary for the earth to be a balanced habitat, one would be astonished to note that they simply could not have been produced by random chances. There are millions of causative factors and reasons which, in unison with each other, create this single desired effect. The scientists are unable to explain why all these factors have gathered to join hands. Even if a small causative factor were to be out of step with the rest, the earth would lose its quality of being a balanced habitat. To achieve this goal, whenever and wherever an exception to the rule was needed, that exception was provided. Some specific examples of the same have been presented before. There is nothing to indicate that all this could have been achieved without there being a Powerful

and Wise Designer. Hence the above verses mention
that:

$$وَجَعَلَ خِلَلَهَآ أَنْهَٰرًا$$

He made rivers to flow amidst it.

$$وَجَعَلَ لَهَا رَوَاسِيَ$$

And He made such mountains as were essential for
stablizing earth and maintaining a life-support system
as mentioned above.

$$وَجَعَلَ بَيْنَ الْبَحْرَيْنِ حَاجِزًا$$

And it is He who created a partition between two
oceans.

$$ءَإِلَٰهٌ مَّعَ اللّٰهِ$$

Is there another God besides Allah who is performing
all these other functions?

$$بَلْ أَكْثَرُهُمْ لَا يَعْلَمُونَ$$

But most of them know not.

All these manifestations of creation cannot be born
out of chances colluding together, nor can they be a
creation of different independent gods. If this were so,
undercurrents of negotiation between them for
achieving the same sublime object without discord
should have been detectable in nature. All this can be
quoted as a great example of Allah's justice. Having
purified and raised water from the oceans and having
performed a glorious purpose, the water is returned to

the same ocean again. The Holy Quran has covered all the essential parts in the scheme. When it draws man's attention to ponder over these matters, evidently it means that the people of the Holy Prophet's[sa] age could only have entertained a vague idea of how this system worked. A man at the time of the revelation of the Holy Quran knew of course that the water was raised from the oceans and returned to the same through rains on plains and upon mountains. However, he could not have had the foggiest idea as to what scientific laws were responsible for raising and purifying water from the oceans. Little did he know that during the same process high voltage electricity is created. He was also unaware that the turning of water vapours suspended in the air back to heavy droplets of water, required the interplay of opposed electrical charges.

18 A New Category of Testimony

Now we turn to a completely different type of testimony belonging to human psyche. Normally it seems that all vehement opponents of the Holy Prophet[sa] were united in their opposition, however, the Holy Quran points out that all of them were not alike. Though such exceptions did not always come to surface, some among them secretly began to entertain the possibility of the Holy Prophet's[sa] truth and even wish that they were Muslims. This is a secret of human nature which could only be known to an All-Knowing God. Among the opponents there were certainly some who recognized many signs in favour of the Holy Prophet[sa], but their social bondage did not permit them to accept him[sa] openly. It is to this that the following verse of the Holy Quran refers:

رُبَمَا يَوَدُّ الَّذِيْنَ كَفَرُوْا لَوْ كَانُوْا مُسْلِمِيْنَ ☐

Many a time those who disbelieve have a deep yearning *in their hearts* that they were *also* Muslims. (Sūrah al-Ḥijr; Ch.15: V.3)

Sometimes upon the disbelievers descend such calamities as strike awe in their hearts; similar calamities befall other disbelievers like them. This subject is discussed in numerous verses of the Holy

Quran in different contexts. The following example should suffice:

وَلَا يَزَالُ الَّذِيْنَ كَفَرُوْا تُصِيْبُهُمْ بِمَا صَنَعُوْا قَارِعَةٌ... اَوْتَحُلُّ قَرِيْبًا مِّنْ دَارِهِمْ حَتَّى يَأْتِيَ وَعْدُ اللّٰهِ اِنَّ اللّٰهَ لَا يُخْلِفُ الْمِيْعَادَ ◻

An explanatory translation of this verse would be:
> ...And as for those who disbelieve a knocking[43] disaster shall not cease to knock at the doors of their hearts (to awaken them) or at the doors of their neighbours until the promise of Allah comes to pass. Surely, Allah fails not in His promise.
> (Sūrah al-Ra'd; Ch.13: V.32)

In another verse, Allah addresses the Holy Prophet[sa], saying:

لٰكِنِ اللّٰهُ يَشْهَدُ بِمَا اَنْزَلَ اِلَيْكَ اَنْزَلَهُ بِعِلْمِهِ ۚ وَ الْمَلٰٓئِكَةُ يَشْهَدُوْنَ ۚ وَ كَفٰى بِاللّٰهِ شَهِيْدًا ◻

> Allah bears witness, whatever He has revealed to you, He has revealed it based on His knowledge. Likewise, the angels bear witness to it, while Allah is sufficient as a witness by Himself.
> (Sūrah al-Nisā'; Ch.4: V.167)

The testimony of angels refers to the testimony of the laws of nature, run by the angels. Again, when Allah emphasizes that whatever He has revealed, He has revealed with His knowledge, He refers to the same testimony of the laws of nature. In saying this, Allah has opened a window of unlimited research by using the expression *bi'ilmihī* (based on His knowledge). This means that because the Holy Quran is based on His knowledge, whatever the Holy Quran claims has to be supported by the testimony of natural laws.

The Holy Prophet[sa] did not personally possess the knowledge that Allah possesses. According to worldly terminology, to have declared him unlettered was a very appropriate epithet. The fact that he had no personal knowledge of the laws of nature is further supported by the following tradition:

> Ḥaḍrat Anas[ra] narrates from Ḥaḍrat 'Ā'ishah[ra] that once the Holy Prophet[sa] passed by a few farmers who were fertilizing the flowers of female date trees with the pollen of male trees. The Holy Prophet[sa] commented 'even if you do not take this trouble, the trees will be fertilized and bear fruit'. Accordingly, they stopped doing this, but that year the unfertilized trees did not bear any fruit at all. They reported this to the Holy Prophet[sa] to which he responded: 'If you have a worldly affair to decide, do it among yourselves. Only if the work is religious in nature refer it to me'.[44]

From this incident, it is definitely proved that the Holy Prophet's[sa] personal knowledge of science was so meagre that he did not even know how date trees were fertilized. Despite this, the repeated uncovering of scientific mysteries by the Holy Quran most certainly proves that the Holy Quran is the word of God and not that of the Holy Prophet[sa].

Evidence of Prophets[as] in Favour of other Prophets[as]

The category of evidence presented before is like a double-edged sword. On the one hand, the person who claims to have been spoken to by God must carry an incontrovertible proof. That proof lies in prophecies which he makes about the future. Similarly it speaks of the unknown past, that is to say, the past in relation to him. Although the knowledge of the time does not support such a claim, the claimant is proved right by the discoveries in the future as it is beyond his personal power to dominate the world of the unknown. This category of evidence is double-edged in the sense that it also serves as a proof of God's existence. If the claimant is right, then there has to be an All-Knowing, All-Powerful God who possesses the knowledge of the past as well as of the future alike, imparting the same to the claimant.

Now we turn to a new category of evidence which also works as a double-edged sword, vindicating the truth of past Prophets[as] and the Prophets[as] to come. This category of evidence is mentioned in the following verse:

وَمِنْ قَبْلِهٖ كِتٰبُ مُوۡسٰٓى اِمَامًا وَّرَحۡمَةً ؕ وَ هٰذَا كِتٰبٌ مُّصَدِّقٌ لِّسَانًا عَرَبِيًّا لِّيُنۡذِرَ الَّذِيۡنَ ظَلَمُوۡا ۖ وَ بُشۡرٰى لِلۡمُحۡسِنِيۡنَ ☐

> And before him *the Holy Prophet^sa* there was the book
> of Moses as a source of guidance and blessing. This,
> the Holy Quran, *works as* a testifier in a manifestly
> clear language to warn the people who have
> transgressed, and give glad tidings to those who do
> good deeds.
> (Sūrah al-Aḥqāf; Ch.46: V.13)

This verse connects Moses^as and the Holy Prophet^sa,
as testifying to each other's truth. In the same way, all
the Prophets^as of the past and future are
interconnected, each one bearing testimony to the
truth of the other. The whole import of this verse is
that the Prophet^sa about whose appearance Moses^as
had prophesied did come exactly as he had predicted,
and when he came he also testified to the truth of
Moses^as. In the same manner, the Torah testified to the
Holy Quran and the Holy Quran testified to the
Torah's truth. This works as a double bondage link
between the past Prophets^as and Books and the
Prophets^as and Books to come.

In addition to this, the Quran observes that
Moses^as was also testified to be true in his own
lifetime, by someone who bore a powerful testimony
in his favour. The verse reads:

قُلْ أَرَءَيْتُمْ إِنْ كَانَ مِنْ عِنْدِ اللّٰهِ وَكَفَرْتُمْ بِهٖ وَشَهِدَ
شَاهِدٌ مِّنْ بَنِيٓ إِسْرَآءِيْلَ عَلٰى مِثْلِهٖ فَأٰمَنَ وَاسْتَكْبَرْتُمْ إِنَّ اللّٰهَ
لَا يَهْدِى الْقَوْمَ الظّٰلِمِيْنَ ☐

> Say, have you ever considered that if he was from
> God and you had rejected him, while a person from
> the Children of Israel had testified to the truth of the
> advent of one similar to him, then while he believed
> you have rejected him out of arrogance. Verily, Allah
> does not guide the transgressors.
> (Sūrah al-Aḥqāf; Ch.46: V.11)

The Holy Quran refers to many of the followers of Moses[as] who, with reference to the Bible, had believed that one like Moses[as] would certainly come. This statement implies that the Jews at the time of the Holy Prophet[sa] did not only reject him but virtually rejected Moses[as] as well and those knowledgeable people who followed him. Pointing to the Jews of the Holy Prophet's[sa] time, the Holy Quran accuses them of their rejection only because of their arrogance, despite the testimony in his favour being very clear and precise.

A similar situation is often observed in the worldly courts. Some judges are fully convinced of the truth of the evidence but others find many excuses to reject the same evidence. They are either sadly mistaken or intentionally corrupt. Both these possibilities applied to some section of the Jews of the Holy Prophet's[sa] time. Many of those who were mistaken, ultimately rectified their attitude and finally declared their belief in him. Allah permits the wilful wrongdoers to wander in the wilderness of doubts because of their own wrongdoings.

The way the believers are so mercilessly treated

can be looked at from another aspect as well. The question genuinely arises whether the wrongdoers and the enemies of truth were ever treated like this by the Prophets[as] and their followers. The answer would be NEVER.

Once, a judge of the trial court at Quetta put the same question to the chief mullah of *Khatm-e-Nubuwwat* in Baluchistan. He specifically asked him if he could quote any example when the Holy Prophet[sa] and his followers treated their enemies as mercilessly and cruelly as the mullahs of this age are treating the Ahmadis. His answer which is recorded in the court, was, no, never. When further asked what was the attitude of the Holy Prophet's[sa] opponents, was it not similar to your attitude towards Ahmadis? The shameless answer was, yes, it was exactly the same. There ends the story of the so-called *Khatm-e-Nubuwwat*!

A Universal Principle Applicable to All Cases where a Testimony is Accepted or Rejected

Verse 3 of Sūrah al-Baqarah is a very comprehensive verse dealing with all similar situations:

$$ ذٰلِكَ الْكِتٰبُ لَا رَيْبَ ۛ فِيْهِ ۛ هُدًى لِّلْمُتَّقِيْنَ $$

This is a perfect book; there is no doubt in it; *it is* a guidance for the righteous.
(Sūrah al-Baqarah; Ch.2: V.3)

277

Commentators have offered many alternative explanations of this verse which depend on the stress made on a particular word during recitation. Although the book is without doubt the same as promised, but also there is no doubt that it would guide only the righteous ones. This is a universal principle that applies not only to the books but also to the Prophets[as]. It is universal also in the sense that it is applicable to the worldly courts equally.

The Holy Prophet[sa] is also presented as a universal witness of the truth of all the Prophets[as] of the world of every age. This is something special about him which one does not find in the case of Moses[as] and any other Prophets[as]. They testified to the truth of a future Prophet[as] but never testified to the Prophets[as] appearing in all other parts of the world in all other ages. This distinction of the Holy Prophet[sa] cannot be denied by the followers of any other religion. They monopolize the truth but the Holy Prophet[sa] did exactly the opposite. He taught his followers, according to the Holy Quran, that if they did not believe even in a single Prophet[as] other than him, it would be tantamount to rejecting him as well. That is why the Muslims must believe in the truth of all Prophets[as] appearing all over the world in every age, or they have to sever ties with the Prophet Muhammad[sa] himself. This aspect of the Quranic teaching does not show benevolence alone but also has an air of *Ītā'i Dhil-Qurbā*. To believe in other

Prophets[as] not because they had initially supported the Holy Prophet[sa] is benevolence, but more than that, the attitude of the Holy Prophet[sa] towards them is like that of parents towards their children.

Although, according to the Holy Quran, all previous religions and Prophets[as] had predicted the advent of the Holy Prophet[sa], unfortunately such prophecies were sadly misunderstood. Before his advent, either the said prophecies had already been misapplied to others, or the words were not so clear as to be understood as a prophecy regarding the future advent of a Prophet[as] or a Book. In the light of this, at the time of the Holy Prophet's[sa] advent, hardly any followers of other religions believed in him as the one predicted. So his benevolence to them was not a response to any visible kindness enacted by them towards him.

The followers of other Prophets[as] are virtually bound to reject the Holy Prophet[sa] in view of the aforementioned misunderstandings. Hence if a Jew rejects the Holy Prophet[sa], then according to the Jews, he does so in accordance with the Biblical teachings. If he believes in him, he is bound to reject Moses[as]. The same applies to the Christians, they must either reject the Prophet[sa] of Islam, or they would have to sever their ties with Jesus Christ[as]. This presents an amazing contrast between the two attitudes. This Islamic teaching possesses a comprehensive beauty containing balance, justice, benevolence and kindness towards one's kith and kin. The other religions of the world either do not mention the existence of other religions at all, or they have to believe them to be the product of impostors. As such, according to them, all other religions are the creation of false claimants.

Some Testimonies in Favour of the Holy Prophet^{sa} to be Fulfilled in the Future as many Testimonies were Fulfilled in the Past

The Holy Quran speaks not only of the testimony of Moses[as] and the Torah in favour of the Holy Prophet[sa]; it also speaks of a witness to appear in the future who would be born in his umma and would testify on his behalf. This witness is itself testified to be true by various kinds of evidence belonging to that age.

We present some relevant verses which support each other. The first one is as follows:

أَفَمَنْ كَانَ عَلٰى بَيِّنَةٍ مِّنْ رَّبِّهٖ وَيَتْلُوهُ شَاهِدٌ مِّنْهُ وَمِنْ قَبْلِهٖ
كِتٰبُ مُوْسٰى اِمَامًا وَّرَحْمَةً ؕ اُولٰٓئِكَ يُؤْمِنُوْنَ بِهٖ ؕ وَمَنْ يَّكْفُرْ
بِهٖ مِنَ الْاَحْزَابِ فَالنَّارُ مَوْعِدُهٗ ۫ فَلَا تَكُ فِيْ مِرْيَةٍ مِّنْهُ ۫
اِنَّهُ الْحَقُّ مِنْ رَّبِّكَ وَلٰكِنَّ اَكْثَرَ النَّاسِ لَا يُؤْمِنُوْنَ ⑰

Can he, then, be an impostor, who possesses a clear proof from his Lord, and *to testify to whose truth* a witness from Him shall follow him, and who was preceded by the Book of Moses, a guide and a mercy? Those *who consider these matters* believe therein, and whoever of the *opposing* parties disbelieves in it, Fire shall be his promised place. So be not in doubt about

it. Surely, it is the truth from your Lord; but most
people do not believe.
(Sūrah Hūd; Ch.11: V.18)

Then there are the verses of Sūrah al-Burūj 2-8
carrying the same argument further:

وَالسَّمَآءِ ذَاتِ الْبُرُوْجِ □ وَالْيَوْمِ الْمَوْعُوْدِ □ وَشَاهِدٍ وَّ مَشْهُوْدٍ □
قُتِلَ اَصْحٰبُ الْاُخْدُوْدِ □ النَّارِ ذَاتِ الْوَقُوْدِ □ اِذْهُمْ عَلَيْهَا قُعُوْدٌ □
وَّهُمْ عَلٰى مَا يَفْعَلُوْنَ بِالْمُؤْمِنِيْنَ شُهُوْدٌ □

By the heaven having mansions *of stars,*
And *by* the Promised Day,
And *by* the testifier and the one who is testified,
favour the witness is borne,
Cursed be the people of the trenches,
The fire *fed* with fuel–
As they sat by it,
And they witnessed what they did to the believers.
(Sūrah al-Burūj; Ch.85: Vs.2-8)

These multiple testimonies are required in support of
one whose era was to be continued until the end of
time. If the testimonies in support of him were to be
confined only to the past, their evidence would appear
to the future generations only as confined to history.

The mention in the Holy Quran of a powerful
witness to appear in the future in favour of the Holy
Prophet[sa], further strengthens the testimony of Moses[as]
in his favour. This is not just a prophecy but the
testimonies in favour of that witness comprise many
others which have already been fulfilled by now.

These brilliant testimonies not only work in his favour, they also prove to be dazzling signs in favour of the Holy Prophet[sa]. In the expression *Yatlūhu minhu*, it was automatically implied that the witness to follow would belong to him, being from his own umma.

It is amazing how most Muslims of the latter days are ignoring this great distinction of the Holy Prophet[sa] and do not bother to understand the nature of the witness in his favour. They do not visualize that the great witness would be distinct from all other Muslim divines of that age. Particularly, they fail to observe that the words *Shāhidun minhu* could simultaneously be translated as a witness on behalf of the Holy Prophet[sa] and a witness on behalf of God. This indicates that his testimony would not just be based on his own beliefs, but he would offer his testimony fulfilling the command of God. It means that it would be revealed to him by God to stand up and bear witness in favour of the Holy Prophet[sa].

This multiple interlinked chain of testimonies presented by the Holy Quran is also fully supported by many traditions of the Holy Prophet[sa], indicating the advent of the reformer of the latter days. All the repeated prophecies regarding the advent of a Mahdi and Messiah are only links of the same chain. Such a mutually supported interlinked series of witnesses is hard to find anywhere else.

Another Category of Evidence relating to the Age when the Holy Prophet^{sa} Claimed to be the Messenger from God

This evidence relates to the time when the Holy Quran was being revealed and the Holy Prophet^{sa} was physically present among his opponents. The relevant verse addressing this subject is as follows:

قُلْ لَّوْ شَآءَ اللّٰهُ مَا تَلَوْتُهٗ عَلَيْكُمْ وَلَاۤ اَدْرٰىكُمْ بِهٖ ۖ فَقَدْ لَبِثْتُ فِيْكُمْ عُمُرًا مِّنْ قَبْلِهٖ ؕ اَفَلَا تَعْقِلُوْنَ ☐

Say, 'If Allah had *so* willed, I should not have recited it to you nor would He have made it known to you. I have indeed lived among you a *whole* lifetime before this. Will you not then understand?'
(Sūrah Yūnus; Ch.10: V.17)

In this verse, the Holy Prophet^{sa} is presented as reminding his enemies that he is the same person who spent the larger part of his life among them. They themselves are witness that his long previous life of childhood, early youth and comparatively mature age extending up to forty years, were without blemish. During this long period of time not a blemish was cast on his character and truthfulness. The enemies who declared him to be a liar after his declaration that he was a Messenger of God, had themselves referred to him as the truest person in Arabia. The epithet of being the most trustworthy was showered on him by these very same opponents. How then could it be possible that the same true and trustworthy person, who never spoke a lie about his fellow human beings, was reproached for making a false claim against God? Thus his opponents, who largely belonged to Mecca, were reminded that they themselves were the erstwhile witnesses of his blameless character and truth, an argument which they could not refute.

It is noteworthy that by pointing to his previous life before the claim, the Holy Prophet[sa] implied that after the claim he is no longer spared of all blemishes and accusations. All true Prophets[as] are treated in the same way. During their life prior to the claim and during their life after the claim they are portrayed entirely differently. The same people who were previously lauded for being the best of the true are now being dubbed as the worst of the false. After the claim of Prophethood all are accused of the worst crimes. History relates no exception to this rule.

The enemies of Prophets[as] begin to allege after the claim is made that their life was not blameless even before. They may make these allegations, but they cannot produce the least evidence that they (the Prophets) were ever accused of even the slightest crime in their past life. This Quranic argument applies universally to all Prophets[as] of all ages; none was spared this fate. Another argument of similar nature but even more powerful, is presented in various verses of the Holy Quran. Repeatedly, the opponents of the Prophet[as] of the time blame him for disappointing them. They ask him if he is the same person in whom they had pinned high hopes of emerging as their leader. Now, they accuse him of not being worthy of even being their lowliest slave, let alone their most revered leader.

Another point to be observed is that no person can right from childhood entertain the ambition that one day, at the age of forty or thereabouts, he would claim Prophethood. In view of this ambition he could not have hypocritically posed to be pious throughout his life. It is simply impossible.

If this category of testimony is applied to the life of the Founder[as] of the Ahmadiyya Muslim Community, you would draw exactly the same inference as you could draw while applying this principle to the life of all other Prophets[as]. You can examine the life of the Promised Messiah[as] before his claim, you would inevitably draw the conclusion that he was becoming progressively more popular. Among closer circles in Qadian, the Hindus observed him from near. They saw his childhood, his early youth and decline of that youth until he stepped into the domain of old age. Likewise, the Sikhs, the atheists and the Christians also observed him. Those who knew him personally, whether they were rich or poor people, all saw him closely. All the testimonies you can gather will be found to be testifying to his truth and praising him for his excellent conduct throughout this period. None of the testimonies raised an accusing finger at even a semblance of a vice found in his person. However, there is no dearth of testimonies that since his childhood he was virtually owned by the mosque. His treatment of the poor at this tender age was that instead of eating his share of food at the table, he would take it out to the street and distribute it to whatever poor children he would come across.

In short, all the testimonies borne by friend or foe point out that he was an innocent child of pure soul, loving his God and fellow human beings. Those who make sacrifices for the sake of the poor and serve the cause of humanity as he did, and are never accused of inappropriate behaviour, and hypocrisy, from childhood through to old age, verily, to them applies the Quranic criterion:

$$\square\ \bar{\text{ن}}\text{وُلِقْعَت}\ \text{َلَفَأ}\ \text{ِهِلْبَق}\ \text{نِّم}\ \text{اًرُمُع}\ \text{مُكْيِف}\ \text{ُثْثِبَل}\ \text{ْدَقَف...}$$

...I have indeed lived among you a *whole* lifetime before this. Will you not then understand?
(Sūrah Yūnus; Ch.10: V.17)

19 The Recording System Operative in the Entire Universe

Now in this context, the question arises about the status of testimony by God and the angels on the Day of Judgement. If you peruse the teaching of other religions, you cannot fail to notice that this category of evidence is only prominent by its absence.

The Holy Quran does not claim that you will be committed only on the strength of God's and the angels' testimony. Had this been the Quranic attitude, humans would have objected by declaring that the angels are not like humans. They do not possess the same passions and inner motives to commit sin. Hence, their testimony about human passion and motivations cannot be considered adequate by itself. There also has to be human testimony against humans.

A famous Urdu poet Ghālib raises the same question in one of his couplets:

پکڑے جاتے ہیں فرشتوں کے لکھے پر ناحق

آدمی کوئی ہمارا دمِ تحریر بھی تھا؟

We are being caught without justification by the testimony of angels alone,

Was there any human witness as well, at the time of recording this testimony?

The Holy Quran goes much further than that; it speaks of the testimony of each criminal against himself. Thus he will be convicted not on the evidence of other humans but by his own confession. The unspoken answer by God to such as Ghālib would be: *no other human would be needed to testify against you. You yourselves will testify against your own motives and acts of crime.* A confession such as this requires no outward testimony, be it of angels or humans. This category of testimony by humans against themselves is mentioned in many verses of the Holy Quran. In short, the confession of the criminal would fully support the testimony of God and the angels against him. The Divine recording system is all comprehensive. According to the following verse of the Holy Quran, on the Day of Judgement man will exclaim with awe and wonder as to the all-comprising nature of this testimony. Man will say,

$$ \text{...} \, \text{يَوَيْلَتَنَا مَالِ هٰذَا الْكِتٰبِ لَا يُغَادِرُ صَغِيْرَةً وَّلَا كَبِيْرَةً إِلَّا آحْصٰهَا} \, \text{...} $$

...'O woe to us! What kind of a Book is this! It leaves out nothing small or great but has recorded it'....
(Sūrah al-Kahf; Ch.18: V.50)

This means that the record presented before the criminal would be so perfect that the criminal himself would not remember all these details until reminded by this record. Once a thing happens it can never be obliterated out of existence.

The same subject is further elaborated in the Holy Quran in Chapter Luqmān verse 17, when Luqmān[as] admonishes his son in the following words:

يٰبُنَيَّ اِنَّهَآ اِنْ تَكُ مِثْقَالَ حَبَّةٍ مِّنْ خَرْدَلٍ فَتَكُنْ فِيْ صَخْرَةٍ

اَوْ فِي السَّمٰوٰتِ اَوْ فِي الْاَرْضِ يَاْتِ بِهَا اللّٰهُ ۽ اِنَّ اللّٰهَ لَطِيْفٌ خَبِيْرٌ ☐

'O my dear son! even though it be the weight of a grain of mustard seed, and even though it be in a rock, or in the heavens, or in the earth, Allah will surely bring it out; verily Allah is the Knower of all subtleties, All-Aware.'
(Sūrah Luqmān; Ch.31: V.17)

During the age when the above verses were revealed to the Holy Prophet[sa], no man on earth could imagine by the farthest stretch of his imagination, that all big and small things are being automatically recorded by an unseen Divine system. The verses clearly indicate that Prophet Muhammad[sa] was informed by a Being who knew of what was unknown at that time and what was known.

If you visit a planetarium, you will be able to witness for yourself how the sound of the Big Bang around twenty billion years ago is still vibrating in the atmosphere. When, with the help of delicate scientific instruments, it is enlarged by many hundredfold, the human ear can still catch its resonance.

When archaeologists dig for the past buried remains, they can uncover things that happened millions or even billions of years ago and can hear the unworded tale they tell of the time when they were fossilised. This unravelling of their tales is not yet over. As man progresses, more of the past will continue to dawn upon him. Even those animals who have become extinct have left a complete fossilised record in their skeletons about the age when they were fossilised.

Students of archaeology can read many minute details of the nature of the animal; the diseases it suffered from, its potentials, its capabilities and incapabilities, how fast it could run, how tall it was and what was the nature of its food. Was it carnivorous or herbivorous? What was the nature of its habits—was it brave or cowardly, intelligent or stupid? Thus the animals inhabiting the globe, the way they moved about and rested, and their mode of life are gradually being uncovered, long after they perished (in some cases billions of years later), providing a complete life history.

Similarly, human fossils of the comparatively near past are subjected to minute scientific studies and the scientists can assert with great authority that a fossil of a certain dead person can reveal the minutest detail of the disease which caused his death. For instance, it can be ascertained if the death was caused by some venereal disease such as syphilis or gonorrhoea. In short, everything is inscribed and every inscription is talking.

If man, despite his limited knowledge, can read and comprehend these writings of the past, how stupid it would be of him to live under the misconception that his own personal record has escaped the Divine recording system. Thus he forgets that he will be confronted one day with whatever he had been doing in the past and will be convicted on the strength of this indelible evidence. The One who created this system is far better equipped to read its inherent messages than the archaeologists of today. If man studies this system more minutely, he would be terrified to realise that the hidden voices in the recesses of his heart, as yet in their formative state, are also being recorded. Likewise, the intention of committing evil, as yet dreamily turning over in its bed of creation, does not escape this recording either. How can man run away from the hour of questioning?

Elaborating upon this subject further, the Holy Prophet[sa] adds to it the subject of limitless forgiveness of God when He so desires. The Holy Prophet[sa] spoke in a parable, telling the tale of a sinful person who had crossed every limit of transgression and had completely fulfilled his desire to commit every possible sin. When death was about to overtake him, he admonished his children to burn his corpse to ashes. Having done so they should scatter these ashes on a windy day over land and water to abolish all record of his life. According to the Holy Prophet[sa], when this man will be reconstructed from his apparently irretrievable ashes on the Day of Judgement, he would be quietly questioned by God as to why he did this. His answer would be: 'Only because I feared you'. God would reply: 'I have the power to forgive those who are afraid of me. If I so decide.' Thus God would forgive this greatest sinner on earth after gaining full command over him.[45]

This tradition does not encourage the criminal to commit crimes. It only tells him that God can forgive him if He so pleases, so he should never lose hope of His forgiveness. He should abstain from committing crime as much as he can but he should never permit himself to sink into despair about the crimes he committed, always having faith in God's limitless mercy. During all this one should never entertain the thought that one can escape God's punishment by deceiving Him. Such stupid childish endeavours remind me of a young boy whom I once saw saying his prayer in the mosque so rapidly as though he were a hen pecking at grain. I did not have to wait long till he finished. When I enquired as to why he was behaving like this he answered, 'I am only fulfilling an obligation to God. How can He know that I am only playfully appeasing Him? Who is seriously praying— not me!' He was merely an ignorant child, but woe to the so-called great scholars who claim to believe they know the ins and outs of religion but waste their entire life trying to mislead God. None can mislead Him. Some verses from Chapter Ḥā Mīm al-Sajdah declare:

...شَهِدَ عَلَيْهِمْ سَمْعُهُمْ وَ اَبْصَارُهُمْ وَجُلُوْدُهُمْ بِمَا كَانُوْا يَعْمَلُوْنَ☐ وَ قَالُوْا لِجُلُوْدِهِمْ لِمَ شَهِدْتُّمْ عَلَيْنَا ۚ قَالُوْٓا اَنْطَقَنَا اللّٰهُ الَّذِيْٓ اَنْطَقَ كُلَّ شَيْءٍ وَّهُوَ خَلَقَكُمْ اَوَّلَ مَرَّةٍ وَّ اِلَيْهِ تُرْجَعُوْنَ☐ وَمَا كُنْتُمْ تَسْتَتِرُوْنَ اَنْ يَّشْهَدَ عَلَيْكُمْ سَمْعُكُمْ وَ لَآ اَبْصَارُكُمْ وَ لَاجُلُوْدُ كُمْ وَلٰكِنْ ظَنَنْتُمْ اَنَّ اللّٰهَ لَا يَعْلَمُ كَثِيْرًا مِّمَّا تَعْمَلُوْنَ☐

...their ears and their eyes and their skins will bear witness against them as to what they had been doing. And they will say to their skins: 'Why bear you witness against us?' They will say: 'Allah has made us to speak as He has made everything *else* to speak. And He it is Who created you the first time, and unto Him have you been brought back. And you did not fear *while committing sins* that your ears and your eyes and your skins would bear witness against you, nay, you thought that *even* Allah did not know much of what you used to do.'
(Sūrah Ḥā Mīm al-Sajdah; Ch.41: Vs.21-23)

Most often, man behaves like a pigeon shutting his eyes upon seeing a cat, and imagines that the cat is not observing him. Or like an ostrich who, while he buries his head under the sand, believes he has disappeared from the sight of all around. Such people who waste their life believing that they are not only hidden from the sight of fellow human beings but also from the sight of God, would be roundly condemned by the following verse: 'Nay, you thought that *even* Allah did not know much of what you used to do.'

20 Covenants, their Different Categories, Punishments and Rewards

Covenant of Man with God

As far as covenants are concerned, this subject has also been further discussed in the Holy Quran. In the verses of the Holy Quran, there is such great order as binds them in harmony and, in a beautiful way, interlinks and mutually relates them.

اِنَّ الَّذِیۡنَ یُبَایِعُوۡنَکَ اِنَّمَا یُبَایِعُوۡنَ اللّٰہَ ۟ یَدُ اللّٰہِ فَوۡقَ اَیۡدِیۡہِمۡ ۚ فَمَنۡ نَّکَثَ فَاِنَّمَا یَنۡکُثُ عَلٰی نَفۡسِہٖ ۚ وَ مَنۡ اَوۡفٰی بِمَا عٰہَدَ عَلَیۡہُ اللّٰہَ فَسَیُؤۡتِیۡہِ اَجۡرًا عَظِیۡمًا ☐

Verily, those who swear allegiance to you indeed swear allegiance to Allah. The hand of Allah is over their hands. So whoever breaks *his oath*, breaks *it* to his own loss; and whoever fulfils the covenant that he has made with Allah, He will surely give him a great reward.
(Sūrah al-Fatḥ; Ch.48: V.11)

The first thing that we need to determine here is whether man is authorised to take a covenant on behalf of God at the hand of another man. The wording of this verse resolves this question perfectly. It declares that unless Muhammad's[sa] hand was representing the hand of God, no man has a right to bear an oath of allegiance at his[sa] hand. It presents the Prophet's[sa] hand accepting the oath of allegiance from other humans as a proxy for God. This is because a person who contracts on behalf of another person has to be duly authorised. Throughout the Holy Quran, in the case of the oath of allegiance at the hands of all Prophets[as], the Holy Quran speaks of them as recipients of God's revelation before they were authorised to take the oath of allegiance of other humans. This indicates that man may never bow in religious obedience to another human, unless he has previously prostrated himself to the will of God. Had it not been so, to bow to the will of the Prophet[sa] could have been taken as idolatry. By not comprehending the true import of this verse some people have actually alleged the Holy Quran to be teaching idolatry while in fact it is exactly the opposite.

The Bahais in particular raise this objection and once I had the experience of successfully confronting a Bahai on this issue. In a question and answer session, a Bahai challenged me by referring to the same verse I have quoted. He argued that the statement that 'they are only taking the oath of allegiance to God' cannot be considered as metaphorical because the remaining verse removes this understanding by explaining that: over the hands of those who are taking the oath of allegiance is actually the hand of God and not of Muhammad[sa].

Then I explained everything to him in detail as I have explained before you and hope that he understood because there was no further attempt on his part to rebut my argument. However, whether he understood or not, the people around him present in the session fully understood and vehemently nodded in agreement. If a man falsely claims to be representing God and commands obedience of others on this strength, in reality he is trying to misappropriate the authority of God.

The same is discussed by Allah in relation to all Prophets[as] beginning with Adam[as]. The precondition for obedience to Adam[as] is for him to be obedient to Allah. Only when he bows his head to the revelation he receives is he authorised to expect obedience to himself from others. Hence, obedience to Adam[as] is tantamount to obedience to God otherwise no one is bound to obey Adam[as]. After this explanation if you re-read the verses relating to the obedience to Adam[as], you would comprehend this subject much better.

In Chapter Ṣād, the Holy Quran relates:

اِذْ قَالَ رَبُّكَ لِلْمَلٰٓئِكَةِ اِنِّيْ خَالِقٌۢ بَشَرًا مِّنْ طِيْنٍ ☐ فَاِذَا سَوَّيْتُهٗ وَنَفَخْتُ فِيْهِ مِنْ رُّوْحِيْ فَقَعُوْا لَهٗ سٰجِدِيْنَ ☐

When your Lord said to the angels, 'I am about to create man from clay,
And so when I have fashioned him *in perfection,* and have breathed into him of My Spirit, fall you down in submission to him.'
(Sūrah Ṣād; Ch.38: Vs.72-73)

The perfection of Adam[as] after having been created from clay only indicates the perfection of his physical evolution. Having achieved this, he is still not authorised to rule others. He is only authorised to rule others after Allah has breathed into him. Here 'breathing of my spirit' means revelation and *Sawwaituhū* سَوَّيْتُهُ (fashioned him in perfection) only refers to all the evolutionary stages which gradually transformed clay into a perfected human being.

The medieval Muslim ulema have failed to understand the meaning of perfection. Perhaps they have been influenced by the crude Biblical account. They visualise the creation of first man as an earthen deaf and dumb statue made by a human artist. Like the artist, God moulded and shaped the first man by suppressing some features and highlighting others. Thus, by putting extra touches here and there, He added all the finishing features and gave him a beautiful human form. Until then he remained a statue without a sign of life. Then God said: 'I have breathed into him My Spirit, and suddenly he became alive'. This is a childish explanation of the verse, insupportable by the phrase used in the Holy Quran. How could God breathe His own spirit, or a portion thereof, into him? Alas! the medieval ulema did not realise that nowhere does the Holy Quran mention infusing life into him. Otherwise, at least somewhere, the Holy Quran could have used some other unambiguous expression. It could simply state: then I made him alive.

The true meaning of breathing of spirit can be easily understood by referring to another verse of the Holy Quran throwing light on the process of creation of spirit. The Holy Quran declares:

$$ \text{وَيَسْتَلُوۡنَكَ عَنِ الرُّوۡحِ ۖ قُلِ الرُّوۡحُ مِنۡ اَمۡرِ رَبِّیۡ ...} $$

They enquire from you about the nature of soul. Say 'the soul is by the Command of my Lord'; ...
(Sūrah Banī Isrā'īl; Ch.17: V.86)

The soul is evidently the Word of God and the same idiom is used in the Old Testament, referring to the Word of God to be eternal with Him. The New Testament also refers to Jesus as being the Word of God, which only means the soul granted to him by God's word.

The Covenant of Prophets[as]

As for the Prophets[as] themselves, before they take covenants from others they have to make a covenant with God. This covenant holds no exception; it binds each Prophet[as] with God as well as with each other. This covenant of Prophets[as] is far above the covenants which other humans make with each other. With the blessing of their covenant with God, they are entitled to be called *Khalīfatullāh* or vicegerent of God. After this covenant, it becomes impossible for them to attribute anything to God without His approval. Even in worldly courts, it is the custom that every witness has to take an oath in the presence of the judge that he will tell the truth, the whole truth and nothing but the truth. That same judge, before his appointment, has himself had to take an oath before higher authorities that he would dispense everything with justice.

Addressing Prophet Muhammad[sa], Allah says:

وَ اِذۡ اَخَذۡنَا مِنَ النَّبِیّٖنَ مِیۡثَاقَهُمۡ وَ مِنۡكَ وَ مِنۡ نُّوۡحٍ وَّ اِبۡرٰهِیۡمَ وَ مُوۡسٰی وَ عِیۡسَی ابۡنِ مَرۡیَمَ ۫ وَ اَخَذۡنَا مِنۡهُمۡ مِّیۡثَاقًا غَلِیۡظًا ۟ لِّیَسۡـَٔلَ الصّٰدِقِیۡنَ عَنۡ صِدۡقِهِمۡ ۚ وَ اَعَدَّ لِلۡكٰفِرِیۡنَ عَذَابًا اَلِیۡمًا ۟

And *remember* when We took from the Prophets their covenant, and from you, and from Noah, and Abraham and Moses, and Jesus, son of Mary, and We *indeed* took from them a solemn covenant;
That He may question the truthful about their truthfulness. And for the disbelievers He has prepared a painful punishment.
(Sūrah al-Aḥzāb; Ch.33: Vs.8-9)

The detail of what the covenant of Prophets[as] was, is not mentioned here. However, the purpose of this covenant is clearly specified in the portion of the verse:

لِّیَسۡـَٔلَ الصّٰدِقِیۡنَ عَنۡ صِدۡقِهِمۡ

which means so that Allah will certainly enquire from the true people about the authority of their truth. Whereas the Prophets[as] are authorised to take the covenant from fellow human beings on behalf of God, they must produce the evidence of their own truth. They also require a binding covenant upon them to remain truthful. This is the same covenant as mentioned above. Thus, all heads are bowed before God as a result of this covenant, and they are made answerable to Him because of it. That is why Allah mentions that for each people their own Book would work as the touchstone of the truth. No people would be held answerable by the standard of the Books revealed to other people. This is clearly mentioned in the verse:

$$كُلُّ أُمَّةٍ تُدْعَى إِلَى كِتَابِهَا$$

(Sūrah al-Jāthiyah; Ch.45: V.29)

That is to say, each people will be summoned to their own book and they would be questioned according to that book on the Day of Judgement.

Glory be to Allah that He took one covenant from the Prophets[as] to make them answerable before Him and authorised them to take a covenant from their people about their belief in, and support offered to, the future Prophets[as]. This covenant is not preserved in so many words in Books other than the Holy Quran, but most certainly the implication of this covenant can be traced to those Books. Thus this chain of covenants goes full circle. The actual wording of this covenant is mentioned in the following verse:

301

وَإِذۡ أَخَذَ اللّٰهُ مِيثَاقَ النَّبِيّٖنَ لَمَآ اٰتَيۡتُكُمۡ مِّنۡ كِتٰبٍ
وَّحِكۡمَةٍ ثُمَّ جَآءَكُمۡ رَسُوۡلٌ مُّصَدِّقٌ لِّمَا مَعَكُمۡ لَتُؤۡمِنُنَّ
بِهٖ وَلَتَنۡصُرُنَّهٗ، قَالَ ءَاَقۡرَرۡتُمۡ وَاَخَذۡتُمۡ عَلٰى ذٰلِكُمۡ اِصۡرِيۡ،
قَالُوۡۤا اَقۡرَرۡنَا، قَالَ فَاشۡهَدُوۡا وَاَنَا مَعَكُمۡ مِّنَ الشّٰهِدِيۡنَ ☐

And *remember the time* when Allah took a covenant
from *the people through* the Prophets[as], *saying*:
'Whatever I give you of the Book and Wisdom *and*
then there comes to you a Messenger, fulfilling that
which is with you, you shall believe in him and help
him.' *And* He said: 'Do you agree, and do you accept
the responsibility which I lay upon you in this *matter*?'
They said, 'We agree;' He said, 'Then bear witness,
and I am with you among the witnesses'.
(Sūrah āl-e-'Imrān; Ch.3: V.82)

This shows that for future Prophets[as] to be supported,
they must themselves testify to the truth of the
previous Prophets[as] and to the truth of their
fundamental teachings.

The Book evidently comprises the Divine verses
revealed to a Prophet by God. These verses contain all
the do's and don'ts. The word *Ḥikmah* (wisdom)
refers to discourses of the Prophets[as], who teach the
underlying philosophy of the do's and don'ts of the
Book.

Both these tasks of the Holy Prophet[sa] are
mentioned in the following portion of the verse of
Surah Jumu'ah that he:

$$\cdots \stackrel{\text{\textarabic{ةَمَكْحِلْا}}}{} \text{\textarabic{وَ الْكِتٰبَ}} \text{\textarabic{يُعَلِّمُهُمُ}} \cdots$$

… teaches them the Book and wisdom…
(Sūrah al-Jumu'ah; Ch.62: V.3)

Prophets[as] who do not bring new Books but follow another Law-bearing Prophet, continue this work of explaining the wisdom of the Book to the future generations who face new challenges to justify their teaching. The covenant of Prophets[as] does not leave out the possibility of a non Law-bearing Prophet[as] following a Law-bearing Prophet[as]. The people of the Law-bearing Prophet[as] cannot object to their appearance by declaring; the Book has already been revealed and its wisdom has already been taught to us, what more can you add to this? In answer to this inherent question, the covenant clearly dictates that even the Prophets[as] who do not bring a new Book but testify to the previous one, may not be rejected as superfluous because they would serve the cause of the previous Book and further explain its wisdom in response to the new challenges. To support such a Prophet would be to one's own advantage.

This covenant of the Prophets[as], fully discussed in Sūrah āl-e-'Imrān, is also mentioned to have been taken from the Holy Prophet[sa] in Sūrah al-Aḥzāb. This verse found in the same Sūrah (al-Aḥzāb) speaks of Ḥaḍrat Muḥummad[sa] as being *Khātamun Nabiyyīn*. If the word *Khātam* is to be translated as the last of the Prophets[as] after whom no Prophet of any description can ever come, then why was there any need for taking the same covenant from the Holy Prophet[sa] as well. Evidently, non Law-bearing Prophets[as], fully subordinate to him, were to appear in his own umma (people), fully testifying to his teaching and supporting him. According to this verse, they must also be fully supported by the umma of the Holy Prophet[sa].

It should be remembered that in the covenant taken from the Prophets[as], it is meant that their followers would support the future Prophets[as] because at the time of their appearance, the Prophets[as] from whom the covenant was taken would certainly have died.

The Covenant of the People of the Book

Again, the Holy Quran mentions a covenant as the covenant of the people of the Book, which clearly describes the responsibilities on their shoulders after they have accepted the Book to be from God. It is amazing how the Holy Quran does not leave out any category of religious contracts.

The covenant in question is mentioned in the following words:

وَإِذْ أَخَذَ اللّٰهُ مِيثَاقَ الَّذِيْنَ أُوْتُوا الْكِتٰبَ لَتُبَيِّنُنَّهُ لِلنَّاسِ وَلَا تَكْتُمُوْنَهُ ۖ فَنَبَذُوْهُ وَرَآءَ ظُهُوْرِهِمْ وَاشْتَرَوْا بِهٖ ثَمَنًا قَلِيْلًا ۖ فَبِئْسَ مَا يَشْتَرُوْنَ ☐

> And *remember* when Allah took a covenant from those who were given the Book, *saying*, 'You shall make this *Book* known to the people and not conceal it'. But they threw it away behind their backs, and bartered it for a paltry price. Evil is that which they have purchased.
>
> (Sūrah āl-e-'Imrān; Ch.3: V.188)

The covenant is not an ordinary contract, it is far more binding on those who pledge their allegiance. So the Holy Quran speaks of the people of the Book as a party of the covenant and as such they will be held more strictly responsible for any breach of it on their part. The essence of the covenant was that they would certainly convey the teaching of their Prophets^{as} to the future generations without any change or concealment. Even if they considered some wording of the teaching to go against their held beliefs, they would still convey the full text without interpolation. The matter of the final decision would be left to the people themselves. They could judge after hearing their side as well as hearing the side of the opposite camp. Then, whatever conclusion they could draw would be their responsibility and not that of the scholars. But the Holy Quran declares that the scholars of the Book did not keep their part of the covenant and sold it for a paltry price.

Whenever Messengers^{as} of God are rejected, they are rejected because of the breach of contract of the previous people. The same happened at the time of the

Holy Prophet[sa]. Had the Jews not been guilty of the breach of contract, they would have revealed to the people those Biblical prophecies which the Muslims construe as applicable to the advent of the Prophet[sa] of Islam. They did not do so and concealed some of the prophecies as originally mentioned. Of course, they had every right to interpret them differently, but they had no right to interpolate them as they did. Because most often the common people do not have a personal knowledge of the Book, they trust their religious scholars that their version of the Book must have been right.

In the present times, the mullahs who oppose Ahmadiyyat are guilty of the same breach of contract as the Jews were at the time of the Holy Prophet[sa]. Why do they not speak of the full context of the verse *Khātamun Nabīyyīn* and the verses preceding and following it? They, too, like the Jewish ulema, had every right to interpret those verses to suit their own beliefs; but not to speak of the entire context is like hiding that part which goes against them. Habitually, they never mention the verse which binds the Holy Prophet[sa] to the same covenant of Prophets[as] as taken from all earlier Prophets[as]. This is so because it clearly goes against their interpretation of the verse *Khātamun Nabiyyīn*.

See how the Holy Quran observes human nature so minutely. It warns against the pitfalls of the crookedness of the heart and the faltering of the ego, lest the people should complain of not having been forewarned. The breach of contracts always deprives people of being guided to the right path. This verse equally applies to all ulema who turn their religion into a source of income. They are liable to make grave errors of judgement when their personal gain is at stake. Religious values are most often sacrificed at the cost of their prime object i.e. the earning of their livelihood. The main source of livelihood of a great majority of the Indo-Pakistan ulema is based on whatever is doled out to them by their government of common people. It is a great trial for them to clearly quote the Quranic verses against the distorted common beliefs. The same was the case of the village ulema who had to survive on a piece of bread or two given to them by the landlords of the village. But it is not just a matter of livelihood, many among these so-called religious leaders have an unlimited craving for amassing wealth. No matter what they get, the hell of their avarice can never be satiated. When such is the state of affairs and their degradation sinks to rock bottom, they no longer care for truth. When, for the reformation of such as them, a Prophet or Reformer is raised by God, they turn his rejection into another means of earning wealth. The louder they cry against him, the more popular they become among the masses and the governments of the time.

The Holy Quran describes this transgressive attitude, which is confined to no limits, in the following verse:

وَتَجْعَلُوْنَ رِزْقَكُمْ اَنَّكُمْ تُكَذِّبُوْنَ ☐

And do you make the denial thereof your *means of livelihood*?
(Sūrah al-Wāqi'ah; Ch.56: V.83)

By denial, this verse refers to the denial of the Reformers of the time. Thus, the breaking of covenants is no ordinary crime. It is a progressively fatal disease of the spirit.

Punishment for the Breaking of the Covenant Binding on the Entire People

In the following verse, the Holy Quran speaks of a punishment to the whole people as a result of their breaking their covenant:

فَبِمَا نَقْضِهِمْ مِّيْثَاقَهُمْ لَعَنَّهُمْ وَجَعَلْنَا قُلُوْبَهُمْ قٰسِيَةً ﴿
يُحَرِّفُوْنَ الْكَلِمَ عَنْ مَّوَاضِعِهٖ، وَنَسُوْا حَظًّا مِّمَّا ذُكِّرُوْا بِهٖ
وَلَا تَزَالُ تَطَّلِعُ عَلٰى خَآئِنَةٍ مِّنْهُمْ اِلَّا قَلِيْلًا مِّنْهُمْ فَاعْفُ عَنْهُمْ
وَاصْفَحْ، اِنَّ اللّٰهَ يُحِبُّ الْمُحْسِنِيْنَ ☐

So, because of their breaking their covenant, We have cursed them, and have hardened their hearts. They pervert the words from their *proper* places and have forgotten a *good* part of that with which they were exhorted. And you will not cease to discover treachery on their part, except *in* a few of them. So pardon them

and show forbearance. Surely, Allah loves those who
do good.
(Sūrah al-Mā'idah; Ch.5: V.14)

This verse mentions in detail the reasons resulting in
God's wrath upon them. It does not require much
prudence to infer that the punishment mentioned here
is of such a nature as results in further punishment.
The punishment of this crime hardens their hearts and
emboldens them to commit more crimes, each
bringing a new punishment in its wake. Addressing
such people, the Holy Quran warns them that this
progressive tendency to commit crime would
ultimately lead to destruction.

The curse of God is what initiates this process,
which means that such people as break their
covenants gradually move away from God. Thus, the
signs of nearness to God are ultimately completely
wiped out from their daily life until they fully deserve
to be entitled 'the cursed'. The second characteristic of
these people is mentioned to be the hardening of their
hearts. The same hardening commands their religious
as well as their worldly affairs. The hard-heartedness
of the Jews has become a byword but the same applies
to all those who commit the crime of breaking their
covenant. This hardening is a natural consequence of
their crime. Thus, you will observe that such violators
of covenants do not only incur the wrath of God, but
also that of the people. In turn, they become callous of
the suffering of common people and distance

themselves from their plight. They only show concern for them hypocritically to gain their support.

Apparently, Christian nations are softhearted and so is their original teaching but a different picture emerges when you analyse their national attitude critically. In totality, their attitude to the poor nations is hard-hearted and it is their economic policies towards their nations which continue to make them stricken with greater poverty. The current system of Capitalism and the universal banking system based on interest owes its existence to the two peoples of the Book, i.e. the Jews and the Christians. This merciless set-up continues to widen the gap between the rich and the poor. The third characteristic mentioned in the verse is their tendency to twist words to interpret a covenant or law to their own advantage. This is the essence of diplomacy in the modern world.

In the religious world their clerics show the same tendency. They play the same game with their own Scriptures and their religious followers. They never feel ashamed of distorting the true import of their teaching. Another characteristic of such people is with regard to their discriminative attitude. They do not abandon the Divine Law altogether but only pick and choose between the do's and the don'ts to suit their own advantage.

Thus, the study of the history of such people reveals that they never abandon their Divine Ordinance altogether but stick fast to a part of it and rescind a part thereof. According to the Holy Quran, such people do not break their trust only with God, but do it habitually to each other. There are only a few exceptions of those whom God guards against this disease. The entire people do not become corrupt, only their majority does. Looking at this from another angle, one can conclude that the seeming punishment is a natural consequence of their own diseases rather than something imposed from the outside.

Looking at it from this angle intensifies in the mind of the observer the importance of justice. The breaking of a covenant is a grave disregard of justice which finally results in diseases with multiple fatal consequences. Where these punishments are enumerated, the adherence to justice by God Himself is also highlighted. The verse points out to the believers that they must not condemn an entire people without exception, of corruption, dishonesty and break of trust. The exception is mentioned in the words اِلَّا قَلِيلًا مِّنْهُمْ, 'Except a few from among them'. Allah knows full well that among them are many pious, God-fearing and trustworthy people. Caution is essential for human beings in condemning others because they are not All-Knowing as God is.

Addressing the same subject of violation of covenants, the Holy Quran mentions another ill-consequence of the same, which according to this part of the verse (13:26) اُولٰٓئِكَ لَهُمُ اللَّعْنَةُ وَلَهُمْ سُوٓءُ الدَّارِ 'On them is the curse and they shall have a grievous abode', describes it as a curse of their final abode. The words *Sū'uddār* can be taken to mean their final abode after death or the final abode in their pursuits of earthly life.

A Mutual Balance between Crime and Punishment

God has meted out to every people a punishment for their violation of covenant which is intrinsically linked with their crime. In relation to those who claim to be Christians, the Holy Quran states that because of the violation of a part of their covenant at the hand of Jesus Christ[as], We caused enmity and hatred between them till the Day of Doom. The verse reads:

وَمِنَ الَّذِيْنَ قَالُوٓا اِنَّا نَصٰرٰى اَخَذْنَا مِيْثَاقَهُمْ فَنَسُوْا حَظًّا مِّمَّا ذُكِّرُوْا بِهٖ ۪ فَاَغْرَيْنَا بَيْنَهُمُ الْعَدَاوَةَ وَ الْبَغْضَآءَ اِلٰى يَوْمِ الْقِيٰمَةِ ؕ وَ سَوْفَ يُنَبِّئُهُمُ اللّٰهُ بِمَا كَانُوْا يَصْنَعُوْنَ ☐

And from those *also* who say, 'We are Christians', We took a covenant, but they too have forgotten a *good* part of that with which they were exhorted. So We made mutual enmity and hatred their lot till the Day of Resurrection. And Allah will soon let them know what they have been doing.
(Sūrah al-Mā'idah; Ch.5: V.15)

The import of this verse has already been fulfilled in an amazing manner. The Christian nations, though united in their interest against others, are disunited in their interest regarding each other and repeatedly come to war when their national interest clashes with that of other Christian nations. The same thing happened in the Americas, time and time again, and also in the history of other Christian nations in Europe.

God punishes in accordance with the crime. They (the Christians) violated one aspect of their covenant and were punished accordingly. Although the Holy Quran specifies the punishment it does not specify the crime. It is so because the very punishment speaks of the crime they must have committed.

The punishment imposed on them is that they will nurture a secret hatred against each other and will be mutually targeted by it till Doomsday. This means that the Christian nations will always fight against each other. Consequently, we observed this happening in the Christian world. In the First World War, we saw the same and in the Second World War the same thing happened as well. This was a universal conflict, but they behave the same way in regional conflicts. This mutual animosity is destined to continue forever. Their colonial history reveals that during enslavement of other nations, wherever and whenever their interests clashed, their conflicts flared up into wars. This is so because they do not use the same yardstick for measuring justice, but each claims to be the proponent of justice. The same history was repeated in India during the partition and in all African states when various tribes were pitched against other tribes. It happened in the Americas from North to South which always divided the Christians into two opposing camps. In their political history, their continuous bifurcation into two opposing camps is their punishment mentioned in the Holy Quran. Hence, the inference is not far-fetched that their crime was to split the person of God despite the claim of His Unity. Jesus Christ[as] never claimed that God was a splittable Person. They violated his teaching and created an internal split which became their own destiny. Hence, believing in One God as was admonished by Jesus[as], they attempted to split Him apart internally.

Some more Punishments in Accordance with the Violation of Covenants

The Holy Quran relates many punishments relating to the violation of covenants. Perhaps in no other Divine book can one find the mention of a similar series of interrelated punishments. In the Bible, however, we find some punishments prescribed in relation to the crimes committed. The Holy Quran, while analysing the history of crimes mentioned in the Bible, only chooses such examples as are applicable to all decadent religions in the world. These punishments are not described in relation to any specific religion, but the crimes generally mentioned are those commonly found among the followers of perverted religions.

In this connection, Islam does not specify Judaism, Christianity, Hinduism or any other religion separately, but, during the decadence of religions, whatever psychological diseases raise their heads among them are enlisted as categories. Such violators of covenants are mentioned in the following verse of the Holy Quran, with some additional punishments by way of the wrath of Allah to be incurred by them:

إِنَّ الَّذِيْنَ يَشْتَرُوْنَ بِعَهْدِ اللّٰهِ وَ اَيْمَانِهِمْ ثَمَنًا قَلِيْلًا

اُولٰٓئِكَ لَا خَلَاقَ لَهُمْ فِي الْاٰخِرَةِ وَلَا يُكَلِّمُهُمُ اللّٰهُ وَ لَا يَنْظُرُ

اِلَيْهِمْ يَوْمَ الْقِيٰمَةِ وَ لَا يُزَكِّيْهِمْ ۪ وَلَهُمْ عَذَابٌ اَلِيْمٌ ☐

As for those who take a paltry price in exchange for *their* covenant with Allah and their oaths, they shall have no portion in the life to come, and Allah will neither speak to them nor look upon them on the Day of Resurrection, nor will He purify them; and for them shall be a grievous punishment.
(Sūrah āl-e-'Imrān; Ch.3: V.78)

The people described in this verse who sell the Words of Allah for a paltry price do so for small insignificant worldly gains. They turn their backs on God for the sake of earthly gains. They will be punished accordingly on the Day of Judgement with a most painful punishment. They will not be rewarded by anything, on the contrary God will turn away from them and will not speak to them as though they did not exist. Of all the punishments mentioned in the Holy Quran, this is described as the most grievous.

While reading this verse, usually the mind turns to the Hereafter as though an event only of the Hereafter is being described. That is not the only import of this verse. Here in this world, the same punishment is meted out to such people. All over the world in every religion, God completely severs His ties with them and they never receive His Revelation. The punishment meted out to them in this world will also be their share in the next world but far more intensified.

The expression that God will not even cast a look upon them likewise applies to this world. They would be ignored as they ignored God. Again the expression *Liyuzakki him* indicates that God will never purify them here or count them among the purified in the Hereafter. This part of the verse makes it manifestly clear that the first application of the word *Tazkiyah* (purification) is bound to appear here on earth. Purification is done during the worldly life. If one is not purified here, he cannot be purified in the Hereafter but only can be counted among those who are not purified. 'Not to look upon them' means not to look upon them with care and endearment.

God is All-Powerful and can do what He likes, but He does everything with justice. In verse 41 of Sūrah al-Baqarah, He addresses man by reminding him that:

...وَ أَوْفُوا بِعَهْدِيٓ أُوفِ بِعَهْدِكُمْ وَإِيَّايَ فَارْهَبُوْنِ ☐

...and fulfil your covenant with Me, I will fulfil My
covenant with you, and Me alone should you fear
(Sūrah al-Baqarah; Ch.2: V.41)

The covenant is always two-sided. God says: it is as
binding on Me as it is on you. I promise that I will
continue to keep this covenant as long as you keep
yours.

The Reward for Keeping the Covenant

So far we have discussed the punishment of violation
of covenants, now we turn to another aspect which is
the reward for those who never violate their
covenants. Addressing such faithful people, God says
in Sūrah al-Ra'd:

الَّذِيْنَ يُوْفُوْنَ بِعَهْدِ اللّٰهِ وَلَا يَنْقُضُوْنَ الْمِيْثَاقَ ☐ وَالَّذِيْنَ
يَصِلُوْنَ مَآ أَمَرَ اللّٰهُ بِهٖٓ أَنْ يُّوْصَلَ وَيَخْشَوْنَ رَبَّهُمْ
وَيَخَافُوْنَ سُوْٓءَ الْحِسَابِ ☐ وَالَّذِيْنَ صَبَرُوا ابْتِغَآءَ وَجْهِ
رَبِّهِمْ وَأَقَامُوا الصَّلٰوةَ وَأَنْفَقُوْا مِمَّا رَزَقْنٰهُمْ سِرًّا وَّ عَلَانِيَةً
وَّيَدْرَءُوْنَ بِالْحَسَنَةِ السَّيِّئَةَ أُولٰٓئِكَ لَهُمْ عُقْبَى الدَّارِ ☐
جَنّٰتُ عَدْنٍ يَّدْخُلُوْنَهَا وَمَنْ صَلَحَ مِنْ اٰبَآئِهِمْ وَأَزْوَاجِهِمْ
وَذُرِّيّٰتِهِمْ وَالْمَلٰٓئِكَةُ يَدْخُلُوْنَ عَلَيْهِمْ مِّنْ كُلِّ بَابٍ ☐

Those who fulfil Allah's pact, and break not the
covenant;

And those who join what Allah has commanded to be joined, and fear their Lord, and dread the evil reckoning;
And those who persevere in seeking the favour of their Lord, and observe Prayer, and spend out of that with which We have provided them, secretly and openly, and repel evil with good. It is those who shall have the *best* reward of the *final* Abode—
Gardens of Eternity. They shall enter them and *also* those who are righteous from among their fathers, and their wives and their children. And Angels shall enter unto them from every gate, *saying*:

سَـلْمٌ عَلَيْكُمْ بِمَا صَبَرْتُمْ فَنِعْمَ عُقْبَى الدَّارِ □

'Peace be unto you, because you were steadfast; behold how excellent is the reward of the *final* Abode!'
(Sūrah al-Raʻd; Ch.13: Vs.21-25)

They perform virtuous deeds secretly because they do not want to show off and they promote them openly to promote virtuous deeds among others. Again when they remove evil, they replace it with virtue. Their motto is not to dispel evil and to create a void, the virtue that they replace evil with fills that void. It is like having demolished a hazardous building; they build a new and much better and useful construction for the benefit of the people. Thus, every evil mentioned in the Holy Quran has its antithesis in the form of a virtue which must replace its corresponding evil. They remove falsehood with truth and remove cruelty with beneficence and love. The same principle is mentioned in the verse where God declares:

$$ جَآءَالۡحَقُّ وَزَهَـقَ الۡبَـاطِلُ $$

...The truth has come and falsehood has fled. ...
(Sūrah al-Isrā'; Ch.17: V.82)

It is like saying that light has come and darkness has vanished.

A Similar Code of Ethics given to Humans is made Binding by Allah upon Himself

In another verse of the Holy Quran, Allah makes it binding upon Himself to bring better signs in place of those He has abrogated, or at least signs similar to them. This principle is mentioned in the verse:

$$ مَاتَنۡسَخۡ مِنۡ اٰيَةٍ اَوۡ نُنۡسِهَا نَاۡتِ بِخَيۡرٍ مِّنۡهَآ اَوۡ مِثۡلِهَاۤ ۚ اَلَمۡ $$
$$ تَعۡلَمۡ اَنَّ اللّٰهَ عَلٰى كُلِّ شَىۡءٍ قَدِيۡرٌ ☐ $$

Whatever Sign We abrogate or cause to be forgotten, We bring one better than that or the like thereof.
(Surah al-Baqarah; Ch.2: V.107)

This verse is normally understood to apply to the verses of the Holy Quran. If Allah abrogates some, He binds Himself to replace them with better, if not similar ones. In reality, no verse of the Holy Quran has ever been abrogated. Commenting on this verse, the medieval ulema used to quote up to five hundred

319

verses of the Holy Quran which, in their opinion, abrogated five hundred other verses. Which verses were replaced exactly by the ones abrogated is a question never attempted to be answered. Similarly, the verses which were better than the ones abrogated have not been enumerated with any proof mentioned about their being superior in any way.

This verse of the Holy Quran has nothing to do with the abrogation of the verses of the Holy Quran, but refers to the signs of Allah where earlier religions which were permitted to be obliterated were either brought back with the same beauty they once possessed, or better religions were revealed to replace them. The verse applies to a much wider fundamental principle. When we closely observe the history of religions, we always discover that many religions are allowed by God to have been obliterated. Whenever this happened, other religions similar to them were revealed to replace them. However, if the advanced age required some new and better religions, they were brought in their stead. They were better in the sense that they could cope more efficiently with the changing requirements of the time. Thus, religions have evolved until they culminated in the final evolution of Islam.

Individual Covenants or Contracts

So far we have discussed communal or national covenants. Now we turn to individual ones between person and person. This applies to those covenants which bind man and God as two parties. Likewise, covenants or contracts between two humans are also discussed under this category. Relating to the same, the Holy Quran mentions those fortunate individuals who did not violate their covenants made with God. Their detailed mention is made in the following verse:

مِنَ الْمُؤْمِنِيْنَ رِجَالٌ صَدَقُوْا مَا عَاهَدُوا اللّٰهَ عَلَيْهِ ۚ فَمِنْهُمْ مَّنْ قَضٰى نَحْبَهٗ وَ مِنْهُمْ مَّنْ يَّنْتَظِرُ ۪ وَ مَا بَدَّلُوْا تَبْدِيْلًا ۙ

Among the believers are men who have been true to the covenant they made with Allah. There are *some* of them who have fulfilled their vow, and *some* who *still* wait, and they have not changed *their condition* in the least;
(Sūrah al-Aḥzāb; Ch.33: V.24)

Ḥaḍrat Anas^ra narrates that his uncle Ḥaḍrat Anas bin Naḍr^ra was not present at the Battle of Badr. He called upon the Holy Prophet^sa and said 'O Prophet of God, I was not present during the Battle of Badr, which you fought against the (invading Meccan) idolaters. Hence, I could not participate in it. If God provides me with the occasion to take part in the next battle, He will see how I settle my account'. Hence, to relieve the sorrow of his helplessness he made an individual covenant with God. This verse had been revealed before Ḥaḍrat Anas bin Naḍr[ra] made this covenant with God; so he might have been wondering with the hope that he could have been among those fortunate persons who are mentioned in this verse by Allah. The Battle of Uhud brought ample proof that his hope was more than fulfilled.

It is reported that beating a retreat in defeat after the first victory of the Muslims, suddenly the non-believers re-attacked the Muslim army. The panic which this surprise attack caused made most of the participants flee without realising what they were doing. They were under the false impression that the Holy Prophet[sa] had been martyred and did not hear him calling them back. During that hour of utter despair, Ḥaḍrat Anas bin Naḍr[ra] was reported to be sitting on a rock eating some dates. When he came to learn what had happened he threw away the remaining dates and knew that the time for keeping his covenant had come. At that time, fighting almost alone, the Holy Prophet[sa] had been grievously injured and fell into a ditch with a few Companions who had also been martyred trying to defend him. Thus, he was almost covered with their corpses falling upon him. It was then that Ḥaḍrat Anas bin Naḍr[ra] charged the centre of the enemy, saying 'O Allah, I offer my apology on behalf of other Muslims and express my condemnation of what the idolaters have done'. On his way he met Saʻd bin Muʻāz[ra] and said: 'O by the Lord of Naḍr (i.e. by the Lord of himself), the heaven is before us, beyond the field of Uḥud I am smelling the fragrance of heaven'.

Later on, when the Holy Prophet^{sa} had recovered from his wounds, Sa'd bin Mu'āz^{ra} approached him and reported to him what he had heard from Ḥaḍrat Naḍr^{ra} and said 'O Prophet of God, it is not within my power to do what he did during this crisis'. Ḥaḍrat Anas^{ra} further reports that after the war when we searched for him, his body was found with more than eighty wounds, inflicted by swords, arrows and lances. The idolaters had disfigured his face by cutting off his ears and nose and whatever else they could. His sister only recognised him by identifying marks on his fingers. Ḥaḍrat Anas^{ra} further narrates that we (all the Companions of the Holy Prophet^{sa}) believed that this verse had been revealed about him and other faithful Companions like him.[46]

The Violation of Individual Covenants

and the Punishment

In comparison to this, the Holy Quran also speaks of those unfortunate people who violate their individual covenant with Allah. They are spoken of in the following verses:

وَمِنْهُمْ مَّنْ عٰهَدَ اللّٰهَ لَئِنْ اٰتٰىنَا مِنْ فَضْلِهٖ لَنَصَّدَّقَنَّ
وَلَنَكُوْنَنَّ مِنَ الصّٰلِحِيْنَ ۞ فَلَمَّاۤ اٰتٰىهُمْ مِّنْ فَضْلِهٖ
بَخِلُوْا بِهٖ وَ تَوَلَّوْا وَّ هُمْ مُّعْرِضُوْنَ ۞ فَاَعْقَبَهُمْ نِفَاقًا
فِيْ قُلُوْبِهِمْ اِلٰى يَوْمِ يَلْقَوْنَهٗ بِمَاۤ اَخْلَفُوا اللّٰهَ مَا وَعَدُوْهُ
وَبِمَا كَانُوْا يَكْذِبُوْنَ ۞

And among them there are those who made a covenant with Allah, *saying*, 'If He gives us of His bounty, we would most surely give alms and be of the virtuous'.

But when He gave them of His bounty, they became niggardly of it, and they turned away in aversion.

So He requited them with hypocrisy *which shall last* in their hearts until the day when they shall meet Him, because they broke their promise to Allah, and because they lied.

(Sūrah al-Taubah; Ch.9: Vs.75-77)

Relating to this individual covenant, we read in the traditions that once an extremely poor person* begged the Holy Prophet^sa to pray for him because he was tired of his poverty. He promised that if God be bounteous to him he would be bounteous to others. Allah responded to the prayer of the Holy Prophet^sa and made that man exceptionally rich. Once, when an emissary of the Holy Prophet^sa approached him for his share of Zakat, he grumbled: you do not know the trouble we take to earn our livelihood, but just by observing what we have from outside, you rush to us

---

* Tha'laba bin Ḥāṭib.

324

begging for Zakat. The emissary reported this matter to the Holy Prophet[sa]. He declared that from now on none would ever ask him to pay his share of Zakat. Later on, when the man heard of this he began to repent and came to beg pardon from the Holy Prophet[sa] and promised to give his entire share. The Holy Prophet[sa] rejected this offer and told him that nothing would be accepted from him in future. It is reported that in the remaining years till the demise of the Holy Prophet[sa], that unfortunate man tried every year for his share to be accepted as Zakat but was refused by the Holy Prophet[sa]. He lived long enough to do the same during the caliphate of Ḥaḍrat Abū Bakr[ra] and that of Ḥaḍrat 'Umar[ra], but they both refused by saying that who were they to alter the decision of the Holy Prophet[sa]. It is reported that his share of Zakat grew so much that the entire valley which he possessed was filled with Zakat animals from one end to the other, but thereafter Zakat was never accepted from him.[47]

How can others know that there are some people who even try to deceive God? Yes, occasionally the others also learn about the attempted deception of hypocritical people. It is, however, possible that such hypocrites may succeed in deceiving the people while making tall claims of their purported financial sacrifice for the sake of God. This deception lasts only as long as God does not reveal their secrets.

In the Ahmadiyya Community, there prevails a strong and well-established system of financial sacrifices. Sometimes some people boast of sacrificing everything they possess for the sake of God. They are comparatively few but still they continue to mingle with a large majority of Ahmadis who are sincere in their vows. When at last God decides to expose such hypocrites, their game of deception is revealed. Here such sincere people are not mentioned who cannot keep their vows because of their subsequent financial losses. They are certainly above reproach. Only such are discussed here who, right from the beginning, intend to deceive. Many verses of the Holy Quran also throw light on this subject. The Holy Prophet[sa] also describes the breaking of vows as deception in the following tradition:

اِذَا عَاهَدَ غَدَرَ

When he (the hypocrite) makes a promise, he does not keep it and is guilty of deception.[48]

Although hypocrisy is a matter of hidden intentions, when its signs erupt they pinpoint the hypocrites.

21 Covenants with Non-Muslims, Treaties and Contracts

It is a distinguishing feature of the Holy Quran that all treaties are spoken of as inviolable between all humans, whatever their religion or race be. This is a teaching which is applicable to the entire mankind of every age. The following verse speaks of the Muslims' contracts even with idolaters with the same sanctity:

إِلَّا الَّذِيْنَ عَاهَدْتُّمْ مِّنَ الْمُشْرِكِيْنَ ثُمَّ لَمْ يَنْقُصُوْكُمْ شَيْئًا وَّلَمْ يُظَاهِرُوْا عَلَيْكُمْ اَحَدًا فَاَتِمُّوْا اِلَيْهِمْ عَهْدَهُمْ اِلٰى مُدَّتِهِمْ ۚ اِنَّ اللّٰهَ يُحِبُّ الْمُتَّقِيْنَ ☐

Excepting those of the idolaters with whom you have entered into a treaty and who have not fallen short of fulfilling their obligations to you nor aided anyone against you. So fulfil to these the treaty *you have* made with them till their term. Surely, Allah loves those who are righteous.
(Sūrah al-Taubah; Ch.9: V.4)

This is an exquisite example of absolute justice. Allah admonishes that We do not hold you responsible only for the covenants you have made with Me and My other Prophets[as], We also hold you responsible for the convenants you make even with the idolaters. Again, it is irrelevant whether the party with which you are bound in a treaty is weak or powerful, righteous or evil. You will have to keep your vows in every respect as a basic principle. The importance of any treaty with idolaters is exactly the same as with anyone else. However, if such signs appear as indicate their intended breach of treaty even to the extent that they secretly prepare a surprise attack—you are still not permitted to attack them. In defence, however, you can also make all preparations to defend yourselves against them when attacked.

The following verse also throws light on the same situation.

وَإِمَّا تَخَافَنَّ مِنْ قَوْمٍ خِيَانَةً فَانْبِذْ اِلَيْهِمْ عَلَى سَوَآءٍ ۚ اِنَّ اللّٰهَ لَا يُحِبُّ الْخَآئِنِيْنَ ☐

And if you fear treachery from a people, throw back to them *their covenant* with equity. Surely, Allah loves not the treacherous.
(Sūrah al-Anfāl; Ch.8: V.59)

The example set by the Holy Prophet[sa] also corroborates this. Not even once did he violate his part of the treaty due to the fear that the enemy would break his part. As long as the enemy did not practically violate a treaty, the Holy Prophet[sa] did not do so in response. However, he was always prepared for such an extreme eventuality; so the enemy could never spring a surprise upon the Muslims.

Two Categories of Treaties with Non-Muslims

Now I will explain that the treaties with non-believers are of two categories. One is conducted under duress and the other when the Muslims have the upper hand. The treaty during the Peace of Ḥudaibiya is an example of the former.

During this treaty, the right of the Muslims to perform the pilgrimage was violated by the enemy. It may appear to be a weakness on the part of the Holy Prophet[sa] to accept this violation because the enemy was powerful and there was a likely threat to the safety of his Companions. However, he did not decide to abstain from the pilgrimage because of this. A verse of the Holy Quran clearly prohibits him from performing pilgrimage if the way to Mecca was not clear and he had to fight his way into it. That was the only reason why he stood adamant against the pressure of all his Companions who were ready to offer every sacrifice to gain entry into Mecca.

The Treaty of the Peace of Ḥudaibiya was finally written and signed by both parties. A noteworthy incident took place during the setting of the conditions of this treaty which highlights the Holy Prophet's[sa] adherence to justice regarding treaties.

As far as the fulfilment of the treaties is concerned, the Holy Prophet[sa] was extremely cautious not to violate any condition. During the negotiations at Ḥudaibiya between the two parties, the Meccans emissary was Suhail bin 'Amar and the Muslim camp was represented by the Holy Prophet[sa] himself. Verbal conditions were settled and the treaty was about to be signed. Suddenly Suhail's own son, Abū Jandal, somehow reached the field of Ḥudaibiya. He was bound in chains, occasionally dropping to the ground as he staggered. It was revealed that having accepted Islam, he was tortured and imprisoned by his own father, the same Suhail who was representing the idolaters. He made a piteous appeal to the Muslims to save him from the clutches of his own father. His father reacted strongly to this and said, 'if you give him shelter, no peace treaty will be signed'. The Holy Prophet[sa] repeatedly appealed to Suhail to allow his son to take shelter, but he adamantly refused. At this the Holy Prophet[sa] advised Abū Jandal to return to Mecca because the agreement had already been verbally reached that escapees from the Meccan idolaters could not be given shelter.

Apparently this treaty was against the interest of the Muslims, but the way it was worded by the Holy Prophet[sa], it turned out to be advantageous to the Muslims. He did not commit himself to send all the Muslim escapees who reached Medina seeking shelter back to Mecca. He only committed himself to send them out of Medina so they could settle anywhere they liked. This part of the contract ultimately developed into a grievous threat to the Meccans' trade caravans. Those who had accepted Islam from among them and had escaped from the Meccans imprisonment, gradually grew into a strong band, settling somewhere near the Meccans' trade route. They began to make surprise lightening attacks on their caravans and run away with the booty which they used as their livelihood.

A cursory glance by an observer cannot fathom the depth of wisdom of the Holy Prophet[sa] underlying the wording of this decision. After a while the Meccans began to realise how they had been outdone by the Holy Prophet's[sa] careful wording of the contract. If the idolators had agreed to let the escapees settle in Medina under the strict control of the Holy Prophet[sa], they would never have attacked the Meccans because it was against the treaty. But when settled outside Medina under their own command they could do whatever they liked.

The Treaty of Medina

One category of treaties can be that every participant, regardless of his religion, will enjoy equal rights with the other participants. The treaty of Medina belonged to this category.

The important clauses relevant to this discussion are as follows:

1. The Quraish Immigrants from Mecca and the Anṣār from Medina who gave them shelter and all those who, despite not being Muslims signed

the agreement along with them, would be deemed as a single umma. The treaty required that if Medina was attacked by outsiders, while staying in Medina, they will all defend Medina together. The remaining part of the first clause of the treaty has been omitted because it was not directly relevant to the subject being discussed.

2. No Muslim would become the supporter or friend of a liberated slave without the consent of his previous master if that master happens to be a Muslim.

3. All the believers would join hands against another believer if he perpetrates cruelty or talks sinfully or transgresses against others or tries in any way to create division among believers. This will be adhered to by every believer even if he has to rise against his own transgressing father.

4. No believer would murder another believer for the sake of a non-believer, likewise he would not support a non-believer against his fellow believer.

5. The covers of God's sanctity will include every participant in this treaty. Even the lowest among them would get his share of this sanctity.

6. Even the Jews who enter this treaty would enjoy equal rights with the Muslims. They will

not be tyrannised, nor will an enemy of theirs be aided against them.

7. The security of every believer is equally important for all of them.

8. If a non-believer murders a believer accidentally he will have to pay blood money unless the inheritors of the deceased forgive him. If he does not pay blood money and has not been forgiven, then all participants of the treaty would enforce him together.

9. If the participants of the treaty quarrel against each other in any matter, their quarrel would be presented before God and His Prophet^{sa} for judgement.

10. The idolaters of Mecca and their allies shall not be granted shelter.

11. If anyone invades Mecca, the participants of the treaty would help each other. If an armistice is offered, all participants of the treaty would participate to decide as one party.

12. The believer must grant the same rights to other participants and pay their dues, unless they oppose them because of religious differences.

13. This treaty would not help the transgressor or the sinful.

14. Every Medinite, whether he be on a journey or remains in Medina, has the same right to security.

15. Whoever acts righteously, God and His

Messenger will be on his side.[49]

It is evident from this treaty that it was not a legislation of a government, the clauses of the treaty are in accord with the social requirements of every society, Hence the spirit of this agreement provides the Jews with equal rights with Muslims. According to this treaty every participant, whether he lives in Medina or leaves Medina to dwell elsewhere, will enjoy the right of living in peace. The participants of the treaty will have no right to interfere in their affairs. This treaty is a moral charter which can settle the differences of all disputing nations in the future, justly and amicably.

According to this treaty, the powerful nations can enjoy no exceptional right to force their will upon the weaker nations. However, all signatory nations which are members of the United Nations Charter can use their united might against a belligerent nation which does not abstain from perpetrating aggression against another. During such an eventuality, they should exert a united pressure on both the disputant parties to immediately stop acts of hostility. Then they can settle their issues in accordance with a mutually agreed authority of arbitration.

Although the charter of Medina gives the predominant right of arbitration to the Holy Prophet[sa] during disputes between Muslims and non-Muslims, he never used this clause to impose his religion upon the non-believers. He always offered the non-Muslims three choices. If they had a book of their own they had a right to be judged according to their own book, also they had a right to decide that the dispute should be settled according to Islamic law. The third option was that their dispute should be judged according to the prevalent Arab custom.

The Personal Example of the Holy Prophet^{sa} regarding his Commitment to Contracts

In relation to commitment to contracts, I now present before you some examples of the Holy Prophet's^{sa} virtuous conduct.

Once an emissary of a people came to the Holy Prophet^{sa} to deliver a message. Having met him, he was so impressed that he accepted Islam. Despite the fact that all his family, cattle and property were evidently left behind, he pleaded with the Holy Prophet^{sa} that he should kindly be permitted to remain at his feet as he could not bear to leave him. The Holy Prophet^{sa} responded by saying, 'I cannot be guilty of breach of contract. You, being an emissary, must return.' An emissary is not permitted to bring a message and stay behind without returning to his master with the answer. What a glorious teaching it is! Had it been someone else in the Prophet's^{sa} place, however just he might have been, he would be likely to have greeted him with all his heart, saying, 'With pleasure, it is your own choice, you are a free man to decide whatever you like.' However, the Holy Prophet[sa] would only permit him to return after having delivered his answer. So he went home, and because he was sincere, after some time he came back. This time he was not an emissary but simply an emigrant.[50]

On another occasion, a Meccan by the name of Ḥuzaifa bin Yamān[ra] came to the Holy Prophet[sa] during the Battle of Badr. He told him that he came with the intention of joining him in the battle against the Meccans but the Meccans had somehow sensed it. Therefore they had taken a verbal promise from him not to fight against the Meccans. The Holy Prophet[sa] admonished him to return without participating in the battle to fulfil his promise, adding that his God was sufficient to help them.[51]

Glory be to Allah, what a paragon of virtue he was. He had every right to remind him that because his contract was made under duress it was not binding upon him. But it was far below the dignity of the Holy Prophet[sa] to have taken such a stance. Woe to the so-called Muslim mullahs of today, that their conduct is far removed from that of the Holy Prophet[sa].

The Prophet Muhammad[sa] did not only commit himself to honour his own pledges, but also honoured the contracts of his Companions, despite the fact that they were not authorised by him to make them on his behalf. Here it remains no longer a matter of justice but aquires the higher stage of *Iḥsān*.

A similar incident is narrated by Ḥaḍrat Umm-e-Hānī', the daughter of Abū Ṭālib. She narrates that once she came to the Holy Prophet[sa] after his ultimate conquest of Mecca. Finding the Holy Prophet[sa] engaged in prayer she waited till he finished, then told him that she had given protection to a son of Habira without consulting other Companions, or taking prior permission from the Holy Prophet[sa]. However, her real brother Ali, born of the same mother, was bent upon killing him because her offer of protection had no validity. The Holy Prophet[sa] declared 'O Umm-e-Hānī, whomever have you given protection, I too have given my protection.'[52]

In no way was the Holy Prophet[sa] required to honour Umm-e-Hānī's commitment. No principle of justice could ever impose this on him. Most certainly it was his beneficence that out of regard for a humble member of his family he stood to honour her promise.

A Prophecy Regarding the Moral Decadence of Muslim Political Leaders in the Future

The Holy Prophet[sa] once warned Muslims to honour their commitments to their non-Muslim subjects, if they fail to do so Allah would harden the hearts of the non-Muslim subjects and they will cease to pay the levy.[53] The levy is a tax imposed on non-Muslim subjects in exchange for the promise of protection offered to them.

If Muslim states had paid proper heed to this admonition, they would not have dwindled away. In this respect, the states of the early period were distinctly different from those of the later. Earlier, when Muslim rulers kept their promises and behaved kindly to their subjects, their subjects also responded by obeying them with respect amounting to love. The difference of religion never stood between their mutual cooperation. A people who protect their contracts, their subjects protect them.

In the history of the Muslims, there is one glorious episode which deserves to be told again and again. Once, the Muslim army was forced to beat temporary retreat from the area of Hims under mounting Roman pressure. The retreating Muslims returned the levy they had received from their subjects. They told them that they had failed to protect them and defend their rights, for which the levy was imposed. Now that they were leaving this territory, it had become impossible for them to defend them against the enemy. At this, the reply of the people of Hims is recorded in history in the following golden letters:

'We had become the subject of tyranny at the hands of our own fellow believers. You came during this state of affairs and your justice and grace has completely won us over. Now we will fight together against the enemy under your appointed governor and the enemy will not be able to advance towards you without killing us all.'

It happened exactly as they had promised and Heracles, the Roman Emperor, was forced to withdraw. The Muslims re-entered the territory with the glory of the victorious. The entire people of Hims received them with great jubilation and happily accepted the renewal of contract to pay them the levy of their own accord.[54]

Then came the unfortunate era when the Muslim rulers forgot the teaching of the Holy Quran and ceased to act according to the Quranic teachings regarding their conduct towards the conquered people. At this, their subjects also severed their ties and became oblivious of them. Thus their broken contracts became instrumental in breaking down their empires and eventually caused their downfall.

Some other Examples of the Honouring of Contracts

Personally, the Holy Prophet[sa] was wont to defend the rights of others meticulously. His personal example towards his subjects who paid levy was beyond censure.

Once, Ḥaḍrat 'Umar[ra], a close Companion of the Prophet[sa] and the Second Caliph after him, learned of the murder of a Jew. No trace of the murderer could be found. This news grieved him so much that he called all Muslims to the central Mosque and delivered a heart-rending sermon from his pulpit.

He said 'Look what shall I do? God had rested the reign of His people in my hands. How will I answer God when one of the children of Adam has been murdered? God will inquire from me as to what I was doing'.

His sermon was charged with such emotion that the murderer, who was among the congregation, stood up there and then. Addressing him he said, 'I am the murderer, why are you putting yourself through such pain and misery. O Leader of the Faithful! Punish me instead and sleep in peace.'[55] Of course, the murderer was subsequently executed. May God rest his soul in peace.

Such was the teaching of the Holy Prophet[sa] to his servants regarding the rights of those who had paid levy. It was this teaching of his which brought about such shining episodes as the one given above.

Again, it is narrated that once a Muslim who had murdered a *Dhimmī* (levy-paying subject) was brought to the presence of Ḥaḍrat Ali[ra]. As every evidence was against him Ḥaḍrat Ali[ra] ordered his execution.

The brothers of the murderer promised to pay blood money to the victim's brother in exchange for his pardon. When this was reported to Ḥaḍrat Ali[ra] for his final consent, he refused to do so until he himself had interrogated the brother of the victim. Before the interrogation, he fully informed him of his rights and then proceeded to examine him thoroughly lest he was under any pressure from the Muslims. In response he told him that he was under no duress, the decision was entirely his own. By the death of the culprit his brother would not be returned, but if he accepted blood money it would prove to be of some help to the bereaved family of the victim. After this, Ḥaḍrat Ali[ra] agreed to the pardon of the murderer. Explaining his conduct, Ḥaḍrat Ali[ra] informed him that he had gone through this bother only because, according to the Islamic principles of justice, the blood of the subjects was just like the blood of the rulers.[56]

Publisher's Note

At this, the main address ended, followed by the normal proceedings of wishing a safe journey to the participants and reminding them of their responsibilities.

The meeting was declared closed after the speaker led the congregation in silent prayer. These details are omitted from this book with the permission of the speaker.

References Part III

43. *al-Munjid* & *Mufridāt-i-Rāghib.*
44. *Sunan Ibni Mājah, Kitābur Ruhūni, Bābu Talqīḥin-Nakhli.*
45. *Ṣaḥīḥ Bukhārī, Kitābu Aḥādīthil Ambiyā'i, Bābun* [Imam Bukhari gives no caption after *'Babun'*, But the Hadith follows *Babun Ḥadīthul Ghāri*, in some editions].
46. *Ṣaḥiḥ Bukhārī, Kitābul Jīhādi Was Siyar, Bābu Qaulillāhi 'Azza wa Jalla Minal Mu'minīna Rijālun Ṣadaqū mā 'Āhadullāha 'Alaihi...*
47. *Tafsīr Durri Manthūr* under verse 75 of Sūrah (Chapter) *Taubah* Vol.3, pp.467-468.
48. *Ṣaḥīḥ Bukhārī, Kitābul Īmān, Bābu 'Alāmātil Munāfiqi.*
49. *Sīrat Ibni Hishām, Hijratur-Rasūl,* under the header *'Kitābuhū Bainal Muhājirīna Wal Anṣāri Wa Mawād'atu Yahūdin'.*
50. *Sunan Abū Dāwūd, Kitābul Jihādi, Bābu Fil Imāmi Yustajannu bihī Fil 'Uhūdi.*
51. *Ṣaḥīḥ Muslim, Kitābul Jihād, Babul Wafāi' Bil 'Aḥdi.*
52. *Ṣaḥīḥ Bukhārī, Kitābul Jizyati, Bābu Amānin Nisā'i wa Jiwārihinna.*
53. *Ṣaḥīḥ Bukhārī, Kitābul Jizyati, Bābu Ithmi man 'Āhada Thumma Ghadara.*
54. *Futūḥul Buldān li Imām Aḥmad Bin Yaḥyā bin Jābir Albaghdādī,* pp.143-144.
55. *Usudul Ghābah li Imam Ibni Ḥajar,* Under *Dhikri Bakar Bin Shaddākh* Vol. 1, p.204.
56. *Nasbur Ra'yati li Aḥādīthil Hidāyah,* Vol.4, p.337.

Absolute Justice, Kindness and Kinship

Kindness and Kinship

The Three Creative Principles

Ḥaḍrat Mirza Tahir Ahmad

Part IV

Speech delivered at the Annual Convention
of the Ahmadiyyah Muslim Jamā'at UK
in Islamabad, Tilford, Surrey, United Kingdom
on July 24, 1988

LIST OF CHAPTERS IN PART IV

إِنَّ اللّٰهَ يَأْمُرُ بِالْعَدْلِ وَالْإِحْسَانِ وَ إِيتَآئِ ذِى الْقُرْبِى

Indeed Allah requires you to abide by justice, and to treat with grace and to give like the giving of kin to kin.
(Sūrah al-Naḥl; Ch.16: V.91)

In addition to the previous discussions under this title, there are some further aspects of the same subject which need to be elaborated. The entire teaching that the Holy Quran has given us is also found moulded into the character of the Holy Prophet, peace and blessing of Allah be upon him.

22 Justice in Speech

Many aspects of justice in speech have been discussed previously. Without repeating them, we shall now throw light on some others. From this angle, after dividing human beings into different categories, I have selected some verses of the Holy Quran and the corresponding sayings of the Holy Prophet[sa]. Justice in speech is the root from which this subject stems and further grows and spreads into many branches.

God declares:

وَاِذَا قُلْتُمْ فَاعْدِلُوْا وَلَوْ كَانَ ذَا قُرْبٰى ۚ وَ بِعَهْدِ اللّٰهِ اَوْفُوْا ۚ...
ذٰلِكُمْ وَصّٰكُمْ بِهٖ لَعَلَّكُمْ تَذَكَّرُوْنَ ☐

…And when you speak, observe justice, even if *the concerned person* be a relative, and fulfil the covenant of Allah. That is what He enjoins upon you, that you may remember.
(Sūrah al-An'ām; Ch.6: V.153)

In this regard, it should be particularly noted that the phrase 'Justice in Speech' can be understood differently by different people. But the Holy Quran throws light on every possible meaning of this phrase.

One Specific Aspect of Justice in Speech

Among people, we find many who beautify their speech with tall claims. However, when you examine their speech critically they are found to be false. In this age, most religious, social and political leaders claim that their speech is always based on justice. Thus the entire world is full of justice in speech. The Capitalists as well as the Communists both claim to be its champion. Every leader of the world, whether he belongs to the East or the West, Capitalism or Communism, talks only of justice. He loudly claims that peace cannot be established without justice. Mostly these are just words of mouth and more often than not, when the time for the dispensation of justice comes, they fail. Such people can be easily identified because they only talk of this wordly life and forget altogether the life to come.

According to the Quranic teaching, anyone who forgets the right of God upon himself may also forget the right of Allah's creatures upon him.

In this context, I quote the Founder of the Ahmadiyya Community, Ḥaḍrat Mirza Ghulam Ahmad[as] who relates:

> 'Morality is of two types. The first is the one pursued by many modern educated people. When meeting another person they are soft spoken, their only aim being to please him, while sometimes their heart is filled with hypocrisy and rancour. This apparently moral attitude is contrary to the Quranic concept of morality. The second

type of moral behaviour is to have true sympathy at heart for others without hypocrisy and without adorning one's speech with flattery and false praises. As Allah the Exalted admonishes: اِنَّ اللّٰہَ یَاۡمُرُ بِالۡعَدۡلِ وَالۡاِحۡسَانِ وَ اِیۡتَآئِ ذِی الۡقُرۡبٰی ٥٧

The verse quoted by the Promised Messiah[as], is the same as the title of my address. It categorizes one's speech in three stages. The first is to be just in speech. The second is to be more than just and to be truly kind. The third is to be more than just kind and to speak to others as though they are one's next of kin, like a mother speaks to her beloved child.

As for as the first stage, that is of justice, is concerned, according to the Holy Quran, the quality of justice of a claimant is put to the test when he is required to give evidence against someone or some people close to him. This has been mentioned in the following verse.

وَ اِذَا قُلۡتُمۡ فَاعۡدِلُوۡا وَ لَوۡ کَانَ ذَا قُرۡبٰی ...

…And when you speak, observe justice, *even if the concerned person or persons* be a next of kin…
(Sūrah al-An'ām; Ch.6: V.153)

The phrase *Dhā Qurbā* is generally understood to be applicable to close relatives who are dearer to one than just friends, but this phrase has a wider application. It can be extended to cover one's tribe and the party to which one has sworn allegiance. With this extended meaning this statement can be rightly applied to modern day party politics. In party politics, a member of the party vows to be loyal to the cause of the party. Similarly in international politics, friendly nations form groups and they are loyal only to their common cause. The question of right or wrong is irrelevant. Automatically justice is evaporated from these alliances and what is left is only a partisan spirit. When these alliances are forged their concept of justice is only relative.

For example, when a leader of some political alliance loudly acclaims justice, he still supports one or more of his allies against whom the rest of the world launches a strong protest of transgression. On the other hand, if a group of enemy nations perpetrates transgression against another nation, which may not even be one of their alliance, they unite in their strong and loud condemnation of that aggression. This equally applies both to the Capitalist and Communist alliances. In view of the above, one can easily understand that the Holy Quran does not only support absolute justice but also suggests ways to test the sincerity of such a claimant. Such people as talk of justice only in their temporal relationship are often found false when put to the above-mentioned Quranic test.

Examples of Absolute Justice Dispensed by the Holy Prophet^{sa} of Islam

There are scores of examples that can be and have been quoted, during this series of addresses, where the Holy Prophet^{sa} dispensed justice in its absolute meaning. He is known to have given his verdict in favour of a Jew or even an idolater against a Muslim. According to his personal conduct in matters of financial disputes, not only did the Holy Prophet^{sa} dispense justice but he went a step further to treat a claimant with kindness and paid more than his dues to him. The same he strongly admonished to his Companions. This conduct of his was not only applicable to disputes, but also as a general personal behaviour; he always paid a person more than his dues and he promoted the same in the society of his Companions. At times his financial dealings were amazing and crossed the bounds of kindness into the realm of one's treatment to one's next of kin.

Hence without a doubt, the Holy Prophet^{sa} was not only a man of absolute justice but his conduct revealed many glorious manifestations of kindness and even of treating his servants as though they were his real next of kin.

The First Characteristic of Justice in Speech

As far as justice in speech is concerned, the Holy Quran requires believers not only to express the truth

351

but to express it in a manner which is absolutely straightforward, so in no way can the statement be misconstrued. This has been admonished to the believers in the following verse:

$$\Box\ \text{یَاۤ اَیُّهَا الَّذِیْنَ اٰمَنُوا اتَّقُوا اللّٰهَ وَ قُوْلُوْا قَوْلًا سَدِیْدًا}$$

O ye who believe! fear Allah, and speak straightforwardly.
(Sūrah al-Aḥzāb; Ch.33: V.71)

The expression *Qauli Sadīd* means a speech which has no tilt in any direction but in the direction of truth. The words should be straightforward without any crookedness. Sometimes it is observed that a speech is true but it has many hidden twists and turns which may mislead the listener. The teaching which Allah bestowed upon the Holy Prophet[sa] clearly warned that just to speak the truth is not sufficient. Speak the truth with such purity as may leave no room in the mind of the listener to misinterpret it. But the Holy Quran warns against another danger linked with straightforward truth. Sometimes people express the truth harshly and insultingly, considering themselves to be absolutely straightforward. However, the straightforward truth does not mean rude expression.

When the Holy Quran refers to straightforward speech it has no connotation of throwing something in the face of somebody. The Holy Quran makes a clear difference between straight talk and insulting talk. In

Chapter Ṭā-Hā of the Holy Quran, when Allah advised Moses[as] and Aaron[as] to go to Pharaoh, they were strongly admonished to be gentle in speech despite the fact that the message was very hard. They were to tell him that he had transgressed and rebelled against Allah, yet they were to deliver this message in as mild a tone as possible.

This admonishment is contained in the following verses:

اِذْهَبَاۤ اِلٰى فِرْعَوْنَ اِنَّهٗ طَغٰى ۝ فَقُوْلَا لَهٗ قَوْلًا لَّيِّنًا لَّعَلَّهٗ يَتَذَكَّرُ اَوْ يَخْشٰى ۝

Go, both of you, to Pharaoh, for he has transgressed *all* bounds.
And address him both of you, with gentle words that he might possibly heed or fear.
(Sūrah Ṭā-Hā; Ch.20: Vs.44-45)

The Second Characteristic of Justice in Speech

Then a new aspect of beauty is added to justice in speech. Justice in speech is good but it should be better than that and more beautified. This is mentioned in Chapter Ḥā-Mīm al-Sajdah. The Quran admonishes:

وَ مَنْ اَحْسَنُ قَوْلًا مِّمَّنْ دَعَاۤ اِلَى اللّٰهِ وَ عَمِلَ صَالِحًا وَّ قَالَ اِنَّنِيْ مِنَ الْمُسْلِمِيْنَ ۝

And who is better in speech than he who invites *men*

353

to Allah and does good works and says, 'I am surely
of those who submit?'
(Sūrah Ḥā-Mīm al-Sajdah; Ch.41: V.34)

In this verse, two points are specifically raised: first,
that call towards Allah (the Most Beautiful) and
secondly, who can be more beautiful in speech than
the one who calls towards Allah (the Most Beautiful).
Who can be better than Allah, towards whom a caller
summons. Such people are always the truest and the
best in speech but the condition required is that the
caller should also behave accordingly. Otherwise the
speech cannot be termed beautiful. It can be said here
that such people are hundreds of thousands, nay even
billions in the world, who call towards Allah. So,
according to this definition their invitation should also
be described as beautiful. What is so special that
Islam teaches us to distinguish between the two? It is
the emphasis of the Holy Quran on the conduct of the
caller towards Allah that is special.

The one whose personal conduct manifests satanic
habits is not entitled to call others to Allah. Thus the
Holy Quran makes manifestly clear that what it says
is well-balanced: and balance itself is a characteristic
of justice.

The Third Characteristic of Justice in Speech

After admonishing straightforwardness in 33:71, the
very next verse informs the reader of an extraordinary
blessing gained from it as follows:

يُصْلِحْ لَكُمْ أَعْمَالَكُمْ وَيَغْفِرْ لَكُمْ ذُنُوۡبَكُمْ وَمَنۡ يُّطِعِ اللّٰہَ
وَ رَسُوۡلَهٗ فَقَدۡ فَازَ فَوۡزًا عَظِیۡمًا ☐

He will reform your conduct for you and forgive you
your sins. And whoso obeys Allah and His
Messenger, shall surely attain a mighty success.
(Sūrah al-Aḥzāb; Ch.33: V.72)

This implies that straightforwardness is essential if
you want to rectify your conduct and that of your
society. Not only will your conduct begin to improve
but also your past errors will be forgiven. The highest
achievement of such people mentioned in this verse,
is that whosoever follows the word and example of
the Holy Prophet[sa] of Islam shall surely attain a
mighty success.

Justice of Speech in Household Affairs

Now I will narrate an example of justice in speech as
practised by the Holy Founder[sa] of Islam for the
admonition of his own household.

After his first wife Ḥaḍrat Khadījah[ra], the Holy
Prophet[sa] loved Ḥaḍrat 'Ā'ishah[ra] the most among his
wives. Once, when he observed something in the
speech of Ḥaḍrat 'Ā'ishah[ra] which was against his
own noble concept of justice in speech, he reproved
her there and then. The manner in which he did so
excels in beauty. Ḥaḍrat 'Ā'ishah[ra] herself narrates
that once I complained to the Holy Prophet[sa] that he
holds his wife Ṣafiya[ra] very dear while she is

diminutive in stature. Thus she narrates that while saying this she tauntingly raised her little finger, meaning that Ṣafiya[ra] is as short in stature as this little finger. She goes on to relate that the Holy Prophet[sa], upon hearing her remarks, admonished her by observing: "Ā'ishah[ra] you have said a small thing but if you mix it in the waters of the oceans it will change its character and taste and embitter it further!' See how out of natural jealously when Ḥaḍrat 'Ā'ishah[ra] taunted another wife, the Holy Prophet[sa] did not ignore it and responded with a perfect rebuttal. A better rebuttal than that cannot be imagined.[58]

The Holy Prophet[sa] taught us how to be just in speech and also how to beautify our speech further. These are the basic tenets without following which, the world cannot be cleansed of disorders. It is a reality that unless the diseases hidden within human hearts are cured, the consequent disorders throughout the world cannot be rectified.

Now, having fully understood the various connotations of justice in speech, we turn to another aspect which is universal in nature.

23 The Basic Principle of Establishing Equality Among all the Children of Adam^{as}

This principle is mentioned in the following verse:

يَاۤاَيُّهَا النَّاسُ اِنَّا خَلَقْنٰكُمۡ مِّنۡ ذَكَرٍ وَّ اُنۡثٰى وَجَعَلۡنٰكُمۡ شُعُوۡبًا وَّ قَبَآئِلَ لِتَعَارَفُوۡا ؕ اِنَّ اَكۡرَمَكُمۡ عِنۡدَ اللّٰهِ اَتۡقٰكُمۡ ؕ اِنَّ اللّٰهَ عَلِيۡمٌ خَبِيۡرٌ ☐

O mankind, We have created you from male and female; and We have made you into clans and tribes that you may recognize one another. Verily, the most honourable among you, in the sight of Allah, is he who is the most righteous among you. Surely, Allah is All-Knowing, All-Aware.
(Sūrah al-Ḥujurāt; Ch.49: V.14)

In the world today, all the prevalent disorders and inherent dangers to world peace spring from the concept of national or racial superiority. This is what is termed as 'Racialism' or 'Racism'. This racism, although loudly condemned by every nation of the world, still exists as it once existed in Nazi Germany. This racism is white as well as black. The lava of hatred that erupts from time to time among black nations against the white is but another name of racism which is black in colour. Alas! the world has not as yet been released from the clutches of this demon. This is an extremely poisonous weed which cannot easily be rooted out. All people of truth who see and recognize it, know very well the roots of this deadly weed are found everywhere, as much in the East as in the West. Despite great speeches and loud condemnation of racism, it continues to raise its head in every soil. This weed is so poisonous and hardy that it insidiously creeps into and flourishes in every soil, be it religious, social, political or philosophical.

Those who profoundly observe the relationship between America, Russia and China know full well that the Western powers and Russian block prefer white racism over Communism, if a choice has to be made. Both would join hands in favour of the supremacy of their white race, especially if Communism is linked with Chinese domination. At no cost can they accept the domination of the yellow race of China over the world.

According to the Holy Quran, every form of racism must be stamped out from the world. Without this, world peace can never be established. According to the verse of the Holy Quran we are discussing (49:14), although colours and races differ, it is only to make recognition easy. Otherwise all humans are linked to the same progeny of Adam and Eve. In no way does it create any distinction. Superiority, according to the Holy Quran, is entirely based on the human fear of God. Fear of God causes a person to consider himself as equal to all others, or even lesser. This is an attribute which causes humans to rise in the sight of Allah.

These inferences are drawn from the above mentioned verse.

A Great Charter Proclaimed by the Holy Prophet^{sa} on Racial Equality

The Holy Prophet^{sa} explained this most beautifully in his last sermon during his last pilgrimage, in the following words:

يَـاۤأَيُّهَـا النَّـاسُ اَلاۤ اِنَّ رَبَّـكُمْ وَاحِدٌ وَّاِنَّ اَبَـاكُمْ وَاحِدٌ اَلاۤ
لَافَضْـلَ لِعَـرَبِيٍّ عَلٰى عَجَمِيٍّ وَّلَا لِعَجَمِيٍّ عَلٰى عَرَبِيٍّ وَّلَا
لِاَحْـمَـرَ عَـلٰى اَسْـوَدَ وَلَا لِاَ سُـوَدَ عَلٰى اَحْمَرَ اِلَّا بِالتَّقْوٰى.
اَبَلَّغْتُ قَالُوْا قَدْ بَلَّغَ رَسُوْلُ اللهِ صَلَّى اللهُ عَلَيْهِ وَسَلَّمَ.

'O humankind your Allah is One and your father was also one, so listen carefully that Arabs have no superiority over the non-Arabs nor have the non-Arabs any superiority over the Arabs. Similarly, the white and red races, have no superiority over black races, and black races have no superiority over the white. Yes, only he is superior who transcends in his personal good deeds. O people tell me if I have conveyed my Lord's message to all of you? At this, the entire gathering spoke with one voice: Yes, the Messenger of Allah has conveyed the message of Allah to all of us.'**59**

The Root of the Malady of Racism

Racism, which is the root cause of distinction between different nations, in fact flourishes within every home. The Quran being the word of God pinpoints this root of all evil and throws ample light on this subject.

To help humankind to abstain from every form of racism the following verse of the Quran declares:

يَا أَيُّهَا الَّذِينَ اٰمَنُوْا لَا يَسْخَرْ قَوْمٌ مِّنْ قَوْمٍ عَسَى أَنْ يَّكُوْنُوْا خَيْرًا مِّنْهُمْ وَلَا نِسَاءٌ مِّنْ نِّسَاءٍ عَسَى أَنْ يَّكُنَّ خَيْرًا مِّنْهُنَّ ۚ وَلَا تَلْمِزُوْا أَنْفُسَكُمْ وَلَا تَنَابَزُوْا بِالْأَلْقَابِ ۖ بِئْسَ الِاسْمُ الْفُسُوْقُ بَعْدَ الْإِيْمَانِ ۚ وَمَنْ لَّمْ يَتُبْ فَأُولٰئِكَ هُمُ الظّٰلِمُوْنَ

O ye who believe! let not one people deride *another* people, who may be better than they, nor let women *deride other* women, who may be better than they. And do not slander your own people, nor taunt *each other* with nick-names. It is bad *indeed* to earn foul reputation after *professing the* faith; and those who repent not are the wrongdoers.
(Sūrah al-Ḥujurāt; Ch.49: V.12)

Now this subject has been explained in such detail that no one who reads the Quran even cursorily can put forward the excuse that he was unaware of it.

Unfortunately, however, such vices prevail even in the Muslim countries where these verses are repeatedly recited. They all say we have believed and have testified, but in the world of practice they forget all this. They consider such practices as trivial but from these, apparently trivial practices, grave disorders arise.

Observe how jokes based on racial, professional and religious differences are commonly concocted in the Indo-Pakistan subcontinent. The unskilled workers make jokes about skilled workers like barbers and weavers. In response, the barbers and weavers spin jokes about unskilled people. The skilled people relate jokes about the farmers and the farmers in their turn relate jokes about skilled people. Similarly in Pakistan, to tell jokes about Sikhs is very popular, while in India, the Sikhs and Hindus tell jokes about the Muslims of the subcontinent. If such jokes are told in private gatherings where the people about whom the jokes are cracked are not present to be offended, then, to some extent, this practice is generally considered harmless. This, unfortunately, is not the case. As a reaction to these jokes, racism between different nations, castes and professions freely flourishes.

The Quran has warned to abstain from this practice; otherwise destiny may turn the tables against those who are powerful today. This warning is not confined to any particular region of the world. There was a period in the history of Great Britain when the professionals and traders were looked down on by the landed gentry. Now the landed gentry has lost its previous status of superiority and it is the rich professionals and tradesmen who rule the British

361

society today. It is mostly they who are elected as parliamentarians.

Warfare Incidental to the Lack of Justice

Man is not in danger because of the proliferation of arms throughout the world. Man is in danger because of the ill-intentions of the nations who possess such arms. In the case of eventual warfare between different nations, how should they be resolved according to the Holy Quran? The answer is given in the following verse:

وَإِنْ طَآئِفَتٰنِ مِنَ الْمُؤْمِنِيْنَ اقْتَتَلُوْا فَأَصْلِحُوْا بَيْنَهُمَا ۚ فَإِنْ بَغَتْ اِحْدٰىهُمَا عَلَى الْأُخْرٰى فَقَاتِلُوا الَّتِيْ تَبْغِيْ حَتّٰى تَفِيْٓءَ اِلٰٓى اَمْرِ اللّٰهِ ۚ فَإِنْ فَآءَتْ فَأَصْلِحُوْا بَيْنَهُمَا بِالْعَدْلِ وَ اَقْسِطُوْا ۖ اِنَّ اللّٰهَ يُحِبُّ الْمُقْسِطِيْنَ ☐

And if two parties of believers fight *against each other,* make peace between them, then if *after that* one of them transgresses against the other, fight the party that transgresses until it returns to the command of Allah. Then if it returns, make peace between them with equity, and act justly. Verily, Allah loves the just.
(Sūrah al-Ḥujurāt; Ch.49: V.10)

A question to be raised here is why the verse does not address mankind in general. But this expectation from the believers is in fact tantamount to the high expectation from all of mankind because a better solution for the conflict between nations, religious or otherwise, cannot be visualized. The reason why mankind at large is not directly addressed is because they will not submit to this advice of the Quran. According to them the Quran has no authority over the people of the world. However, the believers who truly submit to the teachings of the Quran can become a model for the whole of mankind. Thus the teaching of the Quran is reflected to the whole world through the mirror of the believers.

The Quran admonishes that nations should not wait until wars erupt. Before this happens remedial measures are essential to resolve the disputes, otherwise it will be too late. However, if despite efforts of reconciliation or establishing peace, two belligerent nations still go to war, then time should not be wasted in resolutions. Instead they are admonished to join forces to raise weapons against the one party considered to be at fault and who has transgressed.

The Quran advises that after establishing peace, when it comes to arbitration, it must be done with absolute justice. Otherwise, it may sow the seeds of future wars.

The Danger of Wars when the Quranic Admonition is Disregarded

After the Second World War the way great powers of

the world joined their heads to arbitrate, and the way they tried to crush the nations they considered to be criminals, was in itself an unjust and criminal attitude. They intended to crush them forever, so that they could never again raise their heads endangering world peace. Similarly, the arbitration after the First World War laid the foundation for the Second World War.

Every serious student of history will testify to this statement. He can easily pinpoint all the cruel decisions which created a strong reaction among the defeated nations and they quietly resolved to take revenge. The same applies to the decisions taken after the Second World War to obliterate the dangers of a third world war. Leave alone all the other wrong decisions and just concentrate upon the one taken unanimously by Roosevelt, Churchill and Stalin during their summit in Turkey. They all believed that the German nation would always pose a danger to world peace. So they cleverly thought that if the Germans are divided in the middle and handed over to opposite ideologies, in due course both the German halves will be polarised against each other. West Germany will always feel threatened by East Germany and vice versa. In this way, the attention of the German people will be distracted from other nations, and, even if their suppressed sense of vengeance erupts, it will erupt against each other. Changes in ideologies are taking place and will always continue to do so. In the future it cannot be ruled out that East and West Germany may unite again.[*] If and when it happens, the German nation will raise to such great power as could never have been imagined before.

This was not the only potentially wrong decision. There were many others like it as a consequence of which the danger of a future war cannot be avoided. To recapitulate, the Quran warns the victorious powers that after establishing peace once again, when they decide punitive measures against the transgressor that is the time for them to be absolutely just. Only then can they be certain that they will be able to establish a lasting peace.

In the last part of the same verse (49:10), the Quran declares that Allah loves those who dispense justice which implies that those whom Allah loves, He does not permit them to fight against each other.

The Quranic Teaching regarding Righteousness in the Affairs of Mankind without Distinction

As far as the early period of the Muslims is concerned, when they were opposed and persecuted by non-believers surrounding them and those who initially invaded them, they were strongly admonished to adhere to justice. That was the time when the might of the idolators of Mecca was pitched against the Holy Prophet[sa] and his Companions with the

---

[*] This prediction was made in July 1988 before the Berlin Wall came down and has since come true. [Publisher]

determination to wipe them out from the face of the earth. The Quranic teaching during that period is not such as could have sprung from the heart of a person who was profoundly emotionally disturbed. Most certainly this teaching is that of a Being Who knows the present and the future and Who is unbiased in relation to all His creatures. The same point is emphasized by the Founder[as] of the Ahmadiyya Community when he wrote that you should remember that God is not a relative of any of His creatures. If He is a relative to one, He is a relative to all, if not, He is related to none.

This point can be verified from the conduct of the Holy Prophet[sa] and his Companions when they were engaged in a war of survival. At that critical period, the Divine teaching bestowed upon the Holy Prophet[sa] was:

لَا يَنْهٰكُمُ اللّٰهُ عَنِ الَّذِيْنَ لَمْ يُقَاتِلُوْكُمْ فِى الدِّيْنِ وَلَمْ يُخْرِجُوْكُمْ مِّنْ دِيَارِكُمْ اَنْ تَبَرُّوْهُمْ وَتُقْسِطُوْٓا اِلَيْهِمْ ۚ اِنَّ اللّٰهَ يُحِبُّ الْمُقْسِطِيْنَ ☐

Allah forbids you not, respecting those who have not fought against you on account of *your* religion, and who have not driven you forth from your homes, that you be kind to them and act equitably towards them; surely Allah loves those who are equitable.
(Sūrah al-Mumtaḥinah; Ch.60: V.9)

According to this verse, Allah does not forbid from fighting those who have waged war against you, merely because of religious differences, and turned you out of your homes. But those who did not do so must be treated with equity.

Then the Quran proclaims:

$$وَلَا تَجْعَلُوا اللّٰهَ عُرْضَةً لِّاَيْمَانِكُمْ اَنْ تَبَرُّوْا وَتَتَّقُوْا وَتُصْلِحُوْا بَيْنَ النَّاسِ ۭ وَاللّٰهُ سَمِيْعٌ عَلِيْمٌ ☐$$

And make not Allah a target for your oaths that you may *thereby* abstain from doing good and acting righteously and making peace between men. And Allah is All-Hearing, All-Knowing.
(Sūrah-al-Baqarah; Ch.2: V.225)

24 The Teaching of Justice and Kindness Regarding Relatives

So far we have discussed relations between different nations and groups. Now I shall turn to the internal relationships among different tiers of society. Such tiers may comprise the relationship of parents with their children, children with their parents, brothers and sisters of a family and the relationship between close relatives and distant relatives etc. The Holy Quran has not disregarded any of these internal social divisions. I will begin with the rights of parents upon their children.

The Rights of Parents upon their Children

The Quran very strongly admonishes children to treat their parents not only with justice but with kindness:

وَوَصَّيْنَا الْإِنْسَانَ بِوَالِدَيْهِ حَمَلَتْهُ أُمُّهُ وَهْنًا عَلَى وَهْنٍ وَّ
فِطْلُهُ فِي عَامَيْنِ أَنِ اشْكُرْ لِيْ وَلِوَالِدَيْكَ إِلَيَّ الْمَصِيْرُ ☐

And We have enjoined on man concerning his parents—his mother bears him in weakness upon weakness, and his weaning takes two years—'Give thanks to Me and to your parents. Unto Me is the *final* return.'
(Sūrah Luqmān; Ch.31: V.15)

In relation to this Quranic admonishment, the following tradition by Abū Hurairah[ra] is quoted:

> Three times the Holy Prophet[sa] declared, 'may his nose bite the dust, may his nose bite the dust.' (This is an Arabic phrase which is used to indicate that the person about whom one is talking has been disgraced and failed in his life.) The Companions inquired 'O Messenger of Allah who is that person?' The Holy Messenger[sa] indicated in response that he is the one who found his parents in old age and failed to earn paradise by treating them with utmost kindness.[60]

This may appear to be a small immaterial thing but if you look at the Western as well as the Eastern societies today, you will discover that children in both the societies are becoming increasingly careless of their parents. This problem is more prevalent in the Western societies and less in the Eastern societies but there, too, it is gradually spreading. As a result of this, society is generally suffering with growing miseries. The Holy Prophet[sa] however, repeatedly admonished his Companions to treat their parents with kindness in accordance with the Quranic teaching. He taught them elaborately and the rights of parents were so clearly explained that as a result, a most beautiful society came into being in the world.

Once, a young Beduin complained in a tactless manner to the Holy Prophet[sa] that his father wanted to misappropriate his wealth. The Holy Prophet[sa] answered him in the same style but not in the same stern and crude tone. Judging him to be hard of heart, the Holy Prophet[sa] told him straight away to return and reminded him that, 'you and all your prosperity belonged to your father and what your children earn that will belong to you, eat it with pleasure.'[61]

No son can genuinely allege that his father is misappropriating his wealth. The father has a right to use the income of his son as though it were his own. On the other hand, the son is not permitted to consume the earnings of his father as he likes. Apparently this is against justice, but if you ponder over it in depth you will come to the conclusion that it is as it should have been. The way a father loves his son, the son cannot love him in the same way and to the same extent. This is so because the son is the future of the father, but the father is the past of the son. Very soon his own future appears before him in the form of his own family whose interest he prefers to that of his father. An honest observer will conclude the same by critically examining any society anywhere in the world. Of course there are exceptions to the rule, but exceptions always prove the rule. Again, the father is one but the sons can be many. If each son enjoys the freedom to treat the father's wealth as he likes, the entire family would fall apart. See now how the Islamic teaching is in accord with human nature and the Holy Prophet[sa] explained it as such. Parents have a right on their children's earnings, and when they grow old, whatever the child spends on them is not to be considered as an act of charity but as his duty. He should not think that he is bestowing any favours.

In another tradition it is reported that once a person appeared before the Holy Prophet[sa] and complained that his father was utilizing his earnings as he pleased. At that time the father was also present. The son requested the Holy Prophet[sa] to stop his father from interfering in his affairs. The father remained silent and did not once utter a single word. The Holy Prophet[sa] detected the signs of sorrow in his eyes and encouraged him to say what was in his heart. In response, the father recited some verses of an Arabic poem which are translated as follows:

> O Prophet of Allah! When he was young and could not walk, I carried him in my arms and moved him from place to place, as though I had become his legs. When he was an infant and felt hunger and he did not have the strength to pick up the milk by his side, I picked it up on his behalf and held it for him to drink. O Prophet of Allah! When he was young, there was no strength in his arms to defend himself, I defended him and taught him archery. Now O my master, when he has learnt the art of archery, he is aiming his arrows at me!

When the Holy Prophet[sa] heard this he was overwhelmed with emotion. He caught the son by his collar and said 'Go, you and whatever belongs to you, is that of your father.'

Being unaware of this teaching the advanced societies are filled with such sorrows that you cannot imagine its true extent. If you read such literature as mentions the consequences of the neglect by children of their old parents, you will be pained to learn that some parents when they grow old are sent to old people's homes. Often it happens they are not visited by their children except once in a blue moon. Some of them are so tired of loneliness that they prefer to commit suicide. Some become mad and no one inquires after them. Occasionally, when some elderly parents are visited by their children, they consider it as an extreme act of kindness and favour and begin to sing their praises.

All are not alike in the West. There are also many who give full respect to their parents and pay them their dues. But those who do not, exceed them by a large margin and are responsible for the ill fame that the West has earned in this respect. Now this social disease has become so wide-spread that experts in England are forecasting that early in the next century the number of homeless old people will increase to the tune of eleven million. Somehow they will drag on to their death with their misery and agony.

The Quran preempts this social disaster by admonishing:

وَ قَضٰى رَبُّكَ اَلَّا تَعْبُدُوٓا اِلَّآ اِيَّاهُ وَ بِالْوَالِدَيْنِ اِحْسَانًا ۚ
اِمَّا يَبْلُغَنَّ عِنْدَكَ الْكِبَرَ اَحَدُهُمَآ اَوْ كِلٰهُمَا فَلَا تَقُلْ لَّهُمَآ اُفٍّ
وَّلَا تَنْهَرْهُمَا وَقُلْ لَّهُمَا قَوْلًا كَرِيْمًا ☐

Your Lord has commanded, 'Worship none but Him,
and *show* kindness to parents. If one of them or both
of them attain old age with you, never say unto them
any word expressive of disgust nor reproach them, but
address them with kind words.'
(Sūrah Banī-Isrā'īl; Ch.17: V.24)

The first part of this verse deals with justice and
describes a fundamental obligation of man, without
paying respect to which no man is worthy of being
called a man. Having said that, in the second part of
the same verse the Holy Quran advises, 'address both
of the parents with a word of great respect.' This is a
step forward from justice and enters the area of
kindness. This implies that to speak rudely to them
should, of course, be out of the question. It behoves
you to address them always with profound respect.
Then moving forward, in the following verse the Holy
Quran teaches how to truly behave towards them like
their next of kin:

وَاخْفِضْ لَهُمَا جَنَاحَ الذُّلِّ مِنَ الرَّحْمَةِ وَقُلْ رَّبِّ ارْحَمْهُمَا كَمَا رَبَّيٰنِيْ
صَغِيْرًا ☐

And lower to them the wing of humility out of
tenderness. And say, 'My Lord, have mercy on them
even as they nourished me in *my* childhood.'
(Sūrah Banī Isrā'īl; Ch.17: V.25)

374

The first part of this verse speaks of the lowering of the wings of mercy over them. It is just like a bird sheltering its fledglings under its wings. Then in the second part, the Holy Quran teaches a prayer for the grown-up children to recite for their elderly parents which reminds them of their own early life. The prayer implies that the children cannot do everything for their parents like they did for them when they were children, treating them with extreme kindness during their early life. The prayer speaks of three important points: First, justice is taught that on no account may children ever speak harshly to their parents. Whatever intolerance they show, the children should remember that they have reached an old age and it is quite natural for them to do this unintentionally. By referring to their early childhood, Allah reminds the children that even they, during their infancy and later on, caused so much inconvenience to their parents which they tolerated with great patience. They are indirectly reminded: You used to dirty your parents' clothes, you used to make their nightly sleep impossible. For your sake they used to wake up all night long and during the day you used to break their precious belongings, making their rest impossible. Sometimes, when they were about to sleep after a tiring day, you suddenly shattered their sleep with your screams. Have you forgotten all this? Thus the

Holy Quran requires them to be tolerant and never to shout at them.

It was the custom of the Holy Prophet[sa] that sometimes he spoke of the Quranic teachings by way of parables and tales. Such parables and tales left a lasting impression upon his Companions and they became emotionally charged. Once, he told them the tale of three men on a journey who went into a cave to rest in its shelter. Suddenly a great piece of rock fell from above and blocked the entire mouth of the cave. At this, they consulted each other as to what they should do. They reached the conclusion that only prayer could save them from this catastrophe, but how should they pray to God so that He would have mercy upon them? They decided that each of them should remember some exceptional act of goodness which he might have done purely for the sake of Allah. Among them was one who narrated the following incident. He said, 'When I was young and my parents had grown old, it was my custom to return home with my cattle early enough for me to milk them and feed my parents with that milk before they went to sleep. One day I was rather late returning home and found my parents were already asleep. It was also my habit not to feed my own family members or even my cattle, without first feeding my parents. Hence, all night I kept standing by the bed of my parents with a jug of milk in my hand. I did not even move lest they should be disturbed. The following morning when they woke up

I fed them, after which I fed my hungry family and the cattle. O my Allah, if I did it entirely for your sake, please cause the rock to move aside a little.' It so happened that instantly the rock moved aside so that one-third of the blockage was removed and the light started brightening the dark cave. After this, the Holy Prophet[sa] related some exceptional good deeds of the other two companions. At the conclusion of each one, the rock slid aside a little more, until after the third anecdote, the rock moved enough to leave a large enough passage for the trapped men to be able to walk out of the cave.[62] I have not related their stories in detail because they are not relevant to this discussion. I have only related the tale of the person who was exceptionally kind to his parents, to remind people that kindness to parents is a virtue exceptionally liked by Allah.

The Holy Quran has not neglected the importance of justice anywhere or in any situation. Sometimes people fail to comprehend this subject and think that occasionally kindness clashes with the dictates of justice. However, it is possible to do kindness while adhering to the dictates of justice. According to the Holy Quran, of course it is highly essential to pay each person his dues, but after that the higher floors of kindness and of treatment like the treatment to the next of the kin can be built without contradiction.

Allah declares, of course He has strongly admonished people to be extremely kind to their parents. However, when the requirements of this kindness apparently clash with obedience to Allah you may, kindly, reject your parents' desire to offend Allah. Apart from this, in all wordly matters you must remain obedient and kind to them. Obedience to Allah is the highest degree of justice one can attain and even if the parents quarrel with their children to obey them and call partners with Allah of which they have no knowledge, they may never obey them in this.

وَوَصَّيْنَا الْإِنْسَانَ بِوَالِدَيْهِ حُسْنًا ۖ وَإِنْ جَاهَدَاكَ لِتُشْرِكَ بِي مَا لَيْسَ لَكَ بِهِ عِلْمٌ فَلَا تُطِعْهُمَا ۚ إِلَيَّ مَرْجِعُكُمْ فَأُنَبِّئُكُمْ بِمَا كُنْتُمْ تَعْمَلُونَ ☐

And we have enjoined on man kindness to his parents; but if they contend with you so that you *too* may associate partners with Me; of which you have no knowledge whatsoever, then obey them not. Unto Me is your return, and I shall inform you of what you did. (Sūrah al-ʿAnkabūt; Ch.29: V.9)

Allah declares, of couse He has strongly admonished people to be extremely kind to their parents. However, when the requirements of this kindness apparently clash with obedience to Allah you may, kindly, reject your parents' desire to offend Allah. Apart from this, in all wordly matters you must remain obedient and kind to them. Obedience to Allah is the hightest degree of justice one can attain and even if the parents quarrel with their children to obey them and call partners with Allah of which they have no knowledge, they may never obey them in this.

In the above verse Allah does not teach children to show disrespect to their parents, nor does He encourage them to harshly enquire as to who are they to teach them to respect God? Or to reply, I will listen to Allah and not to you! Here, incidentally, humans are taught only to believe what they know to be correct. This is their fundamental right. That which they do not know personally they cannot be forced to believe.

Sa'd bin Abī Waqqāṣ narrates:

I used to pay my dues most respectfully to my idolatrous mother. When I converted to Islam she said to me, 'O Sa'd, what sort of religion have you accepted? You will have to renounce this faith or I will go into hunger strike till death. Then people will blame you for being the cause of my death.' Sa'd responded by saying, 'O my mother, even if you do that I am not going to renounce my faith.' But his mother disregarded his warning and went into a hunger strike for one day and one night, and suffered immensely. At that, Sa'd addressed her thus: 'O my dear mother, by Allah, I swear that even if you possessed one hundred lives and gave them up one after the other in my presence, I would still not renounce my faith.' Observing this resolution on the part of her son, she gave up the hunger strike and started eating normally again.[63]

This incident is reported authentically and, according to Sa'd, the verse under discussion was revealed after this incident.

The Beautiful Teaching of doing Favours to One's Parents even After their Death

Abū Sa'd narrates that while he was sitting in the company of the Holy Prophet[sa], a person from Banū Salma approached the Holy Prophet[sa] and begged him thus: 'O Messenger of Allah, is there any way for me to show kindness to my parents, which I may follow even after their death?'

The Holy Prophet[sa] responded: 'Yes, after their death, pray for both of them and seek forgiveness for them. Also, pay respect to their promises and vows and respect the friends of both. And treat their relatives and their friends, to whom you are related through them, with kindness.'[64]

One can see to what dizzy heights the subject of benevolence and kinship has been raised. Before this, the teaching on living parents has been mentioned. After their death, the subject of beneficence is dealt with here. Allah teaches that one may serve one's parents as much as one pleases but still one will not be able to repay their favours, which will remain overwhelming. To assuage the feeling of remorse over one's failure to serve one's parents as one ought to have while they were alive, the admonishments of the Holy Prophet[sa] mentioned above comprehensively deal with this. The Holy Prophet^{sa} has made it abundantly clear that if parents die during the lifetime of their children while they still owe debts, it is the duty of the children to repay the unpaid debts as fully as possible. It is tragic that nowadays many children do not respect this admonition. Some children, when they are approached by those who come to demand their unpaid debts, reply insolently by way of stupid joke 'go and demand what is owed to you from the person who has died without paying his debts. We have no obligation to pay them!' This is an affront to the aforementioned admonitions of the Holy Prophet^{sa}.

Ibni Abbās^{ra} narrates that the mother of Saʻd bin ʻUbādah^{ra} died during his absence. When he returned home, he approached the Holy Prophet^{sa} and inquired from him, 'If I want to give anything by way of alms on her behalf, will she benefit from it?' The Holy Prophet^{sa} answered 'yes', she would. At this, he respectfully answered, 'You may be my witness that on her behalf I dedicate such and such garden of mine for the service of the poor.'⁶⁵

To Seek Forgiveness on Behalf of Deceased Parents

A tradition is narrated in *Sunan Ibni Mājah* from Ḥaḍrat Abū Hurairah^{ra} that the spiritual status of some parents will be raised in the heavens and in surprise they would ask 'what is this for?' They will be answered, 'This is because your children are seeking forgiveness on your behalf.'[66] In this way the Holy Prophet[sa] fully assured children that even after the demise of their parents, the seeking of forgiveness on their behalf will not go in vain. It will not be just an emotional exercise but Allah will certainly benefit the deceased parents because of this.

The Rights of Children upon their Parents

Apart from the parents' rights over their children, the Holy Quran also clearly mentions the rights of the children upon their parents. It declares:

قَدْ خَسِرَ الَّذِينَ قَتَلُوٓا اَوْلَادَهُمْ سَفَهًۢا بِغَيْرِ عِلْمٍ وَّحَرَّمُوْا مَا رَزَقَهُمُ اللّٰهُ افْتِرَآءً عَلَى اللّٰهِ ۘ ...

They have suffered heavy loss who have murdered their children without realizing it. Similarly, they declared some food forbidden (unlawful) what Allah has provided for them, forging a lie against Allah (Allah had not forbidden for them)...
(Sūrah al-An'ām; Ch.6: V.141)

On the same subject another verse of the Holy Quran declares:

... وَلَا تَقْتُلُوٓا اَوْلَادَكُمْ مِّنْ اِمْلَاقٍ ۘ نَحْنُ نَرْزُقُكُمْ وَاِيَّاهُمْ ...

...do not murder your children for *the fear of* paucity of food——It is We who provide for you and for them as well....
(Sūrah al-An'ām; Ch.6: V.152)

382

In both these verses, the word 'murder' does not imply physical murder. It is a metaphorical expression meaning, among other things, that you should not bring them up in a manner which is tantamount to their spiritual murder. Again it is implied, do not exercise any family planning fearing you will be overburdened by providing for them for the same reason as has been mentioned before viz., that Allah provides for them as well as for you. In this verse, Allah prepares humans for a universal holy war against family planning in the latter days, where it is carried out for the fear of shortage of food.

Sometimes people abort their children fearing poverty. Such abortion is mentioned here as killing of children. This has many implied meanings. The first right of as yet unborn children is that they should never be aborted for the fear of poverty. Unfortunately the world today is not only ignoring this right, but is taking every measure to oppose it. All these world-wide family planning schemes which are widely spread are a demonstration of the same.

Some people erroneously believe that these verses apply only to the earlier times when some Arabs used to kill their children. This is certainly wrong. It does not refer to the Arab custom of murdering daughters which was never done for the fear of poverty. In their false pride, they thought that to give birth to daughters was shameful. This practice was only rarely exercised by an extremely small number of Arabs. Had it been a common practice, the Arab world would have been completely deprived of women and might have become extinct as a result of that. Again, they never murdered male children, and it should be noticed that the word *Aulād* in Arabic is applicable to both male and female children.

The teaching of family planning which is widespread today is done with the specific warning that if poor countries did not prevent conception by modern means, they would ultimately die of hunger. The Holy Quran raised a holy war against this fourteen hundred years ago when at that time there was no imminent danger of this. According to the Holy Quran, not only is it an objection against God as well as His design, it also means that man alleges that Allah's scheme of things is faulty and He does not know how to create balance in His own creation. Wherever Allah has forbidden family planning in the Holy Quran, He has done so on account of the fear of family planners for shortage of food. The Companions of the Holy Prophet[sa] narrate that the only practice they carried out was not to abort children for the fear of poverty, but to take preventative measures against their conception for other reasons.

The Wisdom Underlying the above Quranic Teaching

Little do the people of poor countries understand that the more children they bear the less will be the fear of hunger for them and there will also be many advantages which are far and wide-reaching. In fact children of poor parents assist them in earning bread instead of becoming a burden upon them. Early in their life they are sent to factories such as carpet weaving factories etc., which helps the economy of the family as well as that of the country. Rich countries raise a hue and cry against this in the name of cruelty to children, but it is only a question of economic survival for the poor countries. Again, the population growth of poor countries compels the population to migrate towards the richer countries where they have better chances of earning higher incomes. It is through the extra income which they send back home that not only do their poor families begin to improve the quality of their life and education but also the country as a whole benefits from the transfer of money from richer countries to the poorer ones.

Another benefit of population growth in the poor countries is a constant mixing of people from the third world with the people of the first. It is similar to the winds carrying dust particles from one country to another; thereby constantly mixing them together. It is for these and many more benefits that Allah must have planned the population growth in poverty-stricken countries, but little do the people know.

This labour force which is spreading far and wide into the rich countries is such that the rich countries cannot stop their legal or illegal immigration. In fact, their economic experts understand that it is to their own advantage in improving their economy by paying less wages to these foreign immigrants. These widening populations of the poor countries are changing the fate of the world. When these poor immigrants see new inventions in foreign countries, they send some of them to their poor families in the countries of their origin. Many among them learn the technology of how to make them and export this knowledge back to their own country. So the technical know-how for making modern devices etc., constantly improves. It is from among the same people that some, when they grow rich enough, install great industries in their own countries. Major changes have taken place in the world and in some conquered countries, new social, cultural, economic and political changes have occurred. In this, the population pressure of the poor countries has played a major role.

Some governments of poor countries, when entrapped by the Western propaganda of family planning, stupidly hurt their own cause without realizing it. It is for this reason that the Holy Quran declares them, 'people at loss.'

In contrast to them, many rich people take measures to improve the rate of reproduction. For instance in Germany, families are encouraged to have a larger number of children. The more children there are in the family, the more benefits the families will earn from the government. Similar measures are taken in England and particularly in Norway. According to experts, if the Norwegian people continuously follow the trend of giving birth to such few children or to no children at all, then in the next 15-20 years the Norwegian people may become a minority in their own country. Thus the immigrants may increase in population to the extent that they may capture the political power there.

The Teaching of Adhering to Justice between One's Own Children

As far as the rights of children upon their parents are concerned, the Holy Quran makes it compulsory upon parents not to give preferential treatment to some of their children over others. When Allah entrusts ownership to people over their properties and children, it does not mean that they possess unlimited rights over them. The absolute owner is only Allah. All human possessions are bestowed by Him.

The philosophy of possession is repeatedly explained in the Holy Quran in the same manner. According to this philosophy, man is made only the temporary possessor and Allah is the All-Possessor. That is why man is answerable to Allah for whatever possession is bestowed upon him. Even his own children are a trust with him and he cannot treat them unjustly.

387

It is narrated by Nu'mān bin Bashīr[ra], that once his father took him to the Holy Messenger[sa] and told him that he had given him, Nu'mān, a slave by way of gift. At this the Holy Prophet[sa] inquired if he had gifted a slave to each of his sons. His father answered, 'No, I have only bestowed one slave upon this son of mine.' At this, the Holy Prophet[sa] told him to take the gift back which he did accordingly. In another narration, it is mentioned that the Holy Prophet[sa] admonished: 'Have fear of Allah and treat your children with justice and equality.' By way of explanation he told the father of Nu'mān, 'When you mentioned this gift to your son before me it was like making me a witness over this false deal. Never dare to make me witness over falsehood. I can never become a witness over any transgression.'[67]

The Reward for Treating Children with Justice

Then, to firmly establish the rights of children, Allah has mentioned a reward for this act. It is a strange glory of Allah that He has fixed a reward for a naturally found trend among parents. Most of them treat their children with equal kindness.

Ḥaḍrat 'Ā'ishah[ra] narrates, 'Once a poor woman came to me. She was carrying two girls in her arms, one on either side. I gave her three dates and she gave one to each girl and put one in her own mouth. But before she could eat it the girls demanded it from her. At this, she took the date out of her mouth, divided it into two halves and gave one to each of her daughters.' Now this behoves only a mother and she does this in accordance with her nature, not for the sake of doing a good deed. She was compelled by her heart and so chose to remain hungry. When this was narrated by Ḥaḍrat 'Ā'ishah Ṣiddīqah[ra] to the Holy Prophet[sa], he said 'in reward for this act of hers Allah has made it essential for Him to grant her paradise.'[68]

How great is this teaching! The teaching of justice is so thoroughly intermingled with the teaching of beneficence that one cannot be separated from the other. Allah does not permit the treating of one's children unjustly, even with the apparent intention of pleasing Allah. Ḥaḍrat S'ad bin Abī Waqqās[ra] narrates, 'during the year of the Last Hajj, I fell seriously ill in Mecca. The Holy Prophet[sa] came to inquire after my health. Having told him the seriousness of my illness, I asked that since I have a large property and except for one daughter, there is no other close relative to inherit from me, may I give two-thirds of my property by way of alms?'

Ḥaḍrat S'ad bin Abī Waqqās[ra] was a very knowledgeable person and had fear of Allah. He did not ask if he should be permitted to give all his property for the sake of Allah. Instead he calculated that two-thirds is the right of a son and one-third that of a daughter. He thought that because he had no son he could dedicate two-thirds of his property (which is the son's share) for the sake of Allah, without depriving his daughter of her due right. In answer, the Holy Prophet[sa] replied, 'No'. Then he beseeched again 'permit me to dedicate one-third of my property for the sake of Allah.' The Holy Prophet[sa] said, 'Yes, you may dedicate one-third for the sake of Allah, but actually even one-third is more than enough.' Thereby he implied that the daughter should be given even more than two-third of one's property. He also said that it is better to leave your children well-to-do, rather than poor, so that they may not be compelled to beg from others. He again admonished that whatever you spend on your children, or poor next of kin, or the poor who are not related to you, Allah will most certainly reward you for that.[69]

The Holy Prophet[sa] possessed such great wisdom that his traditions should not be read cursorily, but one should dive deep into the ocean of his words in search of the underlying treasures of wisdom.

Once, the Holy Prophet[sa] told his Companions 'My Allah has promised me that if your umma will spend on their own children, Allah will reward such people as He rewards those who spend for the cause of the poor.' The Holy Prophet[sa] was deeply aware of fine causative psychological factors. Sometimes when he answered, apparently his reply was not related to the question but in fact not a single word in his answer was unrelated. It contained every word which was required. Some narrators report that, once the Holy Prophet[sa] promised that if we fed our wives with our own hands, not out of love for them but to please Allah, then Allah would reward us for that.

Now we return to the previously discussed narration by S'ad bin Abī Waqqās[ra]. He reports, that 'after the admonition by Rasūlullah[sa], I expressed my fear that this disease of mine could prove fatal and I may not return with the other companions to Medina. Thus my migration would be left incomplete and I may not get full reward for it.' At this he assured me 'you will certainly not be left incomplete in reward. Whatever you do for the sake of winning the pleasure of Allah, you will most certainly receive full reward for it and also, it is possible that you may not be left behind.' In fact it was a prayer. He further narrates, 'Allah showed mercy upon me in response to that prayer and I became completely well and was able to return to Medina. Then I lived long after the demise of Ḥaḍrat Rasūlullah[sa] and was bestowed the opportunity to relate this narration.' Incidentally it is worth mentioning that the credit of the victory over Qādsiyah and Iran also goes to Ḥaḍrat Sa'd bin Abī Waqqās.[70]

The Teaching of Beneficence in Addition to the Teaching of Justice concerning one's Children

The Holy Prophet[sa] did not leave any aspect of beneficence to children untouched and taught us how to treat children with kindness and beneficence. Nowadays one can claim that these are ordinary

391

natural things and everybody knows how to be kind to one's own children. The reality is that even in the most advanced societies many children remain deprived of receiving their parent's kindness. A large proportion of these deprived children suffer from mental illnesses. The parents remain concerned with only their own pleasures and do not pay the children their due rights.

According to Ḥaḍrat 'Ā'ishah[ra], once a Bedouin inquired from the Holy Prophet[sa], 'Why do you kiss children?' (as if it were contrary to manly characteristics). He further added, 'We do not kiss them.' The Holy Prophet[sa] responded, 'If Allah has uprooted kindness from your heart, what can I do about it?'[71]

Once, a granddaughter of the Holy Prophet[sa] was in her death throes and his daughter begged him to come. At his arrival she put the child into his lap. The child's breathing was stertorous. Tears began to flow from his eyes. Ḥaḍrat Sa'd bin 'Ubādah[ra] narrates that he also accompanied him. He inquired, 'O Messenger of Allah, what do we see, why are you shedding tears?' The Holy Prophet[sa] answered:

$$\text{هٰذِهِ الرَّحْمَةُ يَضَعُهَا اللّٰهُ فِى قُلُوبِ مَنْ يَّشَاءُ مِنْ عِبَادِهِ}$$
$$\text{وَاِنَّمَا يَرْحَمُ اللّٰهُ مِنْ عِبَادِهِ الرُّحَمَآءُ.}$$

'Lo! what you apparently believe to be tears of weakness are signs of Allah's blessing. Whosoever's heart He chooses, He fills with blessing and Allah bestows mercy upon those of his servants who show mercy to others.'[72]

Once the Holy Prophet[sa] was carrying the little child Umama in his arms. He started praying while still carrying her. When he bowed for *Ruku'* he slid her to the ground, when he got up he lifted her again.[73] According to the jurisprudence taught to pupils nowadays, if someone carries something during his prayer or does something else distracting his attention, his prayer is broken. It is said that once a simple-minded pupil was being taught hadith by a mullah. When this narration was mentioned he said, 'Oh! So the prayer of the Holy Prophet[sa] was broken!' However, this exceptional conduct of Rasūlullāh[sa] cannot be acquired as a general practice. If all people carry children on their shoulders or in their arms while praying, they certainly cannot maintain their concentration like the Holy Prophet[sa] could.

No one can Dedicate one's own Child without his Consent

Regarding the dedication of one's children, the Holy Quran further advances this subject and admonishes that even one's own children are not the parent's property and they cannot be sacrificed on the altar of Allah without their consent. Narrating the incident of Ḥaḍrat Ibrāhīm's[as] readiness to slaughter his child for the sake of Allah the Holy Quran declares:

فَلَمَّا بَلَغَ مَعَهُ السَّعْيَ قَالَ يٰبُنَيَّ اِنِّیْ اَرٰی فِی الْمَنَامِ اَنِّیْۤ اَذْبَحُكَ فَانْظُرْ مَاذَا تَرٰی ، قَالَ يٰۤاَبَتِ افْعَلْ مَا تُؤْمَرُ ، سَتَجِدُنِیْۤ اِنْ شَآءَ اللّٰهُ مِنَ الصّٰبِرِيْنَ □

And when he was old enough to work with him, he said, 'O my dear son, I have seen in a dream that I am slaughtering you. So consider, what you think *of it!*' He replied, 'O my father, do as you are commanded; you will find me, if Allah please, of those who are patient.'
(Sūrah al-Ṣāffāt; Ch.37: V.103)

Remember that Ḥaḍrat Ibrāhīm[as] saw this dream during the early childhood of Ḥaḍrat Ismael[as]. In fulfillment of that dream he had taken Ḥaḍrat Ḥājirah and Ḥaḍrat Ismael[as] to the buried remains of the Khāna Kaaba and left them alone in a desert land which had no water or greenery. In fact, this was the interpretation of the dream which he had already fulfilled then. Yet he had a disquieting feeling in his heart, wondering if the dream had to be realized literally. Despite this, he did not consider it permissible to slaughter his own son without receiving his prior consent. So when Ḥaḍrat Ismael[as] grew old enough to become mature of mind, only then did he inquire from him.

This implies that as a principle, it is required that when parents dedicate their own children, they cannot implement their decision until the children have grown to maturity and have shown their own willingness to be dedicated in the path of Allah. For the same reason in the *Waqf-e-Nau* of children the same principle is applied. After having grown to maturity, if the children do not agree with the decision of their parents to dedicate themselves, their dedication is not accepted.

The Beautiful Teaching of Treating One's Children with Respect

The Holy Prophet[sa] always admonished to treat one's children with respect. This is a teaching which requires to be fully implemented in the world of today. By disregarding the Holy Prophet's[sa] admonishment, the world appears to be filled with the evil that often children do not pay full respect to their old parents and leave them to their own fate as though they did not exist. Most often, the parents are themselves responsible for this. In modern society, most parents indulge in their own pursuit of luxuries and neglect their children. This causes a reaction among the younger generation to be disrespectful towards them when they grow old. The growing tendency to employ babysitters is, in many cases, a genuine necessity. When both the parents have to go out to work, they may need to employ someone to take care of their children during their absence. But when, having discharged their duties, they go out in the evening for recreation, they need babysitters once again. In reality, this is not fully justified. They should take their children along, and share their enjoyment with them. Psychologists observe that when children are willfully neglected in their early childhood, they sometimes begin to suffer from grave psychological disturbances, which may be incurable. Some of the same children grow up to become criminals and vagrants. In some cases, such children as are neglected by parents are so mentally disturbed that they commit suicide. Some facts and figures published by American experts indicate that in America alone, 400,000 deprived children commit suicide every year because they are so tired of their deprivations. This vice is ever on the increase.

The Rights of Orphans

The Holy Quran repeatedly warns about the rights of orphans. Those children whose parents are alive can be looked after to some extent by their parents, but who would take care of the orphans? The Holy Quran lays this responsibility on the entire society and takes special care of the rights of orphaned children. In no Divine Book of the world, other than the Holy Quran, one can find such teachings about orphans as are given by the Holy Quran. The Holy Quran declares:

وَأَنْ تَقُوْمُوْا لِلْيَتْمٰى بِالْقِسْطِ ۚ وَمَا تَفْعَلُوْا مِنْ خَيْرٍ فَإِنَّ اللّٰهَ كَانَ بِهٖ عَلِيْمًا ☐...

'...And *He enjoins you to* observe equity towards the

orphans. And whatever good you do, surely Allah knows it well.'
(Sūrah al-Nisā'; Ch.4: V.128)

Allah declares that because this order is given to the whole society, so society is responsible that no orphan should be left without proper care. Allah also declares:

وَ يَسْئَلُوْنَكَ عَنِ الْيَتْمٰى ، قُلْ اِصْلَاحٌ لَّهُمْ خَيْرٌ ، وَ اِنْ تُخَالِطُوْهُمْ فَاِخْوَانُكُمْ ، وَاللّٰهُ يَعْلَمُ الْمُفْسِدَ مِنَ الْمُصْلِحِ ، وَلَوْ شَآءَ اللّٰهُ لَاَعْنَتَكُمْ ، اِنَّ اللّٰهَ عَزِيْزٌ حَكِيْمٌ ☐

And they ask you concerning the orphans. Say: 'Promotion of their welfare is *an act of* great goodness. And if you intermix with them, they are your brethren. And Allah knows the mischief-maker from the reformer. And if Allah had so willed, He would have put you to hardship. Surely, Allah is Mighty, Wise.'
(Sūrah al-Baqarah; Ch.2: V.221)

There are many societies where orphans are left to shift for themselves and as a result they suffer from many problems. That is why the Holy Quran stresses that orphans should not be neglected. Like all the younger generations who have their parents to look after them, orphans also have a right to be looked after. So the Holy Quran declares, if you can harmonize them well with your own family that would be the best measure. They are your brothers, do not treat them as strangers. It is not sufficient to build orphanages and just provide them with the daily requirements of life.

Then Allah warns that He knows very well those who spread disorder and those who reform the society. Some people keep orphans in their houses with the purpose of enslaving them and taking menial tasks from them. They address them as their own children, but treat them like servants. Thus, Allah observes human nature in depth and continues to point at every hidden danger.

The Teaching of Benevolence concerning Orphans

Then, warning the whole of society, Allah declares:

كَلَّا بَل لَّا تُكْرِمُونَ الْيَتِيمَ

Nay, but you honour not the orphan,
(Sūrah al-Fajr; Ch.89: V.18)

This means that just to take pity on orphans is not sufficient. You must treat them with honour and deep respect. Incidentally, it reminds one of an admonishment of the Holy Prophet[sa], reminding parents to treat their own children with honour. So in fact, orphans should be treated like one's own children.

Here, the teaching enters from the domain of justice into the domain of beneficence. After this, some other deadly moral diseases are mentioned. So, the Holy Quran is a book of comprehensive cure which analyses every moral disease in detail, then speaks of the remedial measures to be taken.

Chapter al-Māʿūn warns by way of raising a question:

اَرَءَيْتَ الَّذِيْ يُكَذِّبُ بِالدِّيْنِۭ ⬜ فَذٰلِكَ الَّذِيْ يَدُعُّ الْيَتِيْمَ ⬜

Have you seen him who rejects religion?
That is the one who drives away the orphan,
(Sūrah al- Māʿūn; Ch.107: Vs.2-3)

This means that the people who drive away the orphans are those who, as a consequence, reject their faith as well.

Noble Conduct of the Holy Prophet[sa] towards Orphans

In this regard, I quote a tradition of the Holy Prophet[sa] in which we are informed of the great reward that will be granted to the person who behaves nobly towards orphans.

Ḥaḍrat Suhail bin Saʿd[ra] narrates:

Ḥaḍrat Rasūlullāh[sa] mentioned that he and the one who cares for the upbringing of orphans will be together in paradise like the index finger is close to the next finger. Saying this, he demonstrated by tightly pressing the two fingers so there was no space left between them.[74]

When we invite the world towards Islam, our intention is not just to increase our number. One should only keep the fact in mind that Islam is really a truth from which the world is deprived. It is a blessing and without it the world is suffering from many evils. Unfortunately people stand up to oppose this truth, not knowing that they are being called to their own welfare.

The Rights of Close Relatives

In addition to the rights of one's own family and that of the orphans, the Holy Quran also lays stress upon the rights of relatives and the circle of fraternity. Most often, instead of being more careful about their rights, people tend to ignore them and commit many transgressions against them. Fraternity is referred to in the Punjab as *Sharīka* and instead of promoting their welfare, people take false pride in belittling and disgracing them. In the West, this problem cannot be fully comprehended. This is because in the West contact with distant relatives is no longer kept. Sometimes they have no concern for their neighbour, nor ever think of other relatives, except maybe for a few. The Holy Quran does not ignore these moral diseases and speaks of remedial measures regarding them. For this reason, I have dealt with the subject of the rights of near relatives in a separate sub-chapter. The Holy Quran declares:

فَاٰتِ ذَاالْقُرْبٰى حَقَّهٗ وَالْمِسْكِيْنَ وَابْنَ السَّبِيْلِ ۚ ذٰلِكَ خَيْرٌ
لِّلَّذِيْنَ يُرِيْدُوْنَ وَجْهَ اللّٰهِ ۚ وَاُولٰٓئِكَ هُمُ الْمُفْلِحُوْنَ ☐

So give to the kinsman his due, and to the needy, and
to the wayfarer. That is best for those who seek the
favour of Allah, and it is they who will prosper.
(Sūrah al-Rūm; Ch.30: V.39)

Here, Allah has enjoined us to take care of a wide
range of rights of humankind. Hence it is required that
when Allah expands one's resources, O reader of the
Quran, give relatives their due rights and also give
rights to the poor who do not beg. Similarly, give due
rights to the wayfarer. This is a beautiful teaching for
those who require Allah's favour and always look
towards him, wondering how Allah treats them and
whether He is happy with them or angry with them.
People who do accordingly are the ones who are truly
redeemed.

Again the Holy Quran declares:

وَاعْبُدُوا اللّٰهَ وَلَا تُشْرِكُوْا بِهٖ شَيْئًا وَّ بِالْوَالِدَيْنِ اِحْسَانًا
وَّ بِذِى الْقُرْبٰى وَالْيَتٰمٰى وَالْمَسٰكِيْنِ وَالْجَارِذِى الْقُرْبٰى وَ الْجَارِ
الْجُنُبِ وَالصَّاحِبِ بِالْجَنْبِ وَ ابْنِ السَّبِيْلِ وَمَا مَلَكَتْ اَيْمَانُكُمْ ۚ
اِنَّ اللّٰهَ لَا يُحِبُّ مَنْ كَانَ مُخْتَالًا فَخُوْرَا ☐

And worship Allah and associate naught with him,
and *show* kindness to parents, and to kindred, and
orphans, and the needy, and to the neighbour that is a
kinsman and the neighbour that is a stranger, and the

companion by *your* side, and the wayfarer, and those
whom your right hands possess. Surely, Allah loves
not the proud *and* the boastful,
(Sūrah al-Nisā'; Ch.4: V.37)

In this noble verse, the subject of justice and
benevolence is being presented in a much wider range
than in the previous one. Hence, apart from the
prohibition of calling partners with Allah and paying
due respect to the rights of parents, benevolence
towards close relatives, orphans, poor people who do
not beg, relatives who are also neighbours and
neighbours who are strangers, are being discussed in
this verse. Similarly, benevolence towards those who
are under your command is also included.

The Great Teaching of Benevolence towards Close Blood Relatives

Ḥaḍrat Anas bin Mālik[ra] narrates from the Holy
Prophet[sa] that he admonished to treat close relatives
with benevolence, if one requires expansion in his
provisions. That is to say one should maintain an
excellent relationship with one's relatives.[75]

Ḥaḍrat Abū Hurairah[ra] narrates that once a person
appeared before the Holy Prophet[sa] and said, 'O
Messenger of Allah, my relatives are such as when I
pay attention to their due rights they completely sever
their ties with me. If I treat them with kindness they
treat me ill. If I show forbearance towards them they
show me arrogance, that is to say they try to inflame

me.'

To this the Holy Messenger[sa] responded by enjoining, 'even if they are not good to you and do not pay you your due rights, you must always pay them their due rights and treat them with benevolence.' Then he said, 'As long as you are doing this, that is, treating them well while they do ill to you and showing benevolence despite their transgression, you will be filling their mouths with dust, meaning you will be putting them to shame. So it is better for you to stick to this stance.'

Then he said, 'Beware, you face no danger; as long as you conduct yourself like this, Allah will continue to help you against their excesses and transgression.'

The Relationship between those Connected through their Mother's Uterus and Allah's Attribute of Raḥmān

It should be noted that 'uterus' in Arabic is called *Riḥam* (رِحَم) and Allah's attribute *Raḥmān* (رَحْمٰن) is also derived from the same root. According to a Ḥadith the Holy Prophet[sa] said that Allah metaphorically addressing the human uterus declares: 'O uterus (that is *Riḥam*), whoever is connected through you, I will be connected with him. And he who breaks his ties with you, I will break my ties with him.'[76]

Thus when we declare the Holy Prophet[sa] to be the best of all Prophets[as], we do so because his teaching is

403

the best of all teachings as brought by other Prophets[as] and the excellence of this teaching over all other teachings is proved with powerful arguments.

References Part IV

57. *al-Badr*, December 8, 1903, Vol.2, No.46.

58. *Sunan Abu Dāwūd, Kitāb-ul-Adab, Bābu fil Ghībah.*

59. *Musnad Aḥmad bin Ḥambal*, Hadith No.22978, Vol.6, p. 570, published by *Dār Iḥyā'it Turāthil 'Arabi*, Third Edition 1994.

60. *Ṣaḥiḥ Muslim, Kitābul Birri waṣ Ṣilah, Bābu Raghima Anfu man Adraka Abawaihi...*

61. *Musnad Aḥmad Bin Ḥambal, Musnad 'Abdullah bin 'Amr*, Hadith No.6640, published by *Dār Iḥyā'it Turāthil 'Arabi*, Third Edition 1994.

62. *Ṣaḥiḥ Bukhārī, Kitābul 'Ijārati, Bābu Man Ista'jara Ajīran.*

63. *Ad-Durrul Manthūr, Fit Tafsīri Bil M'athūri*, Vol.5 p.165, published by *Dārul M'arifati*, Bairut Lebanon.

64. *Sunan Ibni Mājah, Abwābul Adab, Bābu Sal Man Kāna Abūka Yaṣilu.*

65. *Ṣaḥiḥ Bukhārī, Kitābul Waṣāyā, Bābun Idha Qāla Arḍī Au Bustānī.*

66. *Sunan Ibni Mājah, Abwābul Adabi, Bābu Birril Wālidaini.*

67. *Ṣaḥiḥ Bukhārī, Kitābul Hibati wa Faḍlihā Wattaḥrīḍi 'Alaihā, Bābul Ishhādi fil Hibati.*

68. *Ṣaḥiḥ Muslim, Kitābul Birri Waṣ Ṣilati, Bābu Faḍlil Iḥsāni Ilal Bināti.*

69. *Ṣaḥiḥ Bukhārī, Kitābul Janā'iz, Bābu Rathā'in Nabiyyi Ṣallallāhu 'Alaihi Wasallam.*

70. *Ṣaḥiḥ Bukhārī, Kitābul Farā'iḍi, Bābu Mīrāthil Bināti.*

71. *Ṣaḥiḥ Bukhārī, Kitābul Adab, Bābu Raḥmatil Waladi wa Taqbīlihī wa Mu'ānaqatihī.*

72. *Sharḥus Sunna Lil Imām al-Baghawī, Kitābul Janā'iz, Bābul Bukā'i 'Alal Mayyiti Wa Mā Rakhkhaṣa Fīhi min Irsālid Dam'i.*

73. *Ṣaḥiḥ Bukhārī, Kitābul Adab, Bābu Raḥmatil Waladi wa Taqbīlihī wa Mu'ānaqatihī.*

74. *Ṣaḥiḥ Bukhārī, Kitābul Adab, Bābu Faḍli Mańya'ūlu Yatīmān.*

75. *Ṣaḥiḥ Muslim, Kitābul Birri Waṣ Ṣilati, Bābu Ṣilatir Raḥimi wa Taḥrīmi Qaṭī'atihā.*

76. *Ṣaḥiḥ Bukhārī, Kitābul Adab, Bābu Man Waṣalahū Waṣalahullāh.*

Epilogue

Whatever has been observed in these addresses is based on the short verse of the Holy Quran which declares:

$$\text{اِنَّ اللّٰهَ يَأْمُرُ بِالْعَدْلِ وَالْاِحْسَانِ وَ اِيْتَآئِ ذِى الْقُرْبٰى...}$$

Verily, Allah requires you to abide by justice, and to treat with grace, and give like the giving of kin to kin;…
(Sūrah al-Naḥl; Ch.16: V.91)

This verse is the title of this series of addresses. I have attempted my best to do justice to the wide meanings contained in this short verse but the more I try to delve deeper into its meaning, the less capable I find myself to do so. Allah bless all those who have helped me in this task for the collection of all relevant material and also bless those who have helped me in this English translation.

May Allah be with them herein and hereafter–Āmīn.